Teaching *Daughters of the Dust* as a Womanist Film and the Black Arts Aesthetic of Filmmaker Julie Dash

This book is part of the Peter Lang Humanities list.
Every volume is peer reviewed and meets
the highest quality standards for content and production.

PETER LANG
New York • Bern • Berlin
Brussels • Vienna • Oxford • Warsaw

Teaching *Daughters of the Dust* as a Womanist Film and the Black Arts Aesthetic of Filmmaker Julie Dash

Edited by
Patricia Williams Lessane

PETER LANG
New York • Bern • Berlin
Brussels • Vienna • Oxford • Warsaw

Library of Congress Cataloging-in-Publication Data

Names: Lessane, Patricia Williams, editor.
Title: Teaching Daughters of the dust as a womanist film and the black arts
aesthetic of filmmaker Julie Dash / edited by Patricia Williams Lessane.
Description: New York: Peter Lang, 2020.
Includes bibliographical references and index.
Identifiers: LCCN 2019036539 | ISBN 978-1-4331-6648-8 (hardback: alk. paper)
ISBN 978-1-4331-8299-0 (paperback: alk. paper) | ISBN 978-1-4331-6649-5 (ebook pdf)
ISBN 978-1-4331-6650-1 (epub) | ISBN 978-1-4331-6651-8 (mobi)
Subjects: LCSH: Dash, Julie—Criticism and interpretation. | Daughters of
the dust (Motion picture) | African American women in motion pictures.
Classification: LCC PN1997.D313343 T43 | DDC 791.43/72—dc23
LC record available at https://lccn.loc.gov/2019036539
DOI 10.3726/b15275

Bibliographic information published by **Die Deutsche Nationalbibliothek.**
Die Deutsche Nationalbibliothek lists this publication in the "Deutsche
Nationalbibliografie"; detailed bibliographic data are available
on the Internet at http://dnb.d-nb.de/.

The paper in this book meets the guidelines for permanence and durability
of the Committee on Production Guidelines for Book Longevity
of the Council of Library Resources.

This book is dedicated to my mother, Annie Ruth Williams, who taught me to believe that I could become whatever I dreamed I could be, and to the countless other women who have mothered me along the way: Cleo "Big Mama" Bowman, Deborah Harrington, Lucy Lessane Fiering, Lorna Wilson, Joyce Ann Joyce, Alaka Wali, Ayana I. Karanja, Marcia Blair, Henrietta Snype, Cynthia McCottry-Smith, Ruth Rambo, Lucille Whipper, Mary Dunson, Wilma Vaughn, Juanita Williams, Iya Valdate Britto, and of course, Julie Dash, my mentor, my sister, my friend.

It is also dedicated to my sister and friend, the late, Dr. Conseula Francis.

And to Thing One and Thing Two, my two best things.

We carry these memories inside of we.

—Nana Peazant, *Daughters of the Dust*

Table of Contents

Figures

Acknowledgements

Thank you to the Avery Research Center staff for making the 2011 conference, "We Carry These Memories Inside of We: Celebrating the 20th Anniversary of *Daughters of the Dust* and the Black Arts Aesthetic of Julie Dash," the colossal success that it was! Thank you Daron Lee Calhoun II, Valentina Rebaciuc, Deborah Wright, Savannah Frierson, and David Rothsmund for helping me bring this project to fruition. Thank you to all of the contributors to the anthology, your patience and belief in me. Finally, thank you, Julie Dash, for your friendship, sisterhood, and for giving us all such a deep well of creativity and cultural and ancestral pride to draw from!

Introduction

PATRICIA WILLIAMS LESSANE

At the 2019 Sundance Film Festival, Black feminist filmmaker Julie Dash announced she will direct the upcoming Lionsgate biopic of Black feminist freedom fighter, Angela Davis. Dash, whose seminal work is *Daughters of the Dust*, has directed other films since the 1991 debut of this feature film, including *Funny Valentine* and *The Rosa Parks Story* starring Angela Bassett, as well as recent episodes of Ava Duvernay's OWN series *Queen Sugar*. However, her latest dramatic narrative, and current documentary project *Travel Notes of a Geechee Girl* (about the life of Gullah Geechee writer, journalist, and chef Vertamae Grosvenor and for which she was recently awarded a $500,000 National Endowment for the Humanities grant to produce), signal a new chapter in her life: a new beginning and a renewed recognition of her talent and creativity as writer and director. That she is directing a film about Davis, a Black woman whose revolutionary life and life's work have had such a colossal impact on the way we as Black people see ourselves and envision liberation, is appropriate as Dash's debut dramatic narrative film, *The Rosa Parks Story*, situates Black women squarely within the longue durée of Black struggles for freedom, agency, and self-determination—from slavery, through the turn of the 20th century, and then again during the turbulent civil rights era of the mid-20th century.

Dash and Davis occupy unique roles in African American history and Black feminist thinking, both as truth-tellers and high priestesses of Black consciousness. Davis, with intellectual brilliance and defiant spirit, became a rallying figure for Black youth and freedom fighters across the world when she was indicted and then acquitted by an all-white jury of charges that included conspiracy, murder, and kidnapping in connection to a courtroom shooting that left a federal judge and two prison inmates dead.

Davis's courage and brilliant testimony in which she, instead, indicted the United Sates of horrendous crimes against Black people not only proved her innocence, but also exposed a flawed legal system designed to ensnare and enslave freedom-seeking Black Americans. Her triumphant victory signaled to America that it could not go about business as usual in its oppression of Black and Brown people.

Similarly, with *Daughters of the Dust*, Dash rejects the American cinematic tradition of obscuring/distorting/menstrilizing/marginalizing Black people, and looks to African American filmmaking pioneers and other Third World and European filmmakers who bucked the cinematic parameters set during the 19th and 20th centuries. And while *Daughters of the Dust* broke barriers as the first film by an African American woman to debut with a national release, the film occupied a place on the margins of mainstream American cinema for years in both reception and acclaim.

In an early review of the film, writer Valerie Boyd acknowledged the beauty and relevance of the film and aptly predicted what would ultimately be the celebrated destiny of the film:

> *Daughters* is too exquisite a film to not be seen. And African Americans should not depend solely on marketing executives to get the word out. *Daughters* will likely build its audience through Black America's oldest marketing strategy—word-of-mouth. Imagine that: buppies discussing it in water-cooler conversations at their offices; Black nationalists analyzing it in fireside chats at bookstores; sisters in beauty shops paraphrasing some of the film's sauciest lines. Historically significant and visually sublime, *Daughters of the Dust* is like a sacred secret whispered in your ear. Pass it on. (Boyd 1991)

A keen observer of developing technological trends and emerging cultural shifts, Dash embraced the margins of the cinematic frame, imagining and constructing a cinematic space in which her characters present and embody counter-narratives to those depicted in American media and the dominant culture. Then and now, Dash, like Nana Peazant, looks inward to the past and forward to the future for inspiration and vocational guidance in her developing narratives about Black people and Black spaces, and in her executing cinematic technique. Film scholar Manthia Diawara (2000) contends, "Black films use spatial narration as a way of revealing and linking Black spaces that have been separated and suppressed by White times, and as a means of validating Black culture" (245). The Peazant Family, their extended kin, Mr. Snead, and St. Julian Last Child are Dash's people; Ibo's Landing is Dash's world. Both are, separate and apart from the dominant white gaze.

At the 1991 Sundance Film Festival, Julie Dash was nominated for the Grand Jury Prize and Arthur Jafa won for his cinematography, but it was not until 2016 that Dash was awarded the New York Film Critics Circle Award for the 25th Anniversary Restoration of *Daughters of the Dust*, confirming the enduring impact and legacy of both the film and the filmmaker. In that same year, Beyoncé Knowles-Carter released *Lemonade* a Black feminist, multigenre visual album replete with images reminiscent of characters and scenes from Dash's debut full-feature narrative. Like Dash, Knowles-Carter tackles issues germane to the 21st century Black woman's experiences—rejection, subjugation, familial obligations and ancestral connections, colorism, abuse, motherhood, and the struggle for liberation and personhood. Accordingly, Davis (2017, 9) asserts "*Daughters of the Dust* and *Lemonade*, represent Black feminist approaches to filmmaking that lovingly elevate the particularity of the Black female experiences in the United States on both systematic and interpersonal levels, crossing sexual, class, and even skin color lines." In this manner, both Dash and Knowles-Carter "break the mold" in which Black women have been traditionally portrayed (Bogle 2001, 349).

I first saw *Daughters of the Dust* on a sunny day in August 1992 in Atlanta's Piedmont Park. My cousin Shelley and friend Miles agreed to accompany me to see a film I had been raving about for weeks. I had not even seen a trailer for the film, but friends in Chicago and Washington, D.C., had told me about it and said it was one I just had to see. Shelley and Miles knew of my obsession with film, but also of my burgeoning identity as a Black feminist, or Womanist as I had begun to embrace. They also knew I was a veracious reader, having studied English Literature at Fisk University where I excelled in Negro Literature, Harlem Renaissance Literature, and inhaled any and everything written by Black women. Seeing Dash's film was a cinematic convergence of African American literature, poetry, art, and history on the big screen, live and in technicolor. My friends assumed, and rightly so, that I would be moved beyond words when I saw the movie for the first time. What they did not know—nor did I—was that *Daughters of the Dust* would shape my writing and pedagogy in ways I could not have imagined as a young, twenty-two-year-old Black woman learning to see myself and my people with new eyes. I was awakening, and Julie Dash's film further inspired my appreciation of Black film and literature, as well as my future approach to scholarship that had sparked in me while I was in college.

I had found bits and pieces of myself in the pages of books written by 19th and 20th century African Americans while at Fisk. Yet, it was in *Daughters of the Dust* that I first saw myself wholly, although I did not have the words for this feeling back then—unapologetically Black and beautiful. For me, Julie Dash had channeled the anthropologic spirits of Zora Neale Hurston and Katherine Dunham, as well as the literary genius of every Black woman writer I had read up to that point. At the same time, I saw in her 19th century Black women the same 20th century struggles I was experiencing, along with just about every other Black woman I knew. And although the film follows the experiences of a cloistered Sea Island Gullah family contemplating migration, assimilation, and-transitioning from their traditional agrarian way of life to the bustling modernity awaiting them on the mainland, their hopes, dreams, challenges, and wishes are ones my mother held for my siblings and me. The Peazant women wrested self-determination and agency with the hand they had been dealt and held tightly onto them so they might propel their family and them forward.

Dash positions Black women's agency and liberation as the central focus of the film, thus anchoring the secondary and tertiary storylines in the experiences of three generations of Peazant women. In this manner, *Daughters of the Dust* is a Womanist film, that centralizes 19th century Black women's experiences while documenting and contextualizing, and Black peoples' struggles at the turn of the 20th century. Coming out of the Black Arts Movement and the L.A. Rebellion, global Black struggles for liberation and self-determination punctuate Dash's film aesthetic, thus making it revolutionary and groundbreaking at the same time. Like other Black feminist writers (Collins, Higginbotham, hooks, Guy-Sheftall, Harris, Crenshaw, Smith, Perry, Cooper), Dash employs film as the narrative tableau for uncovering—literally bringing to light and to life—Black women's stories, situating their experiences within the nascent, burgeoning, and expanding African diaspora, contested American history, and Black people's global struggles for liberation and self-determination. This is most evident in the film's progression. The family's impending migration parallels the great discovery of photography and the explosive innovation of the Industrial Revolution, as well as the developing metro poles and the shifting Northern landscapes as urban centers. Dash acknowledges the profound importance of the Great Migration to American history; and like Isabel Wilkerson's Pulitzer-Prize winning opus, *The Warmth of Other Suns* (2010), Dash's characters embody Black peoples' quests for freedom, mobility, and self-determination, thus immortalizing their experiences.

It has been over 25 years since I first viewed *Daughters of the Dust*. Over the years, I have watched the film countless times, using it in my courses Black Bodies in Television and Film, African American Society and Culture, and The Untold Story of the Great Migration. Most recently in 2016, I introduced the film to students studying North American Literature at University of Màlaga in Màlaga, Spain. Yet it was fifteen years after seeing *Daughters of the Dust* for the first time that I had the opportunity to actually speak with Julie Dash, inviting her to give a keynote address at Chicago's Museum of Science and Industry. To say I had a "fangirl" moment is an understatement. Meeting Dash and discussing what was on the horizon for American cinema, and Black film specifically, was life-changing. While I had conducted extensive research on *Daughters of the Dust* and had learned of the familial and cultural impetus for her undertaking the project, listening to

Dash recount her research endeavors, the challenges to securing financing for the film, surviving the oppressive Lowcountry heat, and weathering temperamental storm systems and mercurial talent and crew, made the film that more meaningful for me. It seemed the ancestors old Nana Peazant speaks of—Julie's ancestors—would not let her dream die. The film, then, is a testament not only to Dash's creative vision and film aesthetic, but also to her connection to and reverence for her African past and rich Gullah Geechee roots.

Similarly, this book pays homage to Dash's Black arts aesthetic, one imbued with Black pride; recognition and celebration of West African cultural, linguistic, religious, culinary, ontological, and familial and kinship retentions in Gullah Geechee culture; and the dialectical pull between Western concepts of religion and sacred texts, gender, and individualism, and West African cultural traditions rooted in the collective and communal experiences, which are marked by ancestral reverence and passed down via oral traditions. More importantly, however, this anthology positions Dash's film within the canon of Black feminist scholarship evidenced by the ways in which her film acknowledges, builds upon, and works in concert with the writing of early Black women scholars such as Anna Julia Cooper, Maria Stewart, and Alice Dunbar and 20th century Black feminist writers such as bell hooks, Trudier Harris, Audre Lorde, Frances Beal, Deborah King, Toni Cade Bambara, Kimberlé Williams Crenshaw, and others.

The idea for this anthology was born during "We Carry These Memories Inside of We: A Symposium Celebrating the 20th Anniversary of *Daughters of the Dust* and the Black Art Aesthetic of Filmmaker Julie Dash." The symposium, held at the College of Charleston's Avery Research Center for African American History and Culture in Charleston, South Carolina, convened artists, students, and scholars from the humanities and social sciences, as well as cinemaphiles and devotees of the film for three days of intellectual, artistic, and spiritual exchange centered on Dash's iconic film. The papers assembled in this anthology collectively provide multiple entry points for examining and teaching *Daughters of the Dust* as a Womanist film, building upon investigations of the film by scholars including Pacharee Sudhinaraset, Katherine Silva, Michael T. Martin, Laura Gaither, Joel Coats, Donald Bogle, Daniel Garrett, Foluke Ogunleye, Catherine Cucinella and Renée R. Curry, Ed Guerrero, Judylyn S. Ryan, Anissa Janine Wardi, and Elizabeth J. West.

In course design, each of the essays can be used singularly or in tandem with the others written from an anthropological, critical media, film or literary criticism, Black feminist, critical race theory, queer studies, or a multitude of other interdisciplinary analysis. At the same time, the singular focus of this collection lends to an in-depth analysis of the film. What each of these essays provide is an access point for celebrating, interrogating, witnessing, processing, and more importantly, teaching *Daughters of the Dust* as a Black feminist narrative film. This is the greatest gift of this book. As such, I do not only situate the essays within the aforementioned discourses as theoretical frameworks for examining the film, but also within Black feminist, Africana/African-diasporan/African American and queer epistemologies for teaching Black texts. I contend that by building their examination of *Daughters of the Dust* from a Black feminist/Womanist lens, each writer provides a Black feminist/Womanist framework for teaching the film and the eponymous novel. Additionally, the essays in this anthology written by Black women reflect the intellectual and pedagogical frameworks of Black women scholars who teach Black feminist/Womanist texts to 21st century learners, often, but not always in predominately white spaces. Their willingness, and that of the white contributors to this volume, to teach texts by radical Black women writers and filmmakers like Julie Dash within disciplines historically and largely dominated by white male scholars is evidence of Black women's collective courage to speak truth to power, to reject the imposter syndrome, and to celebrate and acknowledge the power and importance of Black women's scholarship and cultural production as crucial to the cultivation of well-rounded, global students. Take for example the experiences of Claire Oberon Garcia, an English professor at Colorado College and Dean of Faculty whose experiences teaching majority white students speaks to the challenges Black women scholars face teaching narratives written by and about African Americans. Recalling earlier teaching experiences, Oberon Garcia describes the "extra twist or two to already complex problems" teaching African American literature as a Black woman created in her classes (Garcia 1994, 37):

> The other side of this seeming consensus is that many students come assuming that much black literature is not "literary": It does not have universal appeal (because it is too immersed in the problems of a particular people) and it is not "beautiful" (because it is too concerned with cruelty and injustice). Although fewer students have these preconceptions now than at the beginning of my teaching career in the 1980s, a significant number still hold assumptions about the inferiority of black literature. (Garcia 1994, 38)

While Garcia recounts her experiences teaching African American literature, the same is true of Black women who require their students to read/watch/examine work by Black women writers, artists, and scholars.

On a personal level, this book reflects the evolution of my professional obsession with the film, but also the evolution of my friendship and work with Julie Dash. In fact, upon applying for my former position as executive director of the Avery Research Center, I reached out to Julie to see what she knew of it. To my utter surprise, she informed me her father, Julian Dash, and all of his brothers had attended the Avery Institute, the private school that educated Black people in Charleston shortly after the Civil War's end, and from which the research center gets its name. For me, Julie's familial connection to Avery was a sign I would get the job. Before we ended our conversation, I told her if and when I got the job, one of my first priorities would be planning a conference to commemorate the 20th anniversary of *Daughters of the Dust*. I asked her if she would be open to coming, if and when I could pull it off, and she agreed. Luckily, my staff, my colleague Dr. Conseula Francis, and I did successfully pull it off, and Dash became the first Avery Research Center artist-in-residence.

We were all ecstatic by the interest, energy, and sheer Black Girl Magic over that weekend, which culminated with a free screening of *Daughters of the Dust* in Charleston's historic Hampton Park. Over three hundred residents gathered with lawn chairs and picnic baskets to experience *Daughters of the Dust* under the Lowcountry stars.

Julie Dash was in residence for the three weeks leading up to the conference. Over the course of her stay at the Avery Research Center, I got to know her much better and we spent countless hours discussing film, history, literature, politics, family, and of course, food. Julie and I had become fast friends; and right before departing for Los Angeles, Julie invited me to a Lowcountry crab crack at her Uncle Johnny's house on the Ashley River. Though I was honored to be invited to the gathering of Julie's relatives and extended kin, I was most struck by the communal ritual of the *crab crack* and the intergenerational exchange between three generations of the Dash family. The similarities between the colorful and lively Dash clan and friends gathered together for a Lowcountry seafood feast on beautiful but breezy September day, and the Peazants' "Last Supper" were visceral, and I could see for myself just how Julie's family history and Gullah cultural traditions had influenced the creation of her iconic film. And in the midst of it all was one Mrs. Peazant! While she was very different from the film's Nana Peazant, Mrs. Peazant was the matriarch of a line of strong Black Charlestonian women.

Aha! I thought to myself: I was witnessing some of Julie Dash's very own "scraps of memories" that had ignited her curiosity about her Gullah background and propelled her examination of the language, gastronomy, cosmology, African retentions, and cultural and religious syncretism at work. As Julie ushered my children and me into the kitchen—the buzzing epicenter of Gullah culinary, cultural, and familial exchange—I envisioned myself as a 21st century Zora Neale Hurston, a participant-observer conducting fieldwork on African Americans I had only read about before seeing *Daughters of the Dust* and moving to Charleston just one year prior.

Since then, Julie's family has become my extended family. I have been fortunate to witness 21st century Gullah traditions and become a part of kinship networks I would never have had were it not for my friendship with Julie. At the same time, Julie has become a mentor, teaching me about the science of cinema, the intricacies of the film business, the creative process of translating a story into film, and how to capture the subtle nuances that breathe life into complex characters and rich narratives. That Julie's friendship has left an indelible mark on my life goes without saying. That *Daughters of the Dust* changed me in intellectual, political, and spiritual ways is an understatement, as the film has shaped my teaching pedagogy and epistemological approach to engagement with all students, but specifically with African American women who enter my classrooms.

My experience with *Daughters of the Dust* is not atypical. The scholars featured in this anthology provide only a small glimpse of the artists, teachers, researchers, students, film buffs, and filmmakers who continue to be enriched and inspired by the film some twenty-five years after its debut. Using a Black feminist framework, each writer situates the film within overlapping discourses while interrogating the implications of intersectionality regarding Black women's identities and lived experiences. In this manner, *Daughters of the Dust* occupies space as both a liberation text and as an epistemological and pedagogical tool for Black feminist criticism.

This anthology is divided into four sections that underscore three central tropes of the film: Part 1—"Capturing the Canon: Julie Dash and the Black Arts and Black Feminist Traditions," Part 2—"Sensory Ignition and Cultural Memory: Visual Art and Gastronomy in *Daughters of the Dust*," Part 3—"The Sacred Emerge: The Witness, the Healed, and *Daughters of the Dust*," and Part 4—"The Power of Place in Shaping Identity and Artistic Cultivation."

PART 1—CAPTURING THE CANON: JULIE DASH AND THE BLACK ARTS AND BLACK FEMINIST TRADITIONS

In Chapter One, "Memory, Meaning, and Gullah Sensibilities: The Black Art Aesthetics of Julie Dash and Jonathan Green," I discuss what I have termed "Gullah sensibilities"—syncretized African retentions unique to Sea Island Black communities—as captured in Dash's iconic film and artist Jonathan Green's majestic portraits of Gullah people and Lowcountry culture. I suggest Dash and Green's Gullah roots in the region endow them with spiritual tools to understand, preserve, and document Gullah life and cultural traditions. Through their crafts, they act as griots for Gullah people by recalling, documenting, and preserving their stories.

In Chapter Two, Ayana I. Karanja situates *Daughters of the Dust* within a larger discussion of the objectification of and violence against Black women and the space the film occupies within the longue dureè of Black liberation. She writes:

> This singular fact speaks volumes about the violence historically inflicted upon the Black woman, both physically and psychologically, across time and space in America. [...] Social critiques of the Black female include dishonorable views of her body and behavior—too fat, too dark, too white-appearing, too loud—and are always measures of her lack or excess. Whether Black women are considered Jezebels, witches, or societal schemers taking off with taxpayer dollars, this segment of the population continues to be a topic of negative public commentary and sociological discourses. (33-34)

Karanja argues the Black Arts Movement, the L.A Rebellion Group, and the Black feminist theory provided Dash the intellectual and political frameworks to contextualize and celebrate Gullah culture while calling attention to Black women's issues both then and now.

In Chapter Three, "Overcoming the Trauma of the Gaze in Julie Dash's *Daughter of the Dust*," Heike Raphael-Hernandez asserts Black women writers and, by extension filmmakers like Dash, have historically confronted damaging and one-dimensional stereotypes of Black women and created characters and narratives reflective of their complex, full, and lived experiences:

> In their own films, these directors picked up those limiting and often condescending representations of mainstream productions that had portrayed the Black woman either as passive, often naïve supporting sidekicks to white protagonists, or had used her presence as an excuse to gaze at the Black female body. Black women filmmakers took this mainstream's gaze as an inviting challenge for their starting points, turning the passive Black woman, who heretofore had been gazed at, into the active agent who transformed the condescending gaze into a loving and accepting look, and thus offered herself her own empowerment needed to overcome the emotional pain and trauma caused by their memories of injustices done to them and their ancestors. (52)

Raphael-Hernandez goes further, making the connection between the theme of the Black woman's journey to spiritual and physical healing and safety of body, and personhood in literature and film. Thus, African American women writers and filmmakers of the 1970s were intentional in their portrayal of the way Black women used their ancestral and internal spiritual compasses to navigate the systemic barriers of racism, sexism, and classism. And as such, "these writers differ significantly from their predecessors because they do not limit their fiction to descriptions of reality and mere criticism of negative societal circumstances" (Raphael-Hernandez 2019).

PART 2—SENSORY IGNITION AND CULTURAL MEMORY: VISUAL ART AND GASTRONOMY IN *DAUGHTERS OF THE DUST*

In Chapters Four and Five, Katie White and Corrie Claiborne, respectively, examine aesthetic forms of traditional Gullah cooking and quilting depicted in *Daughters of the Dust*. Together, their essays celebrate Dash's ability to bring to life the distinctly Gullah approach to cooking and quilting, which are both cultural retentions from their rice coast ancestors.

White's chapter, "Coming Home to Good Gumbo: Gullah Foodways and the Sensory in Julie Dash's *Daughters of the Dust*," employs ethnographic methodologies

such as personal interviews, oral histories, and participant observation to elucidate the symbiotic way sensory reactions and nostalgic feelings about food conjure
images, desires for, and connections to home for Dash's characters, but especially
Yellow Mary.

In her final analysis, White astutely discerns the important role that food and
cooking have and continue to play within Gullah communities:

> For the Gullah, food is more than a necessity for survival. It is life. Since the beginning of
> the Gullah existence food has played a central role in everyday life. Gullah food cannot be
> found in a store-bought package. It must be prepared with love, and perhaps more impor-
> tantly, with hundreds of years of ritual behind each stir of the pot and pinch of spice. (73)

In "Decorating the Decorations: *Daughters of the Dust* and the Aesthetics of
the Quilt," Corrie Claiborne melds film and art criticism with reflexive ethnography to contextualize her response to the film within her South Carolina familial
roots. For Claiborne, the film offers both context and content for appreciating the
craft of quilting and understanding the Black women fabric artists who preserved
their rich and layered lives through this cultural tradition. Of the connections she
sees between her family's story and that of the Peazants', she writes:

> Although not from one of the coastal Sea Islands, my maternal grandmother's family rec-
> ognized African retentions at work in their culture because of the relative low influence of
> white culture in Johnsonville, South Carolina. It was the pride in these African retentions
> that gave my grandmother, for example, the ability to defy convention and go to college
> and, until very late in her life, to refuse to let a white man or any "buckra" ever step foot on
> her property. It is the same strength and employment of African retentions—spiritual and
> natural—that allows Nana Peazant to reject the movement off the island. (76)

Ultimately, Claiborne contends that Dash, like the quilters of her film and
countless other Gullah quilters, pieces together a colorful and intricate narrative
that documents and preserves the story of her people.

PART 3—THE SACRED EMERGE: THE WITNESS, THE HEALED, AND *DAUGHTERS OF THE DUST*

In Chapter Six, "'I Arrived Late to This Book': Teaching Sociology with Julie
Dash's *Daughters of the Dust*, the Novel," anthropologist, Karen M. Gagne, recounts
her experiences reading Dash's novel of the same title and then later teaching both
the film and novel to college students. Unlike the other contributors to this volume, Gagne "arrived late" to both the novel and the film. She asserts that through
the Peazant story, "Dash makes a critical intervention against Western academia"

(87). Together, the novel, film, and Dash's other text, *Daughters of the Dust: The Making of an African American Woman's Film* make:

> An invaluable contribution towards the understanding of the lives of Africans in the New World. [They make] plain the connection between the Gullah Geechee people of the Sea Islands and all Africans in the diaspora, those who moved North and those who live in the South—in the Caribbean and the Americas. (86)

Chapter Seven, Sharon Johnson's "Conscious Daughters: Psychological Migration, Individuation, and the Declaration of Black Female Identity in *Daughters of the Dust*," explores both the novel, the film, and the Peazant family's migration to the mainland as "a metaphor for psychological migration, the movement of the psyche as it necessarily separates from the Mother, incubates as the Unborn Child, and informs, shapes, and defines the emergent Black female identity" (101).

In her examination of the characters Iona, Eula, and Yellow Mary, Johnson suggests "[t]heir imminent geographical migration from Ibo Landing reveals the more difficult psychological migration away from Mother(s): Nana Peazant, Haagar, and Viola" (101). Using Jungian psychology as a research framework, Johnson speculates intergenerational division between the Peazant women regarding the family's decision to leave Ibo's Landing springs from the "forward-striving libido which rules the conscious mind [and] demands separation from the mother" (Jung quoted in Johnson see page 101). Further through her analysis of the mother-daughter relationship of Haagar and her daughters, Johnson contends, "it is between these tensions of the aspects of the Mother archetype that the Unborn Child incubates" (104).

In Chapter Eight, "Reading Nana Peazant's Palms: Punctuating Readings of Blue," Tiffany Lethabo King takes on the layered meanings and cultural influences infused in Dash's film. For Lethabo King, Dash's cinematic homage to syncretized African-diasporan spirituality acts as a decolonized healing work of art that celebrates the African ancestors and rejects the Western gaze. Of the film she writes the following:

> The stills and moving images of the film enable an alternative form of looking, perceiving, and sensing that calls attention to the limitations of Western colonial vision. Paying close attention to the way Dash uses the camera, styles and marks the bodies of actors, references Yoruba cosmologies, and marshals sound and other senses, one can discern a synesthetic visuality that runs counter to the imperious visual regime of settler colonial North America. (110)

Thus, Dash's film "frustrates and at times ruptures settler colonial modes of sight," rendering message and meaning incomprehensible to those who would objectify and taxonimize her characters. In doing so, "Dash's cinematic eye that uses sight as a synesthetic mode of knowledge production also pushes back against sight as a site of epistemic truth" (113).

PART 4—THE POWER OF PLACE IN SHAPING IDENTITY AND ARTISTIC CULTIVATION

Chapter Nine, Marcella De Veaux's "In Search of Solid Ground: Oral Histories of the Great Migration, from the Carolinas to New England," uses oral histories she collected of Black New Englanders whose families had migrated from different parts of the North and the South, including cities like Charleston, South Carolina, from where her own father had migrated, to examine the spiritual, cultural, and psychological impetus and impact such decisions had on the migrants and their subsequent progeny. Further, for the Peazants and other African Americans who left their homes in the South during The Great Migration, one's connection to geography of origin is often complicated, yielding visceral longing, vivid memories, and varied feelings of joy, pain, and sorrow. De Veaux anchors her understanding of what her informants tell her of their memories of leaving their homes and set-tling in New England in spiritual and psychological frameworks. Accordingly, she argues:

> For Nana, the soil represents her connection to her ancestors. Similarly, for descendants of West Africa, the relationship to the living and spiritual world, the land, the landscape, and its natural resources are a basic condition for such a spiritual connection. (129)

In other words, those who remain behind become the bridge by which those who have left can return when they are longing for home.

In Chapter Ten, "Motherlands as Gendered Spaces: Cultural Identity, Mythic Memory, and Wholeness in Julie Dash's *Daughters of the Dust*," Silvia Castro-Bor-rego employs post-colonial and Black feminist theories to argue Dash "consciously created her characters to challenge the icons of the dominant Western culture" (135). Castro-Borrego contends that both the film and the eponymous novel, *Daughters of the Dust*, "become *motherlands* where identity and family history can be traced through memory, storytelling, ancestry, and myth" (135). Like writer Paule Marshall, Castro-Borrego suggests Dash, too, uses the aforementioned ele-ments as a tool for healing, agency, and empowerment.

Collectively, the essays assembled here pay tribute to Julie Dash's iconic film, which continues to inspire moviegoers, filmmakers, and scholars alike. As the first film by an African American woman filmmaker to open with a national release, *Daughters of the Dust* has earned its place within the canon of American and Inde-pendent film for that reason alone. More importantly; however, is its international influence on people of African and African-disasporan descent, who, for the very first time, really saw themselves in film. Dash's iconic film continues to stand the test of time as one of the greatest films ever made. Julie Dash, like the film, continues to make her mark on not just American cinema, but also in the discourse on Black women's creative expression and lived experiences. For that, we should all be grateful.

REFERENCES

Bogle, Donald. 2001. *Toms, Coons, Mulattoes, Mammies, and Bucks: An Interpretive History of Blacks in American Films*. New York: The Continuum International Publishing Group.

Boyd, Valerie. 1991. "*Daughters of the Dust* (movie reviews)." *American Visions* 6, no. 1 (February): 46–8.

Coats, Joel. 2012. "Travel, Dislocation, and Community in *Daughters of the Dust*." *Film Matters* 3 no. 2 (Summer): 52.

Cucinella, Catherine and Renee R. Curry. 2001. "Exiled at Home: *Daughters of the Dust* and the Many Post-Colonial Conditions." *MELUS* 26, no. 4 (Winter): 197–221.

Dash, Julie, dir. 1991. *Daughters of the Dust*. 1991. New York, NY: Kino International.

———. 1992. *Daughters of the Dust: The Making of an African American Woman's Film*. New York: The New Press.

Davis, Cienna. 2017. "From Colorism to Conjurings: Tracing the Dust in Beyoncé's *Lemonade*." *Taboo: The Journal of Culture and Education* 16, no. 2 (September): 7–28. https://doi.org/10.31390/taboo.16.2.04.

Diawara, Manthia. 2000. "Black American Cinema: The New Realism." *Film and Theory: An Anthology*, edited by Robert Stam and Toby Miller, 236–256. Malden, MA: Blackwell Publishers.

Gaither, Laura. 1996. "Close-up and Slow Motion in Julie Dash's *Daughters of the Dust*." *The Howard Journal of Communications* 7, no. 2 (April–June): 103–112. https://doi.org/10.1080/10646179609361717.

Garcia, Claire Oberon. 1994. "A Black Woman Teaches Black Writers to White Students." *Education Digest* 60, no. 2 (October): 37–38.

Garret, Daniel. 2014. "Where Redemption Is Found: We Are What These Years in This Place Have Made Us, and Must Learn to Live with That." *Film International* 12, no. 2 (June): 58–70. https://doi.org/10.1386/fiin.12.2.58_1.

Guerrero, Ed. 1993. *Framing Blackness: The African American Image in Film*. Philadelphia: Temple University Press.

hooks, bell. (1984) 2000. *Feminist Theory: From Margin to Center*. Boston: South End Press.

Martin, Michael T. 2010. "'I Do Exist': From 'Black Insurgent' to Negotiating the Hollywood Divide—A Conversation with Julie Dash." *Cinema Journal* 49, no. 2 (Winter): 1–16. https://doi.org/10.1353/cj.0.0186.

Ogunleye, Foluke. 2007. "Transcending the 'Dust': African American Filmmakers Preserving the 'Glimpse of the Eternal.'" *College Literature* 34, no. 1 (Winter): 156–173. https://doi.org/10.1353/lit.2007.0008.

Omolade, Barbara. 1993. "A Black Feminist Pedagogy." *Women's Studies Quarterly* 21, no. 3/4 (Fall/Winter): 31–38. http://www.jstor.org/stable/40022003.

Reid, Mark A. 2005. *Black Lenses, Black Voices: African American Film Now*. Lanham, MD: Rowman & Littlefield Publishers, Inc.

Ryan, Judylyn S. 2005. *Spirituality as Ideology in Black Women's Film and Literature*. Charlottesville: University of Virginia Press.

Silva, Kathryn M. 2018. "Daughters and Sons of the Dust: The Challenges of Accuracy in African American." *The History Teacher* 51, no. 2 (February): 247–267.

Sudhinaraset, Pacharee. 2018. "'We Are Not an Organically City People': Black Modernity and the Afterimages of Julie Dash's *Daughters of the Dust*." *The Black Scholar* 48, no. 3 (July): 46–60. https://doi.org/10.1080/00064246.2018.1475836.

West, Elizabeth J. 2011. *African Spirituality in Black Women's Fiction: Threaded Visions of Memory, Community, Nature, and Being*. Lanham, MD: Lexington Books.

Wood, Peter. 1974. *Black Majority: Negroes in Colonial South Carolina from 1670 through the Stono Rebellion*. New York. Alfred A. Knopf.

Capturing the Canon: Julie Dash and the Black Arts and Black Feminist Traditions

CHAPTER ONE

Memory, Meaning, and Gullah Sensibilities

The Black Art Aesthetics of Julie Dash and Jonathan Green

PATRICIA WILLIAMS LESSANE

Take 3: Cinema, 1991. Julie Dash announces early in *Daughters of the Dust* her stance regarding the great American afflictions, amnesia and disconnectedness. The film begins with three injunctions to remember the past: the *Black Gnostic* is quoted, the Ibo phrase for "remember" is chanted, an elder's hand sculling the waters of time is repeated. It is not long before the Ibo tale is recited and begins to function as both evidence of, and argument for, cultural continuity.

—Toni Cade Bambara, Preface to *Daughters of the Dust: The Making of an African American Woman's Film* (Dash 1992, xii)

In her preface to Julie Dash's retrospective on the making of *Daughters of the Dust*, cultural worker and Black feminist Toni Cade Bambara prophesizes that in the near future, *Daughters*[1] would occupy more than cult status, and would one day be deemed a classic. Bambara's wisdom and foresight about the film are rooted in her belief in the power of the African spirit and its influence on pan-African identity, literary, artistic, and cinematic expression for generations to come. Public interest in the film resurged in 2016, with Cohen Media announcing the restoration and global re-release of the film to theaters for its 25th anniversary. Additionally, R&B artist and cultural icon Beyoncé paid tribute to the iconic film in her 2016 award-winning visual album, *Lemonade*. Like Dash, Beyoncé *and* Bambara acknowledge the ancestral, cultural, and ontological impacts Africa has had on cultural production by people of African descent throughout the diaspora. For example, Bambara reminds us of Paule Marshall's memorable character, Avey,[2] who must shirk off her middle-class sensibilities in order to remember and embrace her familial and ancestral bonds to Tatum, South Carolina, and ultimately to West Africa. Only then can she be whole. Memory, therefore, plays an important role not only in the preservation of one's cultural traditions, but also in the preservation of one's whole self. Cultural memory—those lived and those passed down—girds the individual within the non-linear cycle of life, ensuring the guidance, the wisdom, the protection, and the *axé* needed for self-determination and agency. Employing memory as a spiritual and cultural construct is a concept we find throughout West African and African diasporan art, literature, and film. Zora Neale Hurston's *Their Eyes Were Watching God* (1937); Toni Cade Bambara's *The Salt Eaters* (1980); Paule Marshall's *Praisesong for the Widow* (1983); Gayl Jones's *Corregidora* (1975); Toni Morrison's *Beloved* (1987); Ntozake Shange's *For Colored Girls Who Have Considered Suicide/When the Rainbow Is Enuf* (1975); Malidoma Patrice Somé's *Of Water and Spirit: Ritual, Magic, and Initiation in the Life of an African Shaman* (1994); Charles Burnett's *To Sleep with Anger* (1990); Kasi Lemmons's *Eve's Bayou* (1997); Haile Gerima's *Sankofa* (1993); and August Wilson's *The Piano Lesson* (1987) and *Joe Turner's Come and Gone* (1984) all situate memory as a conduit for personal and collective healing.

In *Framing Blackness: The African American Image in Film*, Black film scholar and critic Ed Guerrero praises the complexity and beauty of Dash's film, predicting her film will get the popular reception it demands over time (Guerrero 1993, 176). In 2011, the College of Charleston's Avery Research Center for African American History and Culture, along with countless other cultural centers, film centers, and colleges and universities, celebrated the 20th anniversary of *Daughters*. At the Avery Research Center, over 100 scholars, students, artists, filmmakers, and cinephiles gathered at a symposium to celebrate Dash and her film. It seems Bambara and Guerrero were correct in their assessment of this film's importance in Black film and American cinema, in general.

Black scholars, artists, and film critics continue to note this importance of *Daughters of the Dust* and Dash's place as cultural and spiritual griot. Her film pieces together parts of the disparate African experience on this side of the Atlantic. Judylyn S. Ryan (2005), Elizabeth J. West (2011), and Anissa Janine Wardi (2011) have examined memory and spirituality in the works of African American women's literature and film. According to West (2011, 11):

> In the history of African American literature, we find a legacy of women's writings that draw on the physical and experiential to explore matters of spirituality. This tradition of spiritual musings is guided by four principles central to pre–Middle Passage African cosmology: 1) the value of memory to both individual and group well-being; 2) the belief that community represents the essence of human existence and being; 3) the view that nature—both animate and inanimate—represents divineness; and 4) belief in the interconnectedness of worldly and other worldly beings. These principles are integral to Black epistemological and ontological thought, pre- and post–Middle Passage and are central to

shaping a tradition of spiritual exploration in Black women's writing. African American writers from Wheatley to Morrison integrate these themes in their work, signaling the early maintenance and integration of an African worldview among displaced Africans and the important role of women as carriers of culture.

In her chapter "Between Breath and Death," Wardi expounds on this idea in her examination of water and memory in *Daughters* (2011, 49):

> The disjunction between inheriting the past and moving beyond a life on the water is at the heart of the film, as the family's relocation to the mainland threatens community cohesion by potentially engendering cultural amnesia, a process of forgetting the water and the ghosts that permanently inhabit its shore. Water is not merely the site of history, it is an embodiment of history, a body of water that encarnalizes slavery, the Ibos' act of resistance, and generations of the Peazant family's travails.

By forgetting the sacred water surrounding Ibo Landing, the Peazants run the risk of forgetting their syncretic cultural and spiritual footing. "[Accordingly],[3] the expanded representation of diverse religious practices within this Gullah community is yet another way in which the film expresses an ethos of [familial, ancestral, spiritual, and kinship][4] interconnectedness" (Ryan 2005, 136). Similarly, Jonathan Green's *Gullah Images* embodies another way of remembrance through canvas and paint instead of celluloid and lens.

This essay examines memory, meaning, and Gullah sensibilities in Dash's film and Green's book of 150 paintings through their devotion to the celebration and preservation of this unique African American culture. In the same way Nana Peazant preserves the familial, cultural, ancestral, and spiritual roots of her family, Dash and Green both occupy a similar space of griot and high priesthood. Their work reflects their familial and ancestral connection to Gullah culture exemplified in their depiction of drylongso life, kinship, gastronomy, spirituality, folklore, and traditions and functions as the lens through which we can see and experience Black sea island culture. By returning to their Gullah roots "from off,"[5] Dash and Green bring their unique experiences as worldly, professionally trained "New World" Africans to their interpretation of Gullah culture.

As an anthropologist, I am most interested in the customs, rituals, and real-life experiences of the drylongso and their connection to Lowcountry history and geography. Everywhere I look, I am reminded of the beautiful cinematography of *Daughters* and the people and scenes immortalized in the paintings of Jonathan Green. The Gullah dialect is still spoken in private and public spaces. Grocery store cashiers will often ask *Au una du*,[6] church choirs and funeral attendees can often be heard singing the Gullah hymn, "You Better Answer to Your Name," and Gullah-infused delicacies—including red rice, and shrimp and grits—are commonplace in most, if not all, of Charleston's finest restaurants.

In *Gullah Culture in America*, researcher Wilbur Cross uses historical narratives and oral interviews to examine Gullah culture—past and present—and observes cultural continuities identified by Lorenzo Dow Turner (2002), Peter Wood (1974), and Joseph Opala (1987) still easily identifiable today. In the face of pervasive and systemic racism, rising unemployment, industry loss, gentrification of the peninsula, and the overdevelopment of these pristine Sea Islands, Gullah culture prevails today contrary to predictions made by scholars some years back.

> Only a few years ago observers were warning that Gullah was a dying culture. More than one specialist in this field estimated that there was little chance that this culture could long survive because of the rapid growth of the urban areas, the decline of farming and rural communities, and the influx of outsiders whose interest was mainly in vacationing, leisure homes, and commercial development. The isolation of Gullah communities was steadily breaking down, sparked by young people finding jobs in the cities and older people dying off. But then something happened. Instead of the culture dying as one magazine article after another warned in the direst of terms, cultural activists rose up in the community to extol their culture. These activists pointed to the danger of their cultural roots dying, to be sure, but they also highlighted the community's continuing vibrance. (Cross 2008, 18)

With its tropical weather, sandy beaches, vast marshlands, and exotic wildlife, the South Carolina Lowcountry has become the darling of giant real estate developers hoping to secure another Kiawah Island or Hilton Head Island for the rich and the retired. In both cases, many African Americans fell victim to predatory developers and lost prime heirs' property, which are now sites of neo-Charleston mansions situated on Lowcountry beachfronts. The memories of such insidious behavior on the parts of developers and elected officials are singed onto the memories of Gullah people from Wilmington, North Carolina, to Jacksonville, Florida. Reading the "handwriting on the wall," many in the community have joined together to hold back the tides of big development and the displacement of thousands of Black people living in the Lowcountry. Grassroots activists such as Emory Campbell,[7] Marquetta Goodwine,[8] Ron Daise,[9] and Michael Allen[10] have worked alongside Congressperson James Clyburn to establish the National Gullah Geechee Heritage Corridor.[11] Their work, along with that of Dash and Green, are part of ongoing efforts to preserve and sustain Gullah culture.

In many ways, *Daughters* and *Gullah Images* are complementary creative ethnographies, reflexive examinations of Gullah culture made stronger by memories, oral histories, and cultural traditions still visible throughout the Lowcountry today. Significant work has revealed the place of memory and spirituality in the work of African American women writers and filmmakers. In her investigation of the importance of water and African American memory in *Daughters* and Ntozake Shange's *Sassafrass, Cypress & Indigo* (1982), Wardi positions the Atlantic Ocean as the vehicle through which Gullah culture was born and the actual mechanism

through which and on which communal Gullah memory is inscribed and preserved. Similarly, as a member of the second-wave L.A. Rebellion, Dash invokes
ancestral and collective memory as a counter-narrative to traditional Hollywood
productions. Her narrative and life's work are one born out of a need to tell the
litany of untold Black experiences—the customs, rituals, and traditions—that continue to preserve and sustain African American culture and history. Therefore, it
is not surprising then that with *Daughters*, Dash gives voice to the silenced stories
of her ancestors whose lives add to our understanding of this part of Americana.
Dash's work is layered, vivid, and replete with cultural and spiritual syncretism.
Memory not only resurrects the forgotten past, it girds one firmly in the cycle of
life, establishing an emotional and spiritual foundation from which to draw on. In
this manner, remembering becomes a path for healing each of the women carries
within them, and thus they are the spiritual anchors for the community. Along
these same lines, Ryan (2005, 2) "realized that spirituality was not simply an aspect
of the characters' lives but had explicit functions in advancing the [Black female][12]
artist's vision."

Sheila S. Walker's afrogenic approach and Paul Gilroy's (1995) theoretical
framing of the Black Atlantic inform this investigation of Julie Dash and Jonathan Green. In her edited volume, *African Roots/American Cultures: Africa in the*

Figure 1.1: Nana Pondering

Creation of the Americas, cultural anthropologist Walker (2001, 8) suggests the afrogenic scholar brings all of one's lived and ancestral experiences to bear on one's discovery, examination, understanding, and celebration of African diasporan history and culture.

> Afrogenic simply means growing out of the histories, ways of being and knowing, and interpretations and interpretive styles of African and African Diasporan peoples. It refers to these communities' experiences, priorities, styles, and their articulations of them while acknowledging that most human behavior is not intellectually articulated by the actors who perform it and that plural interpretations of similar behaviors are obviously possible.
>
> Afrogenic also refers to the interpretations and interpretive methods of African and African diasporan scholars as a result of our roles as community members whose academic positionality is necessarily mediated by this belonging. The perspectives and methodologies of these scholars manifest a creative tension resulting from our being products of the epistemologies and hermeneutics—the ways of authoritative knowing and interpreting—of our own communities, and of having also medicated through these primary sources other, sometimes competing or incompatible, epistemologies and hermeneutics encountered in the academy.

Accordingly, the beauty, authenticity, and value of Dash's and Green's interpretations of Gullah life lie in their positions as insiders and by virtue of their experiences "from off." Their travels, academic training, and artistic vision inform their identities just as much as their Gullah roots, and vice versa. What we find in their work reflects the cultural syncretism in Gullah culture, and a Gullah hermeneutics that privileges memory, water, land, color, family, spirituality, agriculture, oral traditions, and utilitarian art. Unlike Mr. Snead's camera that simply captures and preserves the image of the Peazant family, Gullah hermeneutics *is* the kaleidoscope through which we see and interpret Gullah culture. In other words, Dash inculcates the complex spiritual systems, unique cultural sensibilities, and the lived and remembered experiences of Gullah people in every line, scene, and frame, thus endowing the viewer with the spiritual eyes to see, understand, and become her characters. Similarly, the faceless drylongso of Green's canvases reflect the *esprit de corps* of the Gullah people of his childhood and recollections.

Further, while Dash's film informs our appreciation for Green's prolific body of art, his work, likewise, informs our understanding of *Daughters*. Together, their work is the foundation for a Gullah hermeneutics. Examined together, they elucidate the hidden meanings, forgotten memories, and syncretic Gullah sensibilities imbued in Dash's film and Green's canvases. Their position as native/insider artist girds them with the special ability to *see* and to be the conduits through which Gullah memories, sensibilities, and meaning are transmitted, explored, and proscribed. In an article about the work of Green, the late noted art collector Carroll Greene remarks the following:

Green's most vivid memories of Gullah life are culled from the 1960s. "I can remember things as a child that are gone now, such as hair wrapping, men weaving fishing nets, farming, and hunting. There is very little of these activities going on now. What fishing and hunting that goes on is mainly sport and not out of necessity as before." […] Green's background provides him with an insider's understanding of the Gullah people and their traditions. For instance, in *Tales*, the artist shows a group of men at the end of the day gathered under a huge live oak listening in varying degrees to the yarns of the storyteller. The scene is a continuation of the strong African oral tradition transplanted to America. Another painting, *Banking Yams*, illustrates an unusual method of storing yams by putting them in little huts made of dried corn stalks and straw. Through art at least, such traditions will be preserved. (Greene 1990, 47)

Through Dash and Green, we are endowed with the *axé*—the spiritual eyes and tools to remember, see, and discern the Gullah culture. In her autobiographical essay, "Making *Daughters of the Dust*," Dash (Dash 1992, 5) reveals her vision and goals for the film, as well as her family's hesitance to discuss some aspects of the past:

The stories from my own family sparked the idea of *Daughters* and formed the basis for some of the characters. But when I probed relatives for information about the family history in South Carolina, or about our migration north to New York, they were often reluctant to discuss it. When things got too personal, too close to memories they didn't want to reveal, they would close up, push me away, tell me to go ask someone else. I knew then that the images I wanted to show, the story I wanted to tell, had to touch an audience the way it touched my family. It had to take them back, inside their family memories, inside our collective memories.

By invoking memory, Dash and Green preserve and assign meaning to Gullah cultural sensibilities, thereby establishing a Gullah hermeneutics. Their work reflects the diverse influences on and multiple consciousness at work in Black Atlantic identity and cultural production. Dash looked beyond American cinema for inspiration and technical direction, having been inspired by Russian and Latin American film, Black Power, and the liberation movements of African people throughout the continent. Black film critic and scholar Donald Bogle counts Dash amongst a group of African American filmmakers on the 1990s who "invigorate American films with a new perspective" (Bogle 2001, 324). Likewise, Green melds his childhood memories of life in the Lowcountry with an appreciation of Western art to create images of Gullah life that are enchanting, timeless, and robust.

Contemporaries in age, Dash and Green both have roots in the South Carolina rice culture. Dash, born in Long Island City, New York, in 1952. Growing up, Dash spent summers in Charleston, where her extended family regaled her with stories about Black Charleston, Gullah culture, and Sea Island living. These stories would become the foundation and creative inspiration for her first major film:

The original concept for *Daughters* was a short silent film about the migration of an African American family from the Sea Islands off the South Carolina mainland to the mainland and then to the North. I envisioned it was kind of "Last Supper" before migration and the separation of the family. The idea first began to wander throughout my head about 1975, while I was still at AFI. I was making notes from stories and phrases I heard around my family, and became fascinated by a series of James Van Der Zee photos at the turn of the century. The images and ideas combined and grew. (Dash 1992, 4)

Jonathan Green was born "with a veil over his eye," and always knew there was a special calling on his life. Raised in the Lowcountry village of Gardens Corner, a small town between Charleston and St. Helena Island, the "caul" over his eye endowed him with spiritual gifts, including an understanding of visions and the ability to "see" the unseen. Like many youngsters, Green did not gain an appreciation for his culture until he went away and experienced life out in the world. After a stint with the Air Force, Green obtained a Bachelor of Fine Arts degree from the School of the Art Institute of Chicago in 1982. Green has spent his entire career capturing the Gullah culture of his youth amid big developers' growing interest in the pristine southeast coastal landscape who hope to fleece the once-rich bastion of Gullah life for economic gain. Together, Green and Dash enable the viewer to see and experience Gullah culture and the convergence of the past/present and African/African diasporan through their eyes.

THE PAST IS PROLOGUE: THE POWER OF MEMORY IN GULLAH CULTURE

With *Daughters*, Dash acknowledges the non-linear concept of time present in many West African spiritual modalities. Narration by the unborn and unseen child exemplifies the symbiotic relationship between the past and the present, the yet born and those passed on. Dash suggests the experiences and lessons of the past—specifically those shared by the African ancestors—have the power to guide, sustain, and empower Gullah people. In one of the most poignant scenes in *Daughters*, the family matriarch, healer, and griot Nana Peazant admonishes Eli Peazant to call on his ancestors for strength, guidance, and wisdom as he embarks on a new life with his wife and newborn child, on the mainland. More pointedly, Nana suggests such guidance will come through specific, vivid, and surreal memories, both personal and collective, rooted in ancestral connections:

Eli, never forget who we is and how far we done come. Eli! Eli, there's a thought, a recollection, something somebody remembers. We carry these memories inside of we! Do you believe that those hundreds and hundreds of Africans brought on this side would forget once knew? We don't know where the recollection comes from. Sometimes we dream'em, but we carry these memories inside of we.[13]

As Eli struggles with the knowledge that his wife, Eula, has been raped by a white man and is possibly pregnant by her assailant, he questions the folk traditions and cultural beliefs that preserved the Gullah culture and maintained the cohesion of their isolated community. Recognizing his broken spirit and doubt about his own manhood, Nana directs him to his memories and dreams, those places where the ancient ancestors and spiritual guides reside ready for human access. Up until this point, Nana has acted as high priestess, griot, and protector for the Peazant family. Sensing the impeding and rapid changes on the horizon, she reminds Eli of the spiritual and cultural tools he needs for his survival and that of his lineage in the new world. Nana preaches and endeavors to teach Eli how to minister himself and be the spiritual anchor for his family, "Eli [...] I'm trying to teach you how to touch your own spirit. I'm fighting for my life, Eli, and I'm fighting for yours"

Figure 1.2: Eli Pondering

(Dash 1992, 96). Her sermon is inspired by her fears and apprehensions about the emerging changes her family will face when they leave the island. That she directs him to turn within and not to some sacred text, points to the dialectical tension between syncretic Gullah spiritual customs and Christianity—more specifically The Black Church—that is expanding and thriving throughout the mainland and the north at the turn of the 20th century.

Through the Peazant women, Dash channels the stories of their rich history. Their shared memories are encapsulated in casual conversations and emotional testimonies that bear witness to what it means to be a "Gullah 'oman" in 1902. If Nana's assessment that "the ancestors and the womb are one," then women are endowed with a special ability to tap the spirit through "thoughts, recollections, something somebody remembers." Dash acknowledges the untold experiences of Black women and "creates a rich, absorbing tableau in which were cast African American actresses of various colors (Barbara O, Alva Rogers, Kaycee Moore) and perspectives who helped break the mold in which Black women have traditionally been portrayed" (Bogle 2001, 349). Writing in the tradition of her Black feminist predecessors and contemporaries, such as Zora Neale Hurston, Alice Walker, Gloria Naylor, Toni Morrison, Toni Cade Bambara, and bell hooks, Dash recognizes the peculiar religiosity—the spiritual synergy of Christian and pan-African spirituality and cosmology—at work in Black women's lives. Similarly, Mark A. Reid writes, "in the early 1970s, Julie Dash, Alile Sharon, Haile Gerima and other independent Black independent filmmakers established cinematic strategies that used female-centered narratives that articulated a Black womanist vision" (Reid 2005, 86). Through Nana, we witness the power of Black women's religiosity; but through Eula and Yellow Mary, we learn it resides within the deep wells of our memories and is always accessible to us.

Dash situates memory and ancestral reverence as vehicles for cultural and spiritual protection and personal guidance. By invoking a non-linear approach to time in the film, Dash asserts the "ancestors and the womb are one" and life and death are part of our human experiences as spiritual beings. Nana Peazant reminds Eli of this spiritual truth when he visits her in the graveyard.

Eli hands Nana tobacco and she cradles it in her BLUE-STAINED hands.

NANA PEAZANT
(serious now, indicating the grave)
I visit with old Peazant every day
since the day he died.
It's up to the living to keep
in touch with the dead, Eli.
Man's power doesn't end
with death. We just move on to a new
place, a place where we watch over our living family[...]

When Nana is possessed by the spirit, she admonishes Eli to remember his cultural roots and trust the internal spiritual guidance instilled in by his ancestors.

She is being taken into a spiritual possession. We continue to hear Nana Peazants words.

> NANA PEAZANT (O.S.)
> Those in this grave, like those
> Who're across the sea, they're
> With us. They're all the same.
>
> NANA PEAZANT (CONT'D)
> The ancestors and the womb are one.
> Call on your ancestors, Eli. Let
> them guide you. You need their
> strength. Eli, I need you to make
> the family strong again, like we
> used to be (Dash 1992, 94–95).

Conversely, Eula and Yellow Mary represent a modern embodiment of Gullah women's religiosity. Although Eula has always lived on Ibo's Landing, she has come of age during Reconstruction and the Industrial Revolution. By virtue of her age, she represents the dialectic between the traditional ways and modernization. Still, Eula clings to the old customs, and her pregnant body becomes the bridge between the old (Ibo Landing/Nana) and the new (the mainland/her unborn child). Through Eula, Dash underscores the place of ritual, prophetic vision, and spiritual possession in Gullah culture, and by extension, Black women's lives. The following exchange between Eula and Yellow Mary exemplifies the complexities of such synergies at work.

CLOSE ON EULA

> EULA
> (whispering to herself)
> Agua ... Agua.
> (then)
> My Ma came to me last night, you
> Know. She took me by the hand.

ON YELLOW MARY

Lounging in the curve of the tree. Yellow Mary studies Eula a few beats, then

> YELLOW MARY
> (soberly)
> Your titty's been dead
> A long time, Eula.

ON EULA

> EULA
> (explaining)

> I needed to see my Ma. I needed
> To talk to her. So I wrote her
> A letter, put it beneath the bed
> With a glass of water, and I
> Waited. I waited and my Ma
> Came to me. She came to me right
> away (Dash 1992, 119).

Here, Eula invokes a Southern Black folk ritual for contacting one's ancestors. While this ritual is not solely unique to Gullah culture, Dash employs it to emphasize the reverential place of ancestors in Black Sea Island spirituality and sensibilities. Further in the film, Dash reveals the conflict between the old folk ways and the burgeoning modern world on the mainland. Consequently, with modernity comes questions about the veracity of Gullah sensibilities and folk tradition, and these tensions are born out in the women's personal experiences, fears, and hopes for the future.

This is most evident with Yellow Mary, who returns home after years of struggling to survive in the North. She has worked as a domestic, prostitute, and nursemaid for a white family, and has experienced her share of abuse, subjugation, and isolation. Personifying the Yemanja archetype,[14] Yellow Mary has also seen the world and all its splendor, and returns home with her female lover, Trula. Yellow Mary embodies the fluidity of sexual identity and the complexity of Black Atlantic identity. Though she rejects the old ways, Yellow Mary returns to Gullah remedies to "fix the titty" (Dash 1992, 126), liberating herself from the family that has held her captive. And while she mocks Eula's reliance on her Gullah sensibilities, calling her "a real back-water Geechee girl!," she recognizes her own need to return to Ibo's Landing, to return home. Yellow Mary sees herself most in Eula.

Interestingly, Eula comes to Yellow Mary's defense when the other women reject her as one of their own. Eula's testimony about the vulnerability Black women face and the shame they hold as a result of rape, isolation, separation, and slavery speaks to their fears of being "ruin't" themselves. Echoing the wisdom of Nana Peazant, Eula beseeches these women to honor their Gullah roots and respect one another as women bound by sacred and ancestral ties. Here, Dash stands on the work of Black feminists Frances Beale, Deborah King, and Kimberlé Crenshaw to underscore the significance of intersectionality—the convergence of race, class, and gender—on Black women's lives. And though the film is set at the turn of the 20th century, the Peazant women personify the real-life struggles contemporary African American women continue to face. As such, Dash's characters are timely and timeless, giving voice to the ethos of women who have been relegated to the margins of history, literature, and the backdrops of American cinema.

Figure 1.3: Yellow Mary

Furthermore, through Eula, Dash establishes a Gullah hermeneutics rooted in the stories and folk traditions passed down through the Dash family, informed by her own understanding of African and pan-African cosmology and her experience as a Black feminist. Dash is deliberate in her incorporation of conjure—the plastering of newspaper on the walls of Eli and Eula's house, the spiritual "hand" Nana prepares for the family to take with them, and Eula's ritual to access her deceased mother—and of African cosmology, Trula embodying the Yorubu/Vodoun goddess Oshun: Eli as Ogun, Nana as Obatala, Eula as Oya Yansa, and Yellow Mary as the water goddess Yemanja. Dash also interrogates the ideological, methodological, and theological tensions between Christianity and pan-African religion and cosmology. This is most evident when Viola and Haagar reject the power of Nana's protective "hand." While Viola capitulates a bit at the urging of the photographer, Mr. Snead, Haagar refuses to kiss the hand and walks away from Nana, and essentially away from her Gullah past. In the margins of the screenplay, Dash scribbled, "Viola attempts to escape from her history and the trauma of her second-class citizenship within her newfound religious beliefs" (Dash 1992, 45). Viola and Haagar see their liberation only possible through their rejection of Gullah ways. By leaving Ibo's Landing, they hope to experience all the treasures and opportunities modernity offers. However, Nana knows the world they will encounter "won't be no land of milk and honey" as they envision.

Thus, Dash takes us back to the water.

GULLAH IMAGES: FROM MOVING PICTURES TO STILL LIFE

Published in 1995 by University of South Carolina Press, *Gullah Images: The Art of Jonathan Green* is Green's celebration and personal testimony about the Gullah culture that nurtured him as a youth. A compilation of 150 stunning images of Gullah life, it is perhaps Green's most important body of work to date. Green captures the essence of the drylongso, or ordinary folk, in their everyday-ness. There are fishermen, farmers, young children, full-bodied women, virile men, stately exhorters, audacious lovers, pretty girls, and handsome boys. They are dark as night and unapologetically Black. They are working, talking, loving, living, and being laid to rest. They are ensconced on a landscape of "hain't" blues and starched whites, and are everywhere surrounded by water. They are tangible, ethereal, and mythical at the same time. Are these *really* Gullah people of the Lowcountry one might ask? At a glance, they remind us of Paul Gauguin's Tahitian ladies; at others, the migrating masses of Jacob Lawrence's *Migration* series. Yet at all times, they are Green's people—those living, working, and making magic in the deep wells of his memories. In *Solitude*, 12″ × 16″; *Two Girls with Wash*, 24″ × 47″; *Canary Yellow Hat*, 12″ × 16″; *Viewing the Wash*, 12″ × 16″; *White Moon*, 48″ × 60″; *Wind Blown Sheets*, 36″ × 48″; *Broom Grass*, 48″ × 60″; *Sweet Grass Nursery*, 36″ × 48″; *Widow Wash*, 12″ × 24″; *The Black Hat*, 12″ × 24″; and *Flying Hat*, 48″ × 60″, (Green 1996) Green uses oil on canvas to depict the multi-hued Gullah women we see in *Daughters*. With deep colors and rich details reminiscent of Gauguin and Lawrence, Green immortalizes the Gullah women of his youth. Green's women in their starched white dresses recall the Peazant women in *Daughters*. They heal, cajole, proselytize, and serenade us in the fields and in the praise house. Could that be Haagar and her daughters tilling the fields in *Green Tomatoes*? Is that Yellow Mary as a succulent Yemanja in *Blue Shadows*? In *Three Hats*, a young, nubile girl listens attentively to the exchange between two of her elders. Green contrasts her blue-Black skin with that of the lighter-skinned women. Could Green have imagined Eula, Trula, and Yellow Mary in this way?

Green's people are secular, and yet they occupy sacred spaces at the same time. Green implies the cultural dichotomies of work/play, life/death, sacred/profane, religion/spirituality, utility/beauty, water/healing, and memory/survival are complementary binaries at work in Gullah culture. They are tied to their ancestral lands—Edisto, Kiawah, Fripp, and St. Helena Islands, just to name a few—and they are united by the sacred waters that brought their ancestors ashore from as far away as West Africa, Europe, and the Caribbean. Thus, the water and the land both figure prominently in Green's work. It was the water that brought them here, carrying with them the memory and customs of the ancestors, and it is the land that has sustained them.

Figure 1.4: Haagar

Through their efforts to document and celebrate Gullah heritage, Julie Dash and Jonathan Green have established a Gullah hermeneutics for understanding memory, ancestor reverence, and African retentions and sensibilities in Gullah culture. Their personal memories and family stories give birth to the people and the scenes captured in their frames and canvass. Like the unborn child in *Daughters*, they are ushered in on the primordial, gestational waters of their memories. Their magic, strength, and power reside in their willingness and ability to recall, to recollect, and to remember.

NOTES

1. From this point on, I refer to the film simply as *"Daughters."*
2. Avey is the protagonist in *Praisesong for the Widow*.
3. Bracketed text mine.
4. Bracketed text mine.
5. Lowcountry term denoting a place off the island or peninsula.
6. Gullah for "How y'all doing?"
7. Native of Hilton Head Island, Gullah activist, and former executive director of the Penn Center on St. Helena Island.
8. Self-proclaimed chieftess of the Gullah Geechee nation.
9. Actor and developer of *Gullah Gullah Island* television show and former chairman of the National Gullah Geechee Heritage Commission.

10. Founding member of the National Gullah Geechee Heritage Commission.
11. The Gullah Geechee Cultural Heritage Corridor was established by an act of Congress on October 12, 2006, under Public Law 109–338 and was designated as part of the National Heritage Areas Act of 2006.
12. Brackets mine.
13. Nana's monologue as spoken in the film. Further in the paper, I include passages from the actual screenplay.
14. Yoruba female deity that personifies beauty, healing, and motherhood.

REFERENCES

Bogle, Donald. 2001. *Toms, Coons, Mulattoes, Mammies, and Bucks: An Interpretive History of Blacks in American Films.* New York: The Continuum International Publishing Group.

Cross, Wilbur. 2008. *Gullah Culture in America.* Westport, CT: Praeger.

Dash, Julie. 1992. *Daughters of the Dust: The Making of an African American Woman's Film.* New York: The New Press.

Gilroy, Paul. 1995. *The Black Atlantic: Modernity and Double-Consciousness.* Cambridge: Harvard University Press.

Green, Jonathan. 1996. *Gullah Images: The Art of Jonathan Green.* Columbia: University of South Carolina Press.

Greene, Carroll Jr. 1990. "Artist Jonathan Green Comes Home." *American Visions: The Magazine of Afro-American Culture* 5, no. 1 (February): 44–52.

Guerrero, Ed. 1993. *Framing Blackness: The African American Image in Film.* Philadelphia, PA: Temple University Press.

Opala, Joseph A. 1987. *The Gullah: Rice, Slavery, and the Sierra Leone-American Connection.* Washington, DC: United States Information Service.

Reid, Mark A. 2005. *Black Lenses, Black Voices: African American Film Now.* Lanham, MD: Rowman & Littlefield Publishers, Inc.

Ryan, Judylyn S. 2005. *Spirituality as Ideology in Black Women's Film and Literature.* Charlottesville: University of Virginia Press.

Turner, Lorenzo Dow. 2002. *Africanisms in the Gullah Dialect.* Columbia: University of South Carolina Press.

Walker, Sheila S., ed. 2001. *African Roots/American Cultures: Africa in the Creation of the Americas.* Lanham, MD: Rowman & Littlefield Publishers.

Wardi, Anissa Janine. 2011. *Water and African American Memory: An Ecocritical Perspective.* Gainesville: University Press of Florida.

West, Elizabeth J. 2011. *African Spirituality in Black Women's Fiction: Threaded Visions of Memory, Community, Nature, and Being.* Lanham, MD: Lexington Books.

Wood, Peter. 1974. *Black Majority: Negroes in Colonial South Carolina from 1670 through the Stono Rebellion.* New York. Alfred A. Knopf.

CHAPTER TWO

Inspiration in the Dark Space

Julie Dash's Re-Visioning of Time and Place in *Daughters of the Dust*

AYANA I. KARANJA

INTRODUCTION: A PREVIEW—FRAMES FROM A MOVING TRAIN

Between 1879 and 1957, 150 Black women were lynched[1] in America. During this New World epoch, the lynching of Black people was the death sentence of choice executed by white mobs, and state and local officials, particularly in the American South. The drama associated with lynching drew large groups of spectators to this ritualized performance of public murder, all too frequently of Black bodies, because Black people had been enslaved until the 1860s and had been categorized as white property. Black people, having been considered human cargo imported from Africa for their labor, were unprotected by law and a large and productive free labor force devoid of any and all civil liberties. Because of this, lynchings became a brand of capital punishment and a bizarre form of spectator sport, irrespective of the Black body's gender. Some Black women hanged during this era were even pregnant.[2] This singular fact speaks volumes about the violence historically inflicted upon the Black woman, both physically and psychologically, across time and space in America.

In the 21st century, a modernized version of yesteryear's gendered power politics has emerged with the aim to police the Black woman's body.[3] Violence against Black women is widespread across publics and institutions, and many unresolved deaths typically pass unrecorded as "causes unknown."[4] Indeed, various forms of sociopolitical death and danger imperil the Black female body, and the Black woman remains a target of personal violence, denigration, and dissent.[5] Social critiques of the Black female include dishonorable views of her body and behavior—too fat, too dark, too white-appearing, too loud—and are always measures of her lack or excess. Whether Black women are considered Jezebels, witches, or societal schemers taking off with taxpayer dollars, this segment of the population continues to be a topic of negative public commentary and sociological discourses. These and other queries are linked in ongoing conversations and critiques of Black womanhood in America.

However, this essay interrogates the conflagration of three specific sociopolitical forces that my research suggests weighed upon Dash's filmic representation of a particular community of Black women situated at a specific historical moment, *Daughters of the Dust* (1992). I argue these particular historical events and/or social forces profoundly impacted Dash's critical womanist consciousness: The Black Arts Movement in America, the often-called "L. A. Rebellion Group of Black Filmmakers" at UCLA, and Black Feminist theory and thought as represented in Black women's literary productions during the early 1970s through the 1980s.

Daughters of the Dust is a filmic endeavor of indelible cultural and political significance. In her cinematic depiction of this community of Black women, one experiences a wide range of ideational frameworks as represented across the personalities and worldviews of the Peazant women. Dash locates the Peazant family in a historically significant setting, its elegy unfolding in non-linear time 1902. The film's location is one among several island tracts of land—geographically known as the Sea Islands—that runs parallel to North Carolina, South Carolina, Georgia, and Florida in the southeastern portion of the United States. It is significant to note that the importation of Africans to the region in the 17th–19th centuries was an early factor in the cultural development of South Carolina Lowcountry culture.[6] Additionally, this cluster of islands was the site of an American experiment involving newly transported, enslaved Africans to the New World to be the primary workforce on cotton, rice, and indigo plantations on the Sea Islands. Noteworthy, too, is Dash's familial history and her fascination with stories told about these islands. In *Daughters of the Dust: The Making of An African American Woman's Film*, Dash (1992, 5) writes:

> The stories from my own family sparked the idea of *Daughters* and formed the basis for some of the characters. But when I probed my relatives for information about the family in South Carolina, or about our migration north to New York, they were often reluctant to discuss it.[7]

From an ethnographic standpoint, the cultural practices and linguistic uniqueness of the Sea Islands' imported Africans also contribute to the history of Black bodies as sites for American experimental protocols, both medical and social in nature. In one instance, the Port Royal Experiment was conducted on the

Sea Islands beginning in 1862 when Union troops freed some 10,000 formerly enslaved Black people during the American Civil War. The government's stated purpose of this experiment was to determine what might be the social, political, and cultural outcomes for an isolated community of formerly enslaved Africans and their progeny should such a community *remain* relatively isolated from mainland society. Civil War battles between the Union Army in the adjacent states—North and South Carolina, and Georgia—caused nearly all of the white citizens to flee, leaving their enslaved human workforce behind to fend for themselves.[8] Thus, African Sea Islanders were virtually untouched by the day-to-day influences of Euro-American mainstream culture and lifestyle for a significant period of time.[9] Following white flight during the Civil War, the U.S. government was interested in determining whether a community of formerly enslaved Black people possessed the wherewithal to meet the challenges of survival, to sustain life and community in the absence of their former overseers who fled the region in the heat of the Civil War.

An example of the field work with which Africans were tasked on the Sea Islands is evidenced in Dash's cinematic matriarch's stained hands. Nana Peazant's hands are physical remnants of plantation labor in indigo agriculture, a plant product associated with early 20th century Sea Island economy. Nana Peazant's hands also call to mind the ways in which Black bodies were *purposefully* marked or "branded" on slave ships sailing from Africa to the Americas. Such branding also served as an indelible body mark or tracer to aid white authority in tracking and identifying Black runaways from slavery.[10] Thus, branding was a form of hyper-identification to reveal Black people's status and the site to which a specific Black body belonged. Otherwise, Black people were virtually *invisible*, amorphous entities in the landscape.

The setting of Dash's film is 1902, post-Reconstruction America, an era during which thousands of Black people left the American South for Northern urban centers in search of employment and a better way of life. Many Black migrants rightly feared white lynch mobs' anger and terrifying vitriol in the South; still others responded to promises of greater social freedom, wage-based employment, and upward social mobility. Thus, the back-story of Dash's film is rooted in historical reality with lamentable accuracy. By narrowing her lens on a single day in the fictionalized life of one Black family—extrapolated from among the thousands of African American kinship groups and individuals that embarked upon a similar adventure, collectively forming a steady stream northward at the turn of the 20th century—Dash captures the internal dialogue and anxious moments that were, no doubt, the real-life experiences of many migrants whose mass out-migration from the agrarian American South to industrialized Northern and Western urban centers became known historically as the "Great Migration."[11] Dash's cinematic work anticipates this social reality as a socioeconomic and psychological conundrum.[12]

To be sure, Dash's film signifies upon the larger historical experiences of the visual meaning of Blackness in America; that is to say, the nature of the white "gaze" directed at Black bodies—or what bell hooks refers to as the "oppositional gaze"—"one that 'looks' to document" (Browne 10). In a socio-historical context, Black people are rendered invisible to White eyes, or, adversely, highly visible to agents of the state.

In one widely read work of fiction, the writer explores this dichotomous visible/invisible dimension of the Euro-American body politic wherein this dominant class 'sees'/is color-blinded by circumstances and social forms society has created that denigrate human Blackness, quoting Ralph Ellison, Avery F. Gordon (2008, 17)[13] writes:

> In a 1981 introduction to *Invisible Man*, Ralph Ellison wrote: "despite the bland assertions of sociologists [the] 'high visibility' [of the African-American man] actually rendered one *un*-visible. [...] His darkness ... glow[ing] ... within the American conscience with such intensity that most whites feigned moral blindness toward his predicament." (xii)

If Ellison's argument encourages an interrogation of the mechanisms by which high Black visibility may actually become a type of *invisibility*, then Toni Morrison's (1992) assertion that "invisible things are not necessarily 'not there,'" encourages the complementary investigation of how what appears to be absent may indeed bear a seething presence.[14] From an aesthetic standpoint, and unparalleled in modern cinematic history, Julie Dash's *Daughters of the Dust* gives the spectator a powerful array of profoundly *visible* Black, female "in-your-face" beauty grounded in artistic veracity such that many viewers of this visual phenomenon are overpowered by the large-screen images of "unapologetically Black" female Blackness. The women in this filmic treatise represent a plethora of possibilities that comprise Black female physical beauty, consciousness, interiority and "body mindfulness." *Daughters of the Dust* is at once a powerful artistic rendering, a cultural polemic, and a revolutionary powder keg. The artistry, rhapsodic mise-en-scène converges upon the spectator's vision and is nearly overwhelming. The unprepared spectator may well experience a form of *culture shock*—far too much Blackness to consume on a widescreen that envelops the viewer in aesthetic profundity. Dash's *Daughters of the Dust* is experienced through a multiplicity of Black female phenotypes whose moral registers range from the innocent of innocents—the film's central interlocutor, the Unborn Child—to the purveyor of African-centered wisdom, the familial elder Nana Peazant. As a consequence of intersectionalities portrayed as multiple female generations—the Unborn Child, her pregnant mother/vessel, Eula, and Nana Peazant—Dash's storytelling, writ large, displays a reframing of images and discourses that surround the socio-historical meanings attached to cinematic imagery of Black womanhood.

Dash could not have chosen a more appropriate land and seascape as a geographical space in which to record her enigmatically beautiful cinematic work. The Sea Islands are a naturally occurring terrestrial and water-washed land and seascape of undulating sand mounds with an oceanic backdrop and sapphire sky that provide the perfect environment against which Dash superimposes a kaleidoscopic range of Black women's skin hues, representative of the true color palette one might find among a group of randomly selected African American women. The absolute beauty of these women, the colors of nature that feature the soft earth tones that surround human images in this film, soften even the reality of those anxious filmic moments that depict a Sea Island family's "Last Supper"—like picnic together on the afternoon prior to the migration of most members of the clan who will leave the familial compound the next day to begin life anew on the American mainland. Their northward migration will interrupt the linearity and history of this clan's experience of connectedness on the island and their familial oneness across space and time. This, then, is an elegiac moment in the history of the Peazants, a pre-migration, ritual moment, an anxiously contemplated movement of a group of women who are variously centered in African customs, behaviors, and belief systems to American urbanity. Clearly, Dash engaged in extensive research and study of West African ritual behaviors and thought systems dating back distant millennia in preparation for this filmic event.[15] Dash's emphasis of Nana Peazant, the elder and sage of the family, is one such indication, among others.

As a result of early cultural contact with white plantation owners for whom Sea Island Africans labored, and from whom they encountered the English language on a daily basis, there emerged among the enslaved community a creolized version of their West African mother tongues overlaid with the English as spoken by their overseers. These Africans, the early Black inhabitants of the region, are often referred to in everyday nomenclature and in literature concerning the period as "salt water Negroes" or "Geechees." Their language, a patois spoken in this isolated community is a synergetic homology of West African tongues and American English. Dash's filmic island community is also known as part of South Carolina Lowcountry. The film's central interlocutor is the family's matriarch and great-grandmother, Nana Peazant. Nana knows little of mainstream American society, yet she fears the spatial breakup of her family. She implores her children to take their old ways with them to their new urban destination, as she senses it to be a site of danger, a place of wantoness and uncertainty. In times of such peril, she calls on the African deities with which she is familiar and asks for protection of departing loved ones. Nana Peazant summons a pantheon of African gods and goddesses, which were passed down to her from previous generations, that she so deeply honors and cherishes.[16] Her faith shows an embedded sense of relationship between herself and the spirit world of African orishas and ancestral cults. Moreover, Dash inculcates such West African ritualistic traditions and employs a cosmology that is unequivocally West African in origin into her film. For example, Eli, the central male in the Peazant family, suffers great discomfort, anger, and frustration as he fears the child in his wife's womb is the result of a rape by a nefarious white man on the island. As a means to calm his angst and anger, Nana implores Eli to turn to the only protection she has ever known: a West African ancestral cult. Drawing on the pantheon of African deities,[17] she advises Eli, "the ancestors and the womb are one. Call on your ancestors, Eli. Let them guide you. You need their strength" (Dash 1992, 95).[18] Even with change upon the horizon for her family, Nana Peazant manages her own daily life and countenances the future through ancient African forms of thought.

Dash's cinematic work is studied and intentional in its referential treatment of African tradition. The many visual and linguistic references to West African culture and tradition mark this film in ways that reveal a deep knowledge and obvious research into significant African traditional cosmologies, which, for some spectators, are likely *unintelligible* in their filmic grasp of her storytelling and narration strategies. Unless the spectator has the ability to comprehend Nana Peazant's constant references to ancient African cultural beliefs and the power she attributes to these traditions, much of the deeper meaning of the film will be lost. Primary among African-centered references, Dash engages the narrative voice and *consciousness* of the Unborn Child who "speaks," though still in her mother's womb, as a significant storytelling strategy. The Unborn Child is a primary interlocutor of events throughout the film. Thus, Dash makes use of African storytelling technique in the non-linear mode of unfolding life events—fusing the past, present, and future. The Unborn Child, herself, complicates her parents' relationship because her mother's husband, Eli, holds suspicion and angst that his wife's pregnancy is the result of a white man's rape. Miscegenation is also inferred in the film by the presence of the character Yellow Mary, a very light-complexioned Black woman—read mulatto—who years earlier left the familial island compound only to find herself engaged in prostitution on the mainland.

Indeed, an African cultural aesthetic bears heavily upon the spectator of *Daughters of the Dust*, and this aesthetic impacts the *intelligibility* of the predominant visual aesthetic and linguistic patterns engaged throughout the film. Nana Peazant's precious "hand,"[19] the bottle trees, chalked tree trunks, and other preserved pieces of hair and torn fabric are significant storytelling strategies that reference an African past memorialized throughout the film. A mesmerizing musical score, the slowed-down frame sequences—a departure even from urban life in 1902—enhances the film's visual magnificence.

America, is in no way in keeping with the fast-paced life of postmodernity as seen in the Unborn Child's stereoscopic view of urban dwellers rushing about on the mainland. These are among the dynamic aspects of the film. The costuming is reminiscent of times past, as is Dash's emphasis on the use of "Geechee" language rather than standard English. Taken as a whole, these are among the elements that confer a somewhat "foreign film" resonance on Dash's cinematic artistry.

The following three sections express the results of my research on the major forces impacting the film work of Julie Dash, specifically *Daughters of the Dust*.

THE BLACK ARTS MOVEMENT

> Black Art is the aesthetic and spiritual sister of the Black Power concept. [...] Both relate broadly to the Afro-American's desire for self-determination and nationhood. Both concepts are nationalistic. One is concerned with the relationship between art and politics, the other with the art of politics. (Neal 2000, 236)

In the context of independent and non-mainstream oppositional filmmaking, I argue the cultural artist's imagination must push beyond the boundaries of the everyday experiences of its subject towards a projected measure of optimism. Many of the productions rendered by Black and Third World artists align with this notion in one way or another. In this connection, then, one might reasonably posit the range of Black artistic productions available today stretches from representations of imported Africans' early New World experiences with dehumanization to contemporary alternative reality work—the latter of which is often referred to as "the Black fantastic" (Iton 2008, 16). To this point, Iton notes the words of Toni Morrison, award-winning novelist,[20] essayist, and cultural critic, "The work that I do frequently falls, in the minds of most people, into that realm of fiction called fantastic or mythic, or magical, or unbelievable. [...] I'm not uncomfortable with these labels" (Iton 2008, 11).

Indeed, some will argue *Daughters of the Dust* falls into the category of the "mythic" or "unbelievable," or even counter-cultural, particularly for viewers who are underexposed, uninformed, or unstudied in African and African American cultural history and aesthetics. Nevertheless, it is with purpose and intention that Dash uses several culture-historical representations that may be traced even as far back as before Europe's sustained contact with West Africa. Thus, *Daughters of the Dust* may well present an unintelligible narrative read for the underexposed spectator.[21] Further, when one adds this representational challenge to the visually awe-inspiring filmic presentation of diverse Black female phenotypes, few of which align with Euro-Hollywood perceptions of female beauty, a critical point in the deeper meaning and aesthetics of Dash's work may be underappreciated. I want to suggest here the notion that as a student studying independent Black filmmaking at UCLA during the period conterminous with the Black Power and Black Arts Movements in America (1960–1970s), Dash produced a work that falls well within the cultural and political oeuvre of that historical epoch in both

Black independent filmmaking in America and in Third World cinema.[22] An over-whelming number of viewers of *Daughters of the Dust,* however, may lack aware-ness of the sociopolitical environment from which Julie Dash emerged. As one of the more important voices in the world of Black artistic endeavors in the 1960s and 1970s, Larry Neal (1971, 272) asserted:

> Black Art is the aesthetic and spiritual sister of the Black Power concept. [...] Both relate broadly to the Afro-American's desire for self-determination and nationhood. [...] One is concerned with the relationship between art and politics; the other with the art of politics. (Emphasis in text, p. 86)[23]

Other forms of economic and political consciousness were also expressed in the 1960s and 1970s, such as Black Studies programs in colleges and universi-ties, Black-owned and produced journals, and Black arts-based institutions. While leadership and inspiration for these and other endeavors remain somewhat debat-able, on the Black Arts side, Amiri Baraka is often credited for having initiated the Black Arts Movement[24] through his articulated focus on the propagation of a *Black aesthetic.* For example, Richard Iton (2008, 87) writes of Baraka's influence in Black Arts Movement:

> Of all the figures associated with the Black Arts movement, Jones most effectively con-verted his prominence in cultural circles into political capital. [...] Jones was the pacesetter with regard to Black cultural and political developments in the 1960s and early 1970s, and more specifically he was responsible for the alignment of Black politics and popular culture, for their synchronic engagement.[25]

As a Black woman, Julie Dash occupies a distinguishing place within the larger framework of African American independent cinema for the tenacity she demonstrated in successfully pursuing the financial support required to produce a feature-length film.[26] *Daughters of the Dust* complicates notions of Black wom-anhood, providing spectators a view of Black female images that straddle time, space, and phenotype that stand in objection to Hollywood's mythologized, sim-plistic stereotypical images of Black and brown female characters—the nannies, jezebels, and whores.[27] Dash's women represent a range of Black female physical looks, beliefs, and political standpoints, thereby rendering full the true-life, phe-nomenal embodiment of the psycho-social life-worlds inhabited by Black women. Further, as writer and director, Dash collapses the space between fictional repre-sentations and historical truth through Black women's hairstyles, dress design, and speech patterns, and, more importantly, interiority. Formidable, too, is the hom-age this filmic *tour de force* pays to contemporaries and predecessors within the world of Black independent filmmaking while pointing toward the global nature of filmic endeavors by other non-Hollywood filmmakers, such as the works of Third Cinema.[28]

THE "L.A. REBELLION GROUP" OF BLACK FILMMAKERS

When we speak of a "Black aesthetic" several things are meant. First, we assume that there is already in existence the basis for such an aesthetic. Essentially, it consists of an African-American cultural tradition. But this aesthetic is finally, by implication, broader than that tradition. It encompasses most of the usable elements of the Third World culture. The motive behind the Black aesthetic is the destruction of the white thing, the destruction of white ideas, and white ways of looking at the world. (Neal 2000, 237)

Why Julie Dash? Why *Daughters of the Dust*? Notably, while Dash was born in New York City, her father was a migrant from the Sea Islands of Georgia, the geographical site on which *Daughters of the Dust* was filmed. No doubt Dash was familiar with, if not fascinated by, many aspects of Gullah culture, many derived from family memories. If we locate the Civil Rights Movement in the American context, brought to national attention by Rosa Parks, Dr. Martin Luther King Jr., and others in America's South between 1955 and 1968, and acknowledge freedom struggles and anti-colonial, anti-imperialist movements springing up across the African continent and beyond during this same period, it becomes clear civil rights struggles against oppression and racial domination in America were ripe for exploration and resistance within a burgeoning Black independent film school, one such as Julie Dash and other critically conscious filmmakers experienced at UCLA in the 1970s–1980s. Women and men who studied at UCLA film school, in or around the same period as Dash are also counted among producers of counter-hegemonic cinematic work. Collectively, Dash, and several other colleagues are often referred to in the literature[29] as the L.A. Rebellion Group.[30]

The antecedents and major influences on the cultural consciousness of the L.A. Rebellion Group emerged as but one dimension of the artistic parallels born of civil rights initiatives and the Black Power Movement, and from which all manner of Black cultural products grew roots, most especially Black arts.

In this connection, consider the widespread impact of the Civil Rights Movement[31] on the imaginative production among Black artists in America during and following the apex of this social movement. While many nationally highlighted events occurred in the American South, the work of civil rights activists occurred all throughout North America, and extended beyond these borders. Protest marches, freedom rides, and sit-ins at lunch counters and other public spaces found mobs police actions against protestors, many of whom were women, as they endured injuries and even death as they fought for human rights and social justice in this era. The Watts Rebellion in Los Angeles was also a major hot spot in 1965.[32] While some have condemned the larger Civil Rights Movement for the marginalized roles foisted upon many Black women, the influence of women in two other significant forms of social protest also: the Black Power Movement and its ideological artistic twin, the Black Arts Movement. It is with great difficulty that one may totally disentangle the key personalities and *political agendas* of each of these latter organizations, but, unlike the parent Civil Rights Movement, the Black Arts Movement widely embraced and uplifted women's artistic contributions.[33]

In this work, focus is given to the Black Arts Movement—those individuals who as creative artists embraced significant ideological stances, arguing that Black artistic endeavors must encompass revolutionary, life-altering messages against the forces of imperialism and oppression.[34] The Black Arts Movement, as a collective, embraced the fullness of Black creative arts—literature, dance, popular music, and other forms of cultural expression and representation, including independent Black filmmaking. Significant in this connection is the fact that Julie Dash was a student among those filmmakers that became known by some as the L.A. Rebellion Group[35] of Black independent filmmakers. These women and men studied at UCLA Film School at Berkeley in the 1970s–1980s many in the aftermath of the marches, rallies, and other forms of social protest against inequality and violence against communities of color. Clearly, then, Dash's work at UCLA followed shortly after the apex of the social action and political work associated with the Black Arts Movement.

From the standpoint of culture and method, UCLA film school students, many of whom were women of color, acquired or expanded their political consciousness and artistic philosophy—particularly so under the instruction of Teshome Gabriel[36] who articulated a strong philosophy of purpose for oppressed and underdeveloped world communities. For example:

> Gabriel posits four main purposes of an aesthetics of liberation: to decolonize minds, to contribute to the development of a radical consciousness, to lead to a revolutionary transformation of society, and to develop new film language with which to accomplish these tasks. [...] For Gabriel, a key concern of Third Cinema practitioners is not in "aestheticizing ideology" but in "politicizing cinema." [...] 'The principal characteristic of Third Cinema is really not so much where it is made [...] but, rather, the ideology it espouses and the consciousness it displays.' [...] The struggle against imperialism and class oppression was no less important in the United States, even if it was not immediately recognized as such, and the L.A. Rebellion filmmakers sought to align their work with global anti-imperialist fights. (Field, Horak, Stewart 2015, 23)

No doubt Dash's *Daughters of the Dust* displays a filmic sensibility directly reflective of such ideology, as she strongly associates Black, Southern lifeways with West African traditions. In this connection, she also foregrounds the familial and communal conflicts that often prevail between African religious epistemologies and the beliefs that white missionaries to Africa grafted onto extant indigenous belief systems. In this way, Dash participated in the cinematic work and philosophic orientation that guided the anti-establishment, counter-hegemonic principles embraced by Black independent filmmakers in opposition to mainstream Hollywood film productions.

The L.A. Rebellion Group embraced and evidenced influences emergent from the Black Arts Movement with their revolutionary use of historical African art forms, poetry, and theater as agents of social change. Whatever might have been Dash's consciousness of civil rights issues in America, I argue Dash's artistic sensibility and cultural consciousness grew deeper by way of emersion in film study at UCLA, which was strongly reflective of philosophical stances and historical realities embedded in the film school curriculum and the agents of critical, political, and social change that were advanced in an institutional, cyclical manner. As such, both faculty and students were innovative and socially conscious:

> In contradistinction to Hollywood [...] *all* filmmakers in the L.A. Collective deployed *cine-memory* to foreground and memorialize thematic concerns constituting a "form of repository or archive, memory recuperates, documents and parses experience. It comprises images, sounds, meanings, gestures, and aural utterances" in order to illumine and critique the present in the past. (Field, Horak, and Stewart, 203)[37]

JULIE DASH AND BLACK FEMINISM

In 1831 Maria W. Stewart asked, "How long shall the fair daughters of Africa be compelled to bury their minds and talents beneath a load of iron pots and kettles?" (Collins 1990, 3). I want to argue here that the emerging energy from various feminisms and sites of women's consciousness movements of the 1970s and 1990s within and beyond the U.S. was equally as powerful as the influences of the Black Arts Movement and the L.A. Rebellion Group on Dash's filmic work. Specifically stated, *Daughters of the Dust* bears the indelible markings of Black female standpoint theory and literary consciousness as demonstrated in Black women's fictional and nonfictional writing. The presence of a feminist worldview appears central to her artistic perception as she eschews historical unflattering views of Black womanhood. To this point, Patricia Hill Collins's exemplary text, *Black Feminist Thought: Knowledge, Consciousness, and the Politics of Empowerment* (1990) was published a mere two years before Dash completed her film. Beginning in the late 1970s and moving forward to the present era, women of color worldwide have strengthened their voices against various cultural forms of patriarchy, and the world has witnessed their burgeoning and active political stances across the broader artistic terrain. This consciousness and activism exist in the broadest terms—including literatures, film, and many other artistic assemblages. This is not to suggest a level of acceptance of mainstream notions of Black womanhood by the Black female masses in times past, but rather to posit an alignment of Dash's representations of Black womanhood with Black women's artistic renderings, those that reflect either formal or informal engagement with Black feminist standpoint theory. Collins (1990, 227) provides three important levels on which individuals resist domination and with which I find Dash's *Daughters of the Dust* to be well aligned: the level of personal biography; the group or community level of the cultural context created by race, class, and gender; and the systemic level of social institutions.[38] In each of these contexts, Dash's filmic representations of Black women's motivations, beliefs, and evidenced interiority are contiguous with these assemblages.

Dash's cinematic oeuvre, however, pays deep homage to the historical place and power attributed to African women, particularly the works by female literary artists of prior and contemporaneous periods. For example, examining the more widely read products of Black female literary artists' imaginaries—writers such as Zora Neale Hurston, Alice Walker, Toni Cade Bambara, and Toni Morrison—the corpus of their collective literary productions form antecedents to Dash's cinematic women. Indeed, these literary artists' references to and reverence for historical, aural, and oral conventions that assert African female power is abundantly clear. In her own words, Dash asserts these Black female literary influences of the 1970s and 1980s on her filmic sensibility, such as the writings of Toni Cade Bambara. Dash compares the strategies she employed in *Daughters of the Dust* to Bambara's literary artistry, which she notes bears similarity to her own filmic frames:

> [The story would] come in and go out and come in, very much in the way of Toni Cade Bambara's [literary] work one character would be speaking to another and then it goes off on a tangent for several pages and then she brings it back and goes out and back again. (Humm 1997, 121)

Dash goes further in her acknowledgement of the influence of Black women writers on *Daughters of the Dust*. Pointedly, she declared (Humm 1997, 126):

> [H]er debt to Black women's literature and to its celebration of the very special role women play in the work of retrieval. "Discrepancies across space, across the Black Atlantic: in the new world it is the women who have become Griots (religious story tellers) of their culture. It was the literature of Black women in the early 1970s that inspired me to become a filmmaker of dramatic narratives. Before that I made documentaries, but after reading Toni Cade Bambara, Alice Walker, Toni Morrison, *I wanted to tell those kinds of stories. [...]They made me whole.*" (My emphasis).[39]

The tradition of Black and brown women storytellers is to imbue their heroines with salutary strength and character, if not supernatural power. Thus, Dash's Nana Peazant is scripted from within a wider universe of African female wisewomen; and through her aesthetic sense of things, the use of interior monologue, and ritualistic behaviors, *Daughters of the Dust* underscores the historical and cultural repertoires of Black people in the diaspora and points towards a centuries-long history of pre–New World beliefs and practices.

CONCLUSION

This essay is an attempt to draw conclusions about the influences and social forces that were strong in the creation of a particular form of artistic endeavor: the creation of Julie Dash's film, *Daughters of the Dust*. At best, this effort becomes a literary insinuation, for only the artist is truly aware of the absolute impetuses and conditions that have inspired the production of her work. As theorists and others offer opinions about an artist's internal motivation and the external forces that combine in a way such that images or sound may be produced, the authenticity of internal and external forces that are the deepest impulses for an artist's work are known only to the producer of the product. In this instance, I have drawn upon three major sources from which my research suggests Julie Dash's development as a Black female filmmaker draws power: Black female embodiment impacted by Black feminist consciousness; the historic Black Arts Movement; and mentorship and study at the UCLA film school. Most pointedly, this essay infers persistence in the forms of female power and energy Dash aggregates to advance her vision of a political, artful, Black womanist feature-length film. For as is noted in Trinh T. Minha-Ha (1991, 230)[40]:

> Art *is* political. But one also has to understand that the uses to which it is put are not its meaning. Its status as object and commodity is not its meaning: there are many objects and commodities. They are not all art. What makes art different? Exactly the ways in which it is not an object, can never in its nature be a commodity.

NOTES

1. For more detailed information on this tragic circumstance, see, for example: Iya Marilyn Kai Jewett, "Remembering Our Sisters: Black Women Lynched," Henrietta Vinton Davis's Weblog (online blog), February 27, 2015, http://henriettavintondavis.wordpress.com/2015/02/27/remembering-our-sisters.
2. See the following website for names and related information in connection with lynched Black women of this period. Retrieved July 4, 2016: http://www.abibitumikasa.com/forums/oppression-afrikans-socially/42055-black-women-who-were-lynched-america.html.
3. See, for example, Hazel V. Carby, "Policing the Black Woman's Body in an Urban Context," *Critical Inquiry* 18, no. 4 (Summer 1992): 738–755.
4. In a recent report on women in American jails, Melissa Jeltsen of the *HuffPost* writes about the scandalous increase in the number of women, noting that in 1978, fewer than 8,000 women were incarcerated in American jails. "By 2014, that number had skyrocketed to nearly 110,000," according to a report by the Vera Institute of Justice and the Safety and Justice Challenge. Women in jail are mostly Black and Hispanic, and overwhelmingly poor and low income. Melissa Jeltsen, "Women in Jail Are Fastest Growing Segment of America's Incarcerated Population," *Huff-Post*, August 17, 2016, Politics, https://www.huffpost.com/entry/women-jail_n_57b1e69de4b-007c36e4f692f?ncid=engmodushpmg00000004.

5. For example, in *Outlaw Culture: Resisting Representations*, cultural critic bell hooks suggests gansta rap is a reflection of the values in American society, owing to the existence of white supremacist capitalist patriarchy.

6. For a deeper understanding of the enslaved Africans' role in developing Lowcountry culture, see "Africans in the Low Country," National Park Service (website), accessed July 5, 2016, https://www.nps.gov/ethnography/aah/aaheritage/lowCountryA.htm.

7. See Julie Dash, Toni Cade Bambara, and bell hooks, 1992.

8. Although there is rather scant historical evidence of intimate relationships between American Natives and African Americans, Dash's film makes clear that not only were there interactions between African Americans and American Natives in the region, but also points toward the serious nature of some such relationships.

9. During the Civil War, the Union Army liberated the Sea Islands and Port Royal. Most white plantation owners fled, leaving behind 10,000 formerly enslaved Black people. Ultimately, in 1865, President Andrew Johnson ended the experiment and returned the land to its previous white owners. "Port Royal Experiment," Wikipedia (website), accessed June 11, 2019, https://en.wikipedia.org/wiki/Port_Royal_Experiment.

10. See Simone Browne's *Dark Matters: On the Surveillance of Blackness*.

11. The Great Migration was the mass movement of some five million Southern Black people to American Northern and Western cities between 1915 and 1960. See, for example, Stephanie Christensen, "The Great Migration (1915–1960)," BlackPast (website), December 7, 2007, http://www.blackpast.org/aah/great-migration-1915-1960.

12. Many Black Americans whose familial roots are in the American South appear to hold a love/hate relationship with their natal region. Some speak longingly of the connection they and their forebearers held with an agrarian way of life—one more in keeping with the familial ways of West African culture. Other factors that point toward nostalgia include a sentiment related to the beauty of a less denatured landscape, a more leisurely life pace, and a prevailing lifestyle that fosters familial interaction. Apart from the taking of Africans from their ancestral homeland, the separation of Black families during the Great Migration remains a major factor in the disruption of traditional forms of Black family life that prevail even into the present moment.

13. Avery F. Gordon, *Ghostly Matters: Haunting and the Sociological Imagination* (Minneapolis: University of Minnesota Press), 17.

14. Toni Morrison, *Playing in the Dark: Whiteness and the Literary Imagination* (Cambridge: Harvard University Press).

15. From an African socio-historical standpoint, elder women are respected and revered by all members of the community.

16. Dash shows here a line of connection in sacred belief systems brought to the New World by enslaved Africans. The nuances of these belief systems remain a part of some African American religious practices and worship behaviors.

17. The beliefs and ritual behaviors deeply rooted in Dash's film bear strong resemblance to those embraced by the Yoruba of West Africa.

18. Julie Dash, *Daughters of the Dust: The Making of an African American Woman's Film* (New York: The New Press).

19. A "hand" is a good luck charm or amulet. In some African communities, a hand is a small packet of materials such as hair clippings, magic charms, dirt, and other materials derived from the natural environment and are believed to bring good fortune.

20. Morrison's award-winning and haunting novel, *Beloved*, was adapted as a cinematic drama in 1998.

21. For example, among the Wolof women of West Africa (Senegal), women's verbal performances related to identity—*taasu*—and praise are historical. *Taasu* is also an oral meditative practice through which various disputes are resolved. Nana Peazant's verbal performances call to mind Wolof women and *taasu*. See Lisa McNee, *Selfish Gifts: Senegalese Women's Autobiographical Discourses* (Albany: State University of New York Press).

22. For an in-depth discussion of Third Cinema, see, "Introduction, Emancipating the Image" (Field, Horak, and Stewart 2015, 1–55).

23. Larry Neal's essay "The Black Arts Movement" is found in *The Black Aesthetic* (Gayle 1971).

24. Baraka (formerly LeRoi Jones) as discussed in Iton's *In Search of the Black Fantastic: Politics and Popular Culture in the Post–Civil Rights Era* (2008, 85).

25. For a full explication of the impact of the Civil Rights Movement on Black cultural arts, see Richard Iton's *In Search of the Black Fantastic: Politics and Popular Culture in the Post–Civil Rights Era.*

26. While Dash is the focus of this work, she is one among other accomplished Black female filmmakers, such as Zenibu irene Davis, Jacqueline Frazier, and Barbara McCullough.

27. See, for example, Shauna Weides, "Mammy, Jezebel, Sapphire, or Queen? Stereotypes of the African-American Female," Great Plains Skeptic (website), April 28, 2015, http://www.skepticink.com/gps/2015/04/28/mammy-jezebel-sapphire-or-queen-stereotypes-of-the-african-american-female/. Such stereotypes have long prevailed, both in and out of film and fiction. Indeed, since the beginning of West Africa's contact with Europe, the Black woman has been caricatured and deemed more a curiosity than a woman—a strange and exotic thing to be toyed with, duped, and controlled. Two such examples: Sojourner Truth, the African-American heroine who was compelled to publicly bear her breast to *prove* her femininity—her womanhood—as she exclaimed, "aren't I a woman"?, to the so-called "Hottentot Venus," a South African woman whose mother named her Sara Baartman, but who became the caged, 'in-the-flesh' icon of the Black female sexualized savage of 19th-century Europe. See Elizabeth Alexander (2004); also Patricia Hill Collins (1990, 168–169).

28. *L.A. Rebellion* contextualizes an eloquent summarization of Third Cinema by Kim Dodge, "Third Cinema is, above all, to interrogate 'structures of power, particularly colonialism and its legacies'; contribute [...] to the 'liberation of the oppressed, whether [...] based on gender, class, race, religion, or ethnicity'[...]" (Fields, Horak, and Stewart 2015, 201).

29. For names and cinematic productions of others studying at UCLA shortly before or after Dash, see Field, Horak, and Stewart's *L.A. Rebellion: Creating a New Black Cinema.*

30. *Ibid.*

31. For a thorough examination of the Black Arts Movement, see "Chapter 3: Nation Time," in Iton.

32. During a six-day period, August 11–17, 1965, nearly 4,000 protesters were arrested and 34 were killed.

33. See Jacqueline Najuma Stewart, *Migrating to the Movies Cinema and Black Urban Modernity.*

34. Morgan Woosley, "Chapter 5: Re/soundings: Music and the Political Goals of the L.A. Rebellion," in *L.A.Rebellion.*

35. Ntongela Masilela, "The Los Angeles School of Black Filmmakers," in *Black American Cinema.*

36. A major influence on students at UCLA Film School. Cf. *L.A. Rebellion*, p. 23.

37. *L.A. Rebellion.*

38. Patricia Hill Collins, "Multiple Levels of Domination," in *Black Feminist Thought.*

39. Maggie Humm, *Feminism and Film.*
40. See, Minh-Ha. *When the Moon Waxes Red: Representations, Gender and Cultural Politics.*

REFERENCES

Alexander, Elizabeth. 2004. *The Venus Hottentot: Poems.* St. Paul: Graywolf Press, 2004.

—— [1993]. "Daughters of the Dust." *Sight & Sound* 3, no. 9 (September): 20–22.

Alexander, Karen. 1991. "Fatal Beauties: Black Women in Hollywood." In *Stardom: Industry of Desire,* edited by Christine Gledhill, 46–57. London: Routledge.

Bambara, Toni Cade. 1993. "Reading the Signs, Empowering the Eye: *Daughters of the Dust* and the Black Independent Cinema Movement." In *Black American Cinema,* edited by Manthia Diawara, 118–144. New York: Routledge.

Bobo, Jacqueline. 1995. *Black Women as Cultural Readers.* New York: Columbia University Press.

Browne, Simone. 2015. *Dark Matters: On the Surveillance of Blackness.* Durham: Duke University Press.

Butler, Judith. 1993. *Bodies That Matter: On the Discursive Limits of "Sex."* London: Routledge.

Christian, Barbara. 1985. *Black Feminist Criticism: Perspectives on Black Women Writers.* Oxford: Pergamon Press.

Coates, Ta-Nehisi. 2015. *Between the World and Me.* New York: Spiegel & Grau.

Collins, Patricia Hill. 1990. *Black Feminist Thought: Knowledge, Consciousness, and the Politics of Empowerment.* London, Unwin Hyman.

Creel, Margaret Washington. 1989. *A Peculiar People: Slave Religion and Community-Culture among the Gullahs.* New York: New York University Press.

Dash, Julie. 1992. *Daughters of the Dust: The Making of an African American Woman's Film.* New York: The New Press.

Diawara, Manthia, ed. 1993. *Black American Cinema.* New York: Routledge.

Ellison, Ralph. 1952. *Invisible Man.* New York: Random House.

Field, Allyson Nadia, Jan-Christopher Horak, and Jacqueline Najuma Stewart. 2015. *L.A. Rebellion: Creating a New Black Cinema.* Oakland: University of California Press.

Gabriel, Teshome H. 1982. *Third Cinema in the Third World: The Aesthetic of Liberation.* Ann Arbor: University of Michigan Research Press.

Gordon, Avery F. 2008. *Ghostly Matters: Haunting and the Sociological Imagination.* Minneapolis: University of Minnesota Press.

Haraway, Donna. 1989. "A Manifesto for Cyborgs: Science, Technology, and Socialist Feminism in the 1980s." In edited by WoodEd.. London: Routledge.

Hartman, Saidiya V. 2007. *Lose Your Mother: A Journey along the Atlantic Slave Route.* New York: Farrar, Straus and Giroux.

hooks, bell. 1994. *Outlaw Culture: Resisting Representations.* New York: Routledge.

——. 1996. *Reel to Real: Race, Class and Sex at the Movies.* New York: Routledge.

Humm, Maggie. 1997. *Feminism and Film.* Bloomington: Indiana University Press.

Iton, Richard. 2008. *In Search of the Black Fantastic: Politics and Popular Culture in the Post–Civil Rights Era.* New York: Oxford University Press.

Karanja, Ayana I. 1999. *Zora Neale Hurston: The Breath of Her Voice.* New York: Peter Lang.

Marshall, Paule. 1983. *Praisesong for the Widow.* London: Virago.

McKnight, Utz. 2014. "The Fantastic Olivia Pope: The Construction of a Black Feminist Subject." *Souls: A Critical Journal of Black Politics, Culture & Society* 16, nos. 3–4 (July–December): 183–197.

McNee, Lisa. 2000. *Selfish Gifts: Senegalese Women's Autobiographical Discourses*. Albany: State University of New York Press.

Morrison, Toni. 1973. *Sula*. New York: Alfred A. Knopf.

———. 1987. *Beloved*. New York: Alfred A. Knopf.

———. 1992. *Playing in the Dark: Whiteness and the Literary Imagination*. Cambridge: Harvard University Press.

Neal, Larry. 1971. "The Black Arts Movement." In *The Black Aesthetic*, edited by Addison Gayle Jr., 272–90. Garden City, NY: Doubleday.

———. 2000. "The Black Arts Movement." In *A Turbulent Voyage: Readings in African American Studies*, edited by Floyd W. Hayes III, 236–45. Lanham, MD: Collegiate Press.

Raengo, Alessandra. 2013. *On the Sleeve of the Visual: Race as Face Value*. Hanover, NH: Dartmouth College Press.

Steady, Filomina Chioma. 1981. *The Black Woman Cross-Culturally*. Cambridge, MA: Schenkman.

Stewart, Jacqueline Najuma. 2005. *Migrating to the Movies: Cinema and Black Urban Modernity*. Berkeley: University of California Press.

Trinh, T. Minh-Ha. 1991. *When the Moon Waxes Red: Representation, Gender and Cultural Politics*. London: Routledge.

Tuhkanen, Mikko. 2009. *The American Optic: Psychoanalysis, Critical Race Theory, and Richard Wright*. Albany: State University of New York Press.

Walker, Alice. 1989. *The Temple of My Familiar*. London: The Women's Press.

Weheliye, Alexander G. 2014. *Habeas Viscus: Racializing Assemblages, Biopolitics, and Black Feminist Theories of the Human*. Durham: Duke University Press.

CHAPTER THREE

Overcoming the Trauma of the Gaze in Julie Dash's *Daughters of the Dust*

HEIKE RAPHAEL-HERNANDEZ

We can take our pain, work with it, recycle it, and transform it so that it becomes a source of power.

bell hooks (1990, 203)

In her 1998 essay about Black women filmmakers, Gloria J. Gibson-Hudson argued the necessity of creating their own, empowering cinematic images became of fundamental concern for Black women in the latter half of the 20th century.[1] According to Gibson-Hudson, throughout film history, Black women all too often had to observe:

> The Black woman, as presented within mainstream cinemas, [was] a one-dimensional depiction. Black women [were] shown as sex objects, passive victims, and as "other" in relation to males (Black and white) and white females. Worldwide, Black women's images [were] prescribed by narrative texts that reflect patriarchal visions, myths, stereotypes, and/ or fantasies of Black womanhood. Consequently, these representations limit[ed] the probability of an audience seeing Black women as figures of resistance or empowerment. (Gibson-Hudson 1998, 43)

Out of this necessity, in the late 1980s and early 1990s, Black women in the United Kingdom, Canada, the U.S., and the Caribbean began to make their own films, thus offering themselves the empowering images of Black women that had been missing. Among them were filmmakers such as Julie Dash, Alile Sharon Larkin, Monica Freeman, Camille Billops, and Daresha Kyi, with Dash being the most well-known among them.[2]

In their own films, these directors picked up those limiting and often condescending representations of mainstream productions that had portrayed the Black woman either as passive, often naïve supporting sidekicks to white protagonists, or had used her presence as an excuse to gaze at the Black female body. Black women filmmakers took this mainstream's gaze as an inviting challenge for their starting points, turning the passive Black woman, who heretofore had been gazed at, into the active agent who transformed the condescending gaze into a loving and accepting look, and thus offered herself her own empowerment needed to overcome the emotional pain and trauma caused by their memories of injustices done to them and their ancestors.

However, the idea of empowerment through their own cultural productions began earlier, with the Black women writers of the 1970s. Since then, Black women writers have presented empowered Black women in their texts, allowing later filmmakers to follow in their footsteps. Turning this once-degrading gaze into a loving look still offers one of the most appealing challenges for Black women writers and filmmakers today. Julie Dash's *Daughters of the Dust* (1991) demonstrates the continuation of this literary tradition in film.

Concerning literature, many theorists have pointed to the content of healing, hope, and agency in Black women writers' texts that began in the latter half of the 20th century. Black feminist theorist Cheryl Wall, for example, points out that the protagonists of these later texts partook in a mood of righteous anger and triumphant struggle that enabled them to undertake a psychological journey starting from victim to survivor. According to Wall, these characters defined and "position[ed] themselves respectively as potential and active agents of social change" (1989, 3). The concept of the individual's journey to agency can be found in many texts by African American women writers since the late 1970s, such as Alice Walker, Toni Morrison, Nikki Giovanni, Gloria Naylor, Paule Marshall, Maya Angelou, Gayl Jones, Toni Cade Bambara, Sherley Anne Williams, Ntozake Shange, Bebe More Campbell, and Terry McMillan. These writers differ significantly from their predecessors because they do not limit their fiction to descriptions of reality and mere criticism of negative societal circumstances. Preceding writers, such as Nella Larsen, Jessie Fauset, Ann Petry, and Dorothy West, depicted spiritually broken Black women who were unable to liberate themselves from oppression. In comparison with these earlier African American women's texts from the Harlem Renaissance, or the Naturalist and Modernist periods, the later texts allowed struggling protagonists to not only recognize negative circumstances but to find the mental and spiritual power within themselves to change those circumstances. They have provided visions of Black women who, with the help of some form of sisterly communities, have found the self-esteem and self-empowerment necessary either to overcome racist, sexist, and economic oppression, or at least not allow these circumstances to crush them. For example, Barbara Christian argued that in Morrison's novels, the writer "makes an attempt [...] to figure out the possibilities of healing and community for her women characters" (1985, 180). Joanne V. Gabbin, too, claimed because of these writers, a transformation had happened in African American literature; for the first time, African American women were "cleansing, healing, and empowering the images of themselves" (1990, 247). Furthermore, Susan Willis saw the unifying contribution of these texts in the writers' capacities to imagine "the future in the present, [a] future born out of the context of oppression. It produces utopia out of the transformation of the most basic features of daily life" (1987, 159).

The move from passive victim to active survivor and agent in these African American women authors' texts is often connected to an initial process of a spiritual or psychological awakening and subsequent journey. Deborah McDowell (1994, 437) emphasizes the psychological journey motif represents a major modifier for these texts:

> Though one can also find [the journey] motif in the works of Black male writers, they do not use it in the same way as do Black female writers. For example, the journey of the Black male character in works by Black men takes him underground. It [...] is primarily political and social in its implications. [...] The Black female's journey, on the other hand, though at times touching the political and social, is basically a personal and psychological journey.

Toni Cade Bambara's *The Salt Eaters* (1980) serves as an example for this claim. After attempting to commit suicide, the novel's protagonist, Velma Henry, is asked by Minnie Ransom, her spiritual healer, "Are you sure, sweetheart, that you want to be well?" (1980, 3). Minnie asks the question because she realizes Velma can overcome her breakdown only when Velma herself first decides she wants to heal psychologically too. Minnie Ransom's question about self-activated healing points to the idea of self-empowerment in African American women writers' texts. The image of the psychological journey—the protagonists' growing awareness of their own spiritual powers and agency—is essential in the process of empowerment because it serves as the foundation for the next step. Furthermore, these writers' initially struggling and finally succeeding protagonists all improve, more or less, their immediate surroundings. Empowered by their spiritual attitudes, they work on communal improvements, which allow the reader to imagine how a possible future in these fictitious communities could look like. Sandi Russell's explanation of Alice Walker's texts, for example, illustrates the "move from loss to hope" causes the protagonists to participate in the "transformation of society" (1990, 122). Joanne V. Gabbin, too, observes the literary protagonists' active participation in societal changes in these texts. She claims because of an "unabashed confrontation with the past and [a] clear-eyed vision of the future," the texts move from "protest toward revelation and informed social change" (1990, 249).

When trying to locate the nexus between individual empowerment and collective survival, one is able to find a critical engagement of Black women artists not only in literature, but also in film adaptations and original film scripts. Since the 1980s, one has been able to point to a growing body of cinematic empowerment narratives that depict individual journeys toward healing, which are accompanied by communities of sisterhood. Film adaptations and films with original scripts can be regarded as the visual continuation of the written text.

In her essay about Black feminist visual theory, Judith Wilson argues these late 20th century Black feminist cultural productions and interventions became necessary because of "feminists and poststructuralists and the emergence of visual theory in Europe and the U.S. during the 1970s and 1980s," which far too often made the mistake of reducing Black spaces to a preoccupation with the Black female body intersected with the gaze (2010, 21). As I stated earlier, throughout the history of cinematic productions, the Black female body had always been intersected with the gaze; yet now, unfortunately, mainstream feminism addressed the gaze and the female body in an all-embracing discourse without paying any attention to particular circumstances impacted by class or race. Such a one-dimensional discourse simply asked for the intervention of two disciplinary locales, Black feminist artistic productions and Black feminist critical film studies.

In addition, Black women had to struggle with another stereotyping gaze in visual cultural productions during the same period. Since the 1970s, one could observe the arrival and subsequent success of a growing group of Black male filmmakers in mainstream, such as Melvin van Peebles, later his son Mario van Peebles, Charles Burnett, Ernest Dickerson, Spike Lee, John Singleton, and the brothers Albert and Allen Hughes. Yet, as John Williams argues in his review of Black filmmakers, as laudable as their advent was on the commercial film industry scene, their "homeboy style" did nothing to counter the existing stereotypical images of Black women found already in the media. In her 1977 manifesto "*A Place in Time* and *Killer of Sheep*: Two Radical Definitions of Adventure Minus Women*," Black filmmaker Kathleen Collins claimed earlier Black films, such as *Shaft* and *Superfly*, simply reproduced Black women's stereotypical images. Williams maintains the same critique should also be applied to the later Black male filmmakers (1994, n.p.).

According to Judith Wilson, this long-overdue intervention came with the group of Black women filmmakers who have emerged since the late 1980s because:

> They have frequently engaged aspects of current body/gaze discourses. But in doing so, they often push these preoccupations into unfamiliar territory—invoking the intricate, aesthetic [...] their art points to another universe of questions around black self-esteem, cultural heritage, and aesthetic preferences [...] (Wilson 2010, 21)

In her analysis of Black women filmmakers, Jacqueline Bobo calls this a genesis of a tradition (1998, 3).

In her 2012 essay "Tuning into *Precious*: The Black Women's Empowerment Adaptation and the Interruption of the Absurd," Erica R. Edwards highlights an additional format for Black feminist cultural productions that have shifted their focus from mere literary texts to the wider realm of pop art. To find empowerment narratives, one should now also look to the film and television adaptations of novels by Black women writers. Edwards writes, "Adaptations have thus provided the language for the collision of black feminist literary culture and mainstream black popular culture" (2012, 75). Naming the adaptation of Alice Walker's *The Color Purple* (book: 1982/film: 1985) the starting point, Edwards sees a steady continuum with Gloria Naylor's *The Women of Brewster Place* (1983/1989), Terry McMillan's *Waiting to Exhale* (1992/1995), Toni Morrison's *Beloved* (1987/1998), Zora Neale Hurston's *Their Eyes Were Watching God* (1937/2005), and finally, Sapphire's *Push* (1996) as the film *Precious* (2009). Edwards claims:

> Understanding adaptations as a practice and a genre corresponding to the emergence of pop feminism from the 1970s to the 2000s is necessary for understanding how the narrative logics and technologies of salvation in the film contain black women's empowerment within a compensatory frame of individual success and eschew a radical ethos of collective survival. (2012, 74)

With her theoretical suggestions about film adaptations, Edwards echoes the nexus between literature and visual cultural productions.

The "gaze" as a theoretical substructure has been of essential importance for Black feminist discourse from the very start. As bell hooks already maintained in her groundbreaking 1992 essay "The Oppositional Gaze: Black Female Spectators," racist U.S. history taught Black people not to look. During the time of slavery, for example, "the politics of slavery, of racialized power relations, were such that the slaves were denied their right to gaze" (1992, 107). The enslaved Africans very well understood the power dynamics of constantly being gazed at and simultaneously being denied the right to gaze. Referring to Michel Foucault's contemplation of domination and relations of power, hooks argued the enslaved knew "even in the worst circumstances of domination, the ability to manipulate one's gaze in the face of structures of dominations that would contain it, opens up the possibility of agency" (1992, 107).

Locating the gaze and its power dynamics in later 20th- and early 21st-century Black feminist theory, Farah Jasmine Griffin advances this idea by adding the concept of the erotic to power relations born out of the gaze. In her analysis of late 20th century novels of slavery and their use of the erotic as resistance and means of healing, Griffin observes while "white supremacist and patriarchal discourses construct black women's bodies as abnormal, diseased and ugly, black women writers seek to reconstitute these bodies" (1996, 521). Griffin argues Black women writers who started to:

> Explore female bodies as sites of healing, pleasure, and resistance [were] engaged in a project of re-imagining the black female body—a project done in the service of those readers who have inherited the older legacy of the black body as despised, diseased and ugly. (1996, 521)

Griffin regards Audre Lorde's earlier call for nominating the erotic as a resource for empowerment as a vanguard action for later Black feminist theory. In her pioneering essay "Uses of the Erotic: The Erotic as Power," Lorde had encouraged women of color in general and lesbians of color in particular to celebrate the erotic as sensual as well as political resource, a tool for empowerment.[3] While Griffin cautions one to see the essentialism in Lorde's claims—indeed, many scholars have criticized Lorde's text as too essentialist—Griffin, nevertheless, notes the importance of Lorde's contribution by pointing to the historical legacy of Black women bodies. Griffin writes:

> The burden of a historical legacy that deems black women "over-sexed" makes the reclamation of the erotic black female body difficult. Unless the way that body is constructed in history and the continued pain of that construction are confronted, analyzed and challenged, it is almost impossible to construct an alternative that seeks to claim the erotic and its potential for resistance. (1996, 526)

Therefore, it is important, as Griffin insists, to "return to the site of the most formidable violence for black women as slaves" (1996, 526).

The best example for a cinematic return is offered by Julie Dash and her well-known film *Daughters of the Dust* (1991).[4] Here, too, women learn to empower themselves by confronting the physical and psychological violence done to their bodies since slavery. Dash allows and enables her women to finally come to the understanding that the gaze at the enslaved female body had caused violence not only during the times of slavery, but also had created for them a sense of unworthiness and ugliness of their own bodies. The film takes place on a small island off the Atlantic coast of South Carolina in 1902. Here we meet an African American extended family, the Peazants, on the eve of their departure from a Sea Island in the South to a big city in the North. Although at first the setting of the movie seems at first to be unrelated to the Black community of the 1990s, Dash's *Daughters* deals with problems that, according to her, Black people in general and Black women in particular still face today in American society. Like Walker, Morrison, and Naylor, Dash hopes to influence her own community to question current attitudes and circumstances, and consider possible changes. In fact, Dash claims one of her main objectives with *Daughters* was to influence her own community toward political agency. In her interview with bell hooks, she agrees with hooks that the film intends "progressive political intervention" (Dash 1992, 32).

With *Daughters of the Dust*, one can claim the film succeeds with one of the necessities Black feminists have desired to see as major concern for Black women—the struggle with self-love. One of *Daughters of the Dust's* main concerns deals with the self-destructing denial of physical and spiritual beauty by Black women. With her film, Dash intends to convey to Black women that the strength they need for survival in a society still hostile toward them lies in each other and in their unity; yet instead of realizing this necessity, most women in *Daughters of the Dust* are busy hating oneself and each other. Yellow Mary, for example, one of the Peazant women who left the island many years ago and returns to attend the reunion, experiences a tremendous amount of ostracism and hatred by her own family because she has returned as a prostitute. Yellow Mary indeed stretches her family's tolerance to the extreme because she not only comes home as a well-to-do prostitute, but additionally brings with her another prostitute with whom she seems to have a lesbian relationship. Upon encountering Yellow Mary, all the other Peazant women suddenly seem very eager to show off their own spotless and righteous lives. They greet her with degrading and hateful remarks such as "All that yellow, wasted"; "The heifer has returned"; "The shameless hussy." When Yellow Mary offers cookies as a homecoming present, the reactions range from "I wouldn't eat them anyhow, if she touched them" to "You never know where her hands could have been. I can just smell the heifer."

Blinded by their own dreams of self-determination and success in the North, the Peazant women cannot comprehend Yellow Mary's dreams of financial and personal success failed because the mainland's racist and sexist society impeded Yellow Mary and her husband from seeing the fulfillment of their dreams. The subjugation Yellow Mary endured on the mainland is most evident in the abuse she suffered at the hands of her employers. For example, when Yellow Mary worked as a wet nurse for a family, she was treated without any respect or rights, and was subsequently raped repeatedly. During her visit with her family, she reveals to Eula, one of her cousins, this was the way she "got ruined" and this experience turned her into a prostitute. Still, the Peazant women do not allow themselves to see any possible connections between Yellow Mary's failed dreams and their own high hopes because such a realization would carry a dangerous implication for the fulfillment of their dreams. Instead, they blame Yellow Mary for her failed life. Even when Yellow Mary tells them "the raping of colored women is as common as the fish in the sea," they continue to claim it was all Yellow Mary's own mistake, hoping still their own new life in the North will be completely different from hers and that, for once, they and their daughters will no longer be vulnerable to the sexual trauma of the past and the present.

Dash believes such self-hatred can be overcome and unity can be established through the memory of Black history and culture. Emphasizing Dash's ideas on memory in regard to a group vision, Jacquie Jones explains that in *Daughters of the Dust*, "Dash authenticates the collective memory as essential and as necessary" (1993, 21). To illustrate her point, Dash uses the image of the ancestors. According to her, the Peazants can succeed in any society, be it Southern or Northern, only if they begin to remember their ancestors' spirit and their determination to overcome any negative circumstances together as a united group. They should realize their uniqueness as a group by remembering their recent African American history, their ancient African heritage, and the beauty and richness of their own culture. In his discussion of *Daughters of the Dust*, Manthia Diawara explains the movie urges African Americans in the 1990s "to know where we came from, before knowing where we are going" (1993, 14). Toni Cade Bambara supports Diawara's thesis when she lauds the movie's potential by saying "the film, in fact, invites the spectator to undergo a triple process of recollecting the dismembered past, recognizing and reappraising cultural icons and codes, and re-centering and revalidating the self" (1993, 124).

The shift in family members' attitudes toward Yellow Mary happen when Eula, who was raped and "ruined" by a white man herself, observes so much hatred among the Peazant women that she breaks down and cries:

> As far as this place is concerned, we never enjoyed our womanhood. Deep inside, we believed that they ruined our mothers, and their mothers before them. And we live our lives always expecting the worst because we feel we don't deserve any better [...] You think you can cross over to the mainland and run away from it? You're going to be sorry, sorry if you don't change your way of thinking before you leave this place [...] If you love yourselves, then love Yellow Mary, because she's part of you [...] We carry too many scars from the past. Our past owns us [...] Let's live our lives without living in the fold of old wounds.

In this scene, Eula proves she fully understands the Peazant women's dilemma with the past and the present. Using the example of the Black woman's situation in American history, Eula attempts to show her family they have tried for too long to ignore their past and have somewhat blinded themselves with some other fabricated ideas. Therefore, she tells them about their dilemma: "Deep inside we believe that even God can't heal the wounds of our past or protect us from the world that put shackles on our feet."

At Eula's urging, most members finally realize how far their hatred and disrespect have already carried them. They now understand Eula's insistence on seeing how the past really happened rather than how most of them have tried to invent it by simply deleting certain negative memories and events. This specific example of the Black woman's situation in American history helps the Peazants to understand Eula's insistence "we've got to change our way of thinking." They finally realize they have to see themselves as a peculiar people with a unique history and culture that enables them to truly find the love and respect for oneself and each other.

NOTES

1. Parts of my discussion of Julie Dash's *Daughters of the Dust* in this essay have been published before in: Hieke Raphael-Hernandez, "'I am not running, I am choosing': Black Feminist Empowerment and the Continuation of a Literary Tradition in Filmmakers Julie Dash's *Daughters of the Dust* (1991) and Dee Rees' *Pariah* (2011)," *Ostrava Journal of English Philology* 6, no. 2 (2014): 7–20.
2. For a short discussion of their individual films, see John Williams, "Re-Creating Their Media Image: Two Generations of Black Women Filmmakers," *Cineaste* 20, no. 3 (April 1994): n.p.
3. For the entire argument, see the chapter "Uses of the Erotic: The Erotic as Power" in Audre Lorde, *Sister Outsider* (1984; repr., Berkeley, CA: Crossing Press, 2007), 53–59.
4. Parts of my discussion of Julie Dash's *Daughters of the Dust* in this essay have been published before in my monograph *The Utopian Aesthetics of Three African American Women (Toni Morrison, Gloria Naylor, Julie Dash): The Principle of Hope* (Lewiston, NY: The Edwin Mellen Press, 2008).

REFERENCES

Bambara, Toni Cade. 1980. *The Salt Eaters*. New York: Vintage Books.

———. 1993. "Reading the Signs, Empowering the Eye: *Daughters of the Dust* and the Black Independent Cinema Movement." In *Black American Cinema*, edited by Manthia Diawara, 118–144. New York: Routledge.

Bobo, Jacqueline. 1998. "Black Women's Films: Genesis of a Tradition." In *Black Women Film and Video Artists*, edited by Jacqueline Bobo, 3–20. New York: Routledge.

Christian, Barbara. 1985. *Black Feminist Criticism: Perspectives on Black Women Writers*. Oxford: Pergamon Press.

Dash, Julie, dir. 1991. *Daughters of the Dust*. 1991. New York, NY: Kino International.

Dash, Julie. 1992. *Daughters of the Dust: The Making of an African American Woman's Film*. New York: The New Press.

Diawara, Manthia. 1993. "Black American Cinema: The New Realism." In *Black American Cinema*, edited by Manthia Diawara, 3–25. New York: Routledge.

Edwards, Erica R. 2012. "Tuning into *Precious*: The Black Women's Empowerment Adaptation and the Interruptions of the Absurd." *Black Camera* 4, no. 1 (Winter): 74–95.

Gabbin, Joanne V. 1990. "A Laying on of Hands: Black Women Writers Exploring the Roots of Their Folk and Cultural Tradition." In *Wild Women in the Whirlwind: Afra-American Culture and the Contemporary Literary Renaissance*, edited by Joanne M. Braxton and Andrée Nicola McLaughlin, 246–263. New Brunswick: Rutgers University Press.

Gibson-Hudson, Gloria J. 1998. "The Ties that Bind: Cinematic Representations by Black Women Filmmakers." In *Black Women Film and Video Artists*, edited by Jacqueline Bobo, 43–66. New York: Routledge.

Griffin, Farah Jasmine. 1996. "Textual Healing: Claiming Black Women's Bodies, the Erotic and Resistance in Contemporary Novels of Slavery." *Callaloo* 19, no. 2 (Spring): 519–536.

hooks, bell. 1990. *Yearning. Race, Gender, and Cultural Politics*. Boston, MA: South End Press.

———. 1992. *Black Looks: Race and Representation*. Boston, MA: South End Press.

Jones, Jacquie. 1993. "The Black South in Contemporary Film." *African American Review* 27, no. 1 (Spring): 19–24.

Lorde, Audre. (1984) 2007. *Sister Outsider: Essays and Speeches*. Berkeley, CA: Crossing Press.

McDowell, Deborah E. 1994. "New Directions for Black Feminist Criticism." *Within the Circle: An Anthology of African American Literary Criticism from the Harlem Renaissance to the Present*, edited by Angelyn Mitchell, 428–441. Durham and London: Duke University Press.

Russell, Sandi. 1990. *Render Me My Song: African-American Women Writers from Slavery to the Present*. New York: St. Martin's Press.

Wall, Cheryl A. 1989. "Introduction." In *Changing Our Own Words: Essays on Criticism, Theory, and Writing by Black Women*, edited by Cheryl A. Wall, n.p. New Brunswick and London: Rutgers University Press.

Williams, John. 1994. "Re-Creating Their Media Image: Two Generations of Black Women Filmmakers," *Cineaste* 20, no. 3 (April): n.p.

Willis, Susan. 1987. *Specifying: Black Women Writing the American Experience*. Madison: University of Wisconsin Press.

Wilson, Judith. 2010. "One Way or Another: Black Feminist Visual Theory." In *The Feminism and Visual Culture Reader*, edited by Amelia Jones, 19–23. London: Routledge.

Sensory Ignition and Cultural Memory: Visual Art and Gastronomy in *Daughters of the Dust*

CHAPTER FOUR

Coming Home to Good Gumbo

Gullah Foodways and the Sensory in Julie Dash's *Daughters of the Dust*

KATIE M. WHITE

[...] To understand a culture, past or present, we should endeavor to understand how a society feeds itself. It is the ubiquity and everydayness of eating that makes understanding it historically so important. The taste and flavor of food play an important part in social relationships, and a food's taste can embody meanings well beyond what is put into the mouth. (Fitzgerald and Petrick 2008, 393)

This chapter examines ways in which foodways are created and sustained within Gullah communities, paying particular attention to the role of the five senses, especially taste, in transmitting and preserving the culture. Gullah people are the descendants of enslaved Africans from the Senegambia region of West Africa who have created and sustained a culture, particularly on the Sea Islands of North Carolina, South Carolina, Georgia, and Florida, by integrating memories and rituals from Africa with resources found in the Americas. I argue much can be learned from the sounds, smells, touch, and sights of food preparation and consumption. The following research questions are a guide: How does food transmit culture? What can be learned about gender roles, relationships, and power dynamics in Gullah culture through a sensory interrogation of foodways? How do the five senses, particularly taste, aid in the transmission and preservation of foodways?

There are two approaches of discovery applied here to explore the connections of food and culture retention. First, this chapter conveys film and popular culture's power to create fictional referents for culture and society. Second, this chapter explores the role of women in the elaboration and sustenance of Gullah culture, especially that of the fictional character Yellow Mary in Julie Dash's 1991 film,

Daughters of the Dust. This film tells the story of the Peazants, an African American Sea Island family preparing to come to the mainland in 1902, and illustrates the tensions between tradition and assimilation experienced by families during the Great Migration at the turn of the 20th century.

By investigating Yellow Mary's travels away from Ibo Landing, a fictive space in Gullah culture, and what drives her to return home, this project explores taste and the sensory, sustainability of culture and cultural identity, and migratory patterns of Gullah people from the Sea Islands. It argues Yellow Mary assumes the role of what scholar Anita Mannur refers to as a "culinary citizen," asserting her place on Ibo Landing through nostalgic memory (see Mannur 2007). It demonstrates how Yellow Mary operates as a diasporic body, creating a framework for the larger narrative of migration within the film.

To begin answering my research questions, I utilize ethnographic evidence to help explain the relationship between sensuality, food, and cultural identity, including the tensions surrounding our relationships to and around food. Much like the film's characters, the Gullah women whom I interviewed in 2009 also discussed their relationships with food. The information in these interviews fleshed out the history of Gullah cuisine and initiated a discussion about the sensory elements of Gullah foodways (White 2009). The stories of Ms. Grace Thomas, Ms. Sue Hilton, and Ms. Ellen Taylor will inform this paper.[1] As an illustration of the tension, movement, and sensuality around food, I analyze how food operates in film and literary texts, including cookbooks. I also attempt to contextualize Yellow Mary as that diasporic body who cites food as a pull factor toward home. To aid in the contextualization, I unpack gumbo recipes from the Lowcountry to see what sensory elements Yellow Mary may have been missing from gumbo outside of Ibo Landing, and I discuss how Dash's use of sensory elements, such as sounds, gestures, images, and performances, are critical to understanding the history of Gullah people and culture.

POWER, FOOD, AND CULINARY SENSORY COMMUNICATION

Gullah people were not brought to the Americas; rather, Gullah culture was born in diaspora. There is scholarly debate surrounding the reasons why the Gullah ended up on the Sea Islands of North Carolina, South Carolina, Georgia, and Florida (Littlefield 1981; Opala 1987; Carney 2002; Morgan 2004). Nevertheless, enslaved African women from Senegambia and Sierra Leone were brought to Charleston and Savannah—and eventually sold to rich white planters on the Sea Islands—for their specialized knowledge of rice cultivation. These enslaved female rice planters were responsible for filling the coffers of white plantation owners by toiling in humid rice fields every day during the 14-month rice planting season (Morgan 2004, 162) and for educating enslaved males on the rituals of rice cultivation.

The coastal South Carolina Sea Islands, particularly St. Helena Island, Lady's Island and the town of Port Royal in Beaufort County, are Gullah country. This area is very close to Hunting and Fripp Islands where Julie Dash filmed *Daughters of the Dust*. *Daughters of the Dust* illustrates ways food is ritualized in Gullah culture, both in the actual cooking of food, and in its preparation. Women create community while peeling potatoes, preparing rice, and boiling crabs, much like women in the rice fields of Sierra Leone constructed community while fanning and pounding rice.

Daughters of the Dust centers on a Gullah family on the fictive Ibo Landing in South Carolina at the turn of the 20th century. Matriarch Nana Peazant is unhappy some of the younger family members want to leave Ibo Landing for the mainland in search of a new, more successful life. She begs them to hold onto their history and their roots by repeatedly reminding them they owe their ancestors their every breath. The Peazant family lives without electricity, running water, and other "mainland" American luxuries of that era, but Dash, also producer and writer of the film, exposes a self-sufficient familial operation. Peazant family members are clothed well and eat well. They rely on a mixture of African and Christian spiritual traditions, as well as faith in one another, to maintain their relationships with one another and their ancestors, tradition, and culture. There is power in their connectivity to family and to the land.

In Gullah culture, the kitchen is a classroom in which empowerment is taught, albeit indirectly. Food is revered as a blend of old and new traditions and as a crucial element in maintaining and disseminating Gullah traditions. In the foreword to her cookbook *My Gullah Kitchen* (2006), Eva Segar credits her mother and grandmother for teaching her how to cook. They allowed her to observe their methods and "play cook" alongside them in the kitchen. Segar came to cook on her own rather simply:

> One day, Mother came home and said, "Sister, you was home all day. How come you didn't put on the rice? And why didn't you boil the beans or peas or something?" So I went from "play cooking" to cooking for ten or more people just about every day. I've been cooking ever since. (Segar 2006, 9)

In Segar's case, cooking was taught by example. She mentions watching her mother and grandmother, but does not indicate how much of the teaching, if any, was done verbally, through recall, or through written recipes. Segar also fails to mention how the process of cooking is often wrought with frustration, burned dishes, and failure to replicate tastes and memories, all of which may cause cooks to abandon traditional processes or develop new methods.

Gullah heritage is passed on through a kind of ritual presence, not just through stories. Many of the women I interviewed remember pulling up a stool by the stove to watch their mothers, grandmothers, or great-grandmothers cook. Watching an elder cook is also an education in proper relations of authority and respect. Children learned to yield to the women in the kitchen who were in charge of the stove. Watching the techniques and ingredients used by these women often allowed Gullah children to be ready to help when called upon. In "We Got Our Way of Cooking Things: Women, Food, and Preservation of Cultural Identity Among the Gullah," scholar Josephine Beoku-Betts shows that both inside and outside the kitchen, Gullah women take very seriously "the task of transmitting cultural traditions to a rapidly declining younger generation" (1995, 550). This requires not only hard work on the part of tradition bearers, but also the willingness and receptivity of younger generations. To help transfer her knowledge of farming processes and love of the land to Gullah children, Ms. Thomas has implemented an internship program for school-age children on her farm. The students earn a small stipend in exchange for working in the fields, delivering Community Supported Agriculture (CSA) baskets to members, and other jobs necessary to maintain her farm. Per an article written by the Coastal Conservation League, "What they really get is a good, old-fashioned course in hard work, not to mention newer lessons, like money management and job application skills" (The Summer of Food 2011). Ms. Taylor also began a new tradition on holidays such as Christmas. Her grandchildren help her prepare the large family meal from start to finish—from harvesting vegetables and fruits and dredging for oysters, to dressing whatever meat is on the menu (Ellen Taylor, interview with author, January 13, 2009).

Ms. Hilton distinctly remembers frying chicken with her mother at age four; this is her first memory of helping in the kitchen. Before that, she watched from afar, much like Ms. Thomas, who learned by watching the women in her family prepare food over the years (Sue Hilton, interview with author, January 13, 2009). As a vegetarian, Ms. Thomas has learned to replicate the taste of favorite Gullah foods such as Hoppin' John and red rice by replacing the pork with lots of onions, garlic, and a special spice blend she created. "The key to it is the taste buds," she explains. "My taste buds are still in tune to the taste buds of how my mother cooked and how I cooked before I became a vegetarian. So when I cook, I am going to get as close as I possibly can" (Grace Thomas, interview with author, January 15, 2009). She has been able to come so close to the taste of traditional recipes that she has even fooled her brother. At a recent dinner he remarked, "Ah, Sis, that was so good, I almost didn't miss the meat" (Grace Thomas, interview with author, January 15, 2009).

There is more to cooking from memory than is evidenced by Ms. Thomas's claim, judging by the information imparted in other interviews, as well as various Gullah cookbooks. A multi-faceted sensory curriculum goes into the development of such sensitive taste buds. Years of watching, listening, smelling, touching, and tasting have provided the culinary education for Ms. Thomas and countless Gullah women. Many people can likely relate to certain foods feeling like home, but not all can replicate such dishes perfectly. Beyond cooking for oneself, it is also very difficult to find "home" in familiar dishes when traveling, in exile or simply when the person with whom you associate certain dishes has passed on. In "Exiled at Home: *Daughters of the Dust* and the Many Post-Colonial Conditions" (2001), Catherine Cucinella and Renée R. Curry argue that:

> [...] No collective "home"—whether geographical, familial, sexual, marital, religious, or racial—exists for the women characters in *Daughters of the Dust*. They constantly occupy the many varied post-colonial positions of exile while negotiating moves between "homes" old and new. (Cucinella and Curry 2001, 199)

Adding to this argument, I contend that the women in *Daughters of the Dust* (Dash 1991) are also searching for home through food or culinary techniques, much like my informants and their families in Beaufort County.

Like other rural, impoverished people, the Gullah have simple cooking techniques. Technology was limited on the Sea Islands until the mid to late 20th century, when the areas began to attract wealthy builders, vacationers and retirees from other parts of the United States. The Sea Islands, such as St. Helena and Daufuskie, were relatively untouched by "outsiders" until the early 1980s. Bridges were not considered a necessity until wealthy white Northerners identified the Sea Islands as a prime vacation spot. Gullah food was not cooked in stainless steel Kenmore ovens or chopped on Corian countertops. Food was raised, hunted, or trapped by people on the islands and prepared using water from a hand pump (Robinson 2003, 4). Cookbook author Sallie Ann Robinson grew up on Daufuskie Island in the 1960s and 1970s and had to take a boat to the nearest grocery store. She writes in her cookbook, *Gullah Home Cooking the Daufuskie Way*:

> Most of our food came from the land—and water—around our tin-roofed home. We tended a big garden, four seasons of the year in Daufuskie's mild weather. We raised chickens, hogs, and cattle in our yard. We gathered berries and trapped or sometimes shot animals in the woods. We fished, crabbed, shrimped, and picked oysters. We didn't always have a lot, but we always had enough. (Robinson 2003, 4)

Cooking for Robinson was the bringing together of the fruits of a day's physical labor. "Food is life. And the way we lived, life was gathering, growing, and preparing food" (Robinson 2003, 12). Culinary tradition was more than the passing on of recipes; it was a transmission of knowledge of farming, hunting, and fishing.

The preparation called for creative energy. Robinson's writing is about growing up in the mid to late 20th century, but the ingredients and preparations she enjoys are rooted in slavery times, as enslaved women molded old traditions from Sierra Leone with new resources found in America. Enslaved women had to be creative in the kitchen and recipes were passed down. Taste is a matter of opinion and arguably, in the case of the Sea Islands, tradition. The preservation of Gullah culture, then, involves not only the cultivation of certain culinary skills, but also a particular sense of taste. The construction of Gullah culture is a sensory experience, engaging all senses.

COMING HOME

Ms. Thomas came home to St. Helena Island not intending to stay, much like Yellow Mary in *Daughters of the Dust*. Both women claim not to have had good food while they were away. Ms. Thomas described her many years in Atlanta where she disregarded her Gullah culture and did not allow familiar foods and traditions to sustain her:

> I was into my African culture and that African culture superseded my Gullah culture [...] Every now and then a word would slip out and people would ask where I was from, but it was something intangible that I kept that was eating at me and making me want to come back. (Grace Thomas, interview with author, January 15, 2009)

Dash's character Yellow Mary comes back after approximately ten years away from Ibo Landing to a chilly homecoming. She arrives with store-bought cookies in a tin and eschews verbal cuts from her female relatives about her lack of involvement in the kitchen only, to articulate her desire for home-cooked food a short while later. While Yellow Mary is chatting with her female traveling partner, Trula, and her cousin Eula in one of the trees close to the beach, Yellow Mary says she hopes the women are making gumbo. She looks back toward the spot on the beach where a group of women are preparing the picnic food. One can almost see her smelling it or even feeling it in the air. Yellow Mary says, "Y'know, I sure hope they're fixing some gumbo. It's been a long time since I've had some good gumbo. (Looking up at Trula) I had some in Savannah, you know, but they didn't put everything in it. I haven't had some good food in a long time" (Dash 1992, 122).

Food takes on many meanings in this scene. It is sustenance, memory, ritual, and most poignantly, lesbian sexuality, as Yellow Mary's gaze is directed toward Trula when she says she has not had good gumbo in a long time. Trula is Yellow Mary's light-skinned traveling companion. In an interview with bell hooks published in *Daughters of the Dust: The Making of An African American Women's Film* (Dash 1992), Dash explains that in her research for the film, she found prostitutes of that time, which Yellow Mary is, were involved with other women. Their significant others were often women, yet their customers were usually men. Dash comments, "in developing Yellow Mary's character [I] realized that she, as an independent businesswoman would not be traveling alone. In fact, she would have a significant other" (Dash 1992, 66). Given the sexual relationship between the two women, I argue Yellow Mary's comment about gumbo has two meanings. First, she is hungry for a familiar, home-cooked dish. Secondly, Trula no longer provides her with what she desires sexually or in terms of a home and what that implies, such as comfort, family, and stability.

Leading into her comment about gumbo, Yellow Mary mocks the traditions and backwardness of Ibo Landing, as if to create distance between herself and the land only to wish her way back onto it. In her essay "Culinary Nostalgia: Authenticity, Nationalism, and Diaspora," Anita Mannur (2007, 13) writes:

> The desire to remember home by fondly recreating culinary memories cannot be understood merely as reflectively nostalgic gestures .... Discursive and affective aspects of food are valued over their symbolic and semiotic meaning in nostalgic narratives that negotiate the parameters of "culinary citizenship," a form of affective citizenship which grants subjects the ability to claim and inhabit certain subject positions via their relationship to food.

Yellow Mary is arguably assuming the role of culinary citizen in this instance, asserting her place on the island through nostalgic memory.

I also argue Yellow Mary is operating as a diasporic body, creating a framework for the larger narrative of migration. Her voiceover at the beginning of the film sets the tone: "I am the first and the last. I am the honored one and the scorned one. I am the whore and the holy one. I am the wife and the virgin. I am the barren one and many are my daughters. I am the silence that you cannot understand. I am the utterance of my name" (Dash 1992, 75–76). Yellow Mary's uttered words are adapted from the Nag Hammadi Scriptures, a collection of thirteen ancient codices discovered in Upper Egypt in 1945 and previously thought destroyed. The selection Yellow Mary speaks from is "Thunder, Perfect Mind," drawn from writings dealing primarily with the feminine deific and spiritual principle, particularly with the Divine Sophia (The Nag Hammadi Library 2011). According to the Gnostic Society archives, the Divine Sophia—or Holy Wisdom—desired most intensely to know the origin of her own creation (The Nag Hammadi Library 2011). Perhaps Dash is very deliberately placing Yellow Mary in the role of Divine Sophia as she returns home to Ibo Landing to rediscover her origin.

What can be learned about Gullah culture, as well as migration and diasporic bodies, from observing Yellow Mary navigate the space of Ibo Landing after some time away? She is someone who has left the island and stayed away for ten years. The notes in Dash's screenplay (1992) list Yellow Mary as working for a family near Edisto Island, South Carolina, which today is not very far north from the fictional Ibo Landing. At the turn of the 20th century and before bridges existed there, Edisto Island was considered the mainland. Per the screenplay, when Yellow Mary became pregnant in the late 19th century, she lost her baby, so she used her available breast milk to nurse the white children of an Edisto Island family. When Yellow Mary traveled with this family to Cuba to look after the babies, she was assaulted by their father. According to the screenplay, her travels have taken her to Edisto Island, Cuba, and Savannah, where she could have easily found rice-based cuisine. What was missing in the gumbo Yellow Mary ate in Savannah that caused her to crave the gumbo of home?

Gumbo recipes from Beaufort County and Savannah do not differ greatly, but it is difficult to find two recipes that are alike. Dash (1992, ix) writes:

> [She] was raised on Gumbo; in my house it was called Okra Soup. Gumbo has been described as the "poor man's meal," or a "Saturday dish," prepared when you emptied your refrigerator at the end of the week. As far as I'm concerned Gumbo is a luxury. It takes all day to prepare (to do it right) and the fresh okra required to make it can be difficult and expensive.

Many Gullah cookbooks, however, have okra soup and gumbo listed separately with very different ingredients. Virginia Mason Geraty's cookbook *Bittle en' T'ing': Gullah Cooking with Maum Chrish'* (1992) cites Okra Soup as a mixture of okra, fresh tomatoes, corn, onions, and seasonings, while the main component of her gumbo is smoked side-meat cut in such a way that each person will have several pieces (Geraty 1992, 6). Geraty lived for many years on Edisto Island and now resides in Charleston. Jesse Edward Gantt Jr. and Veronica Davis Gerald from St. Helena Island argue in *The Ultimate Gullah Cookbook: A Taste of Food, History, and Culture from the Gullah People* (2003) that gumbo begins with a brown gravy or roux, which Dash and Geraty's recipes do not include. Along with meat, Gantt and Gerald offer crabmeat, oysters, and shrimp as additions. Dash and Geraty's recipes require a lengthy simmering process, whereas Gantt and Gerald's gumbo needs only twenty minutes to simmer before serving, which is likely due to the gravy acting as a thickener (Gantt and Gerald 2003, 30). Searches for Savannah Gumbo return many links to celebrity chef Paula Deen's recipe, which is similar to Gantt and Gerald's, but has more of a chicken base than smoked pig or turkey. Deen's also includes cayenne pepper, which the South Carolina recipes do not (Deen n.d.).

Each of the aforementioned gumbo recipes was published in the latter part of the 20th century, so it is difficult to discern what gumbo components Yellow Mary wished for when she was away from Ibo Landing. As Janet Theophano argues in *Eat My Words: Reading Women's Lives Through the Cookbooks They Wrote* (2002, 50):

> Although recipes remain nearly unchanged through the years, each new cook adapts some recipes to accommodate altered environments and the changes in fashion, and invents new

dishes. Change is constant. The accidental or deliberate modification takes place with the passing of each generation, with the movement of people from one location to another, with periods of crisis or scarcity such as war and natural disaster .... Yet some recipes are not forgiving. Cooks may closely follow the original for the purposes of remembrance. To alter even an ingredient would disrupt the evocative, symbolic qualities of a dish.

Theophano's argument works as a foil for Yellow Mary or any consumer of food. Cooks may be the ones following recipes, but those who are not cooking are often looking for consistency, familiarity, and sensuality when eating specific foods. For example, in Ntozake Shange's novel *Sassafrass, Cypress & Indigo* (1982), food serves as a bridge to home for sisters Sassafrass, Cypress, and Indigo whether they are making familiar recipes in an apartment in Los Angeles or New York, or lapping up Mama's gumbo when they come home for Christmas:

> "Mama, the gumbo is ridiculous." Sassafrass was eating so fast she could barely get the words out of her mouth. "Mama, you know if I told them white folks at the Callahan School that I wanted some red sauce & rice with shrimp, clams, hot sausage, corn, okra, chicken & crab meat, they'd go round the campus sayin, 'You know that Negro girl over-does everything. Can you imagine what she wanted for dinner?'" (Shange 1982, 48)

Through Sassafrass, Shange illustrates that food is nuanced. Taste is subjective, and the tastes, smells, and feelings we crave may not be easily found outside of home.

Yellow Mary's wish for good food and gumbo leads us to the larger feast scene in the film, which is conducted almost entirely without dialogue. The sights and sounds of food being passed and consumed assume center stage. The central role of food in Gullah culture, particularly in celebrations, is implied simply by watching the family prepare their plates and eat. Listening to the sounds of this scene is arguably more important than watching. Gwendolyn Audrey Foster (1997, 49–65) credits Dash for evoking:

> Suppressed signs and sounds of the past. From the beginning of the film, the viewer is presented with a mélange of Gullah culture through sounds, images, and performances. It is the attention to the nuances of rituals, styles, and especially the kinesthetics of gesture, which strongly evokes an Afrocentric visual memory making.

Viewers are invited to migrate back to the Sea Islands at the turn of the previous century to witness common cultural practices that may have made their way north with some of the Gullah people who migrated. Foster's essay praises Dash for her creative use of time, space, and color to tell the story of the Peazant family, focusing on the film and filmmaker rather than issues of migration. Dash offers the viewer the type of sensory experience Fitzgerald and Petrick (2008) argue is important if we are to understand the history of a people and culture.

THE FIVE SENSES

The five senses are dramatically shown during the feast on the beach in *Daughters of the Dust* (Dash 1991). There is no dialogue during this scene, but the viewer can imagine the savory smells of the food and see the pleasure of the people sharing a meal. The wind is whipping and the tide is rolling out on the Sea Island as the Peazant women prepare a delicious meal for their family and visitors. They all are dressed well in suitable attire for that time—white dresses and boots for the women and lightweight trousers, shirts, and suit jackets for the men. Nana Peazant is dressed in blue, the color of her indigo-stained hands. Yellow Mary, Trula, and Viola have on more sophisticated traveling clothes than the others, distinguishing them as travelers outside of Ibo Landing. The only sounds are the clinking of forks against ceramic plates, the crunching of corn on the cob, the shelling of shrimp and the cracking of blue crabs. The family members need no words as they pass plates back and forth between bowls and platters piled high with fish and tomatoes. Generations of sharing allow them to communicate seamlessly and silently.

This scene may be what Yellow Mary is looking for in her travels. The food the Peazant family is enjoying was likely planted, harvested, caught, or shucked by some of their hands. They have created a sustainable life and home by working the land and by passing on skills and traditions to one another. As the women prepared the food, no recipes were recited and narrated from a cookbook. Yellow Mary could not find the good gumbo she was looking for because it can only be made by Peazant women or by people who have watched Peazant women make it in their way. This feast scene demonstrates the benefits of sustainability in terms of defining home for people. Ironically, just as the scene evokes home and sustainability, it also signifies the end of an era and the beginning of a new life for a certain number of Peazants on the mainland.

As we have seen, investigating sensory elements of history, people, and cultures can help us, pun intended, make sense of the world. Current scholarship is invested in the anthropology of smell, hearing, and movement, but least of all on taste (Sutton 2001, 14). As we saw in the scholarship and in the film *Daughters of the Dust* (Dash 1991), this paper is the beginning of an intervention I wish to make to illustrate the intersection between sustainability and the five senses, particularly taste and memory, using film, literature, and ethnography as investigative and theoretical tools.

Valuing all five senses can help to uncover how much lived experience constructs nostalgic memory. What goes into the making of Gullah folklore? Where, how, and by whom are memories created, and what role does each of the five senses play in the creation of memories? What are we missing in retelling Gullah history without a reliance on sensory experience? Is sensory experience the same as lived experience? These questions will continue to inform my future research.

Gullah people, such as Ms. Thomas, assert love and care can be felt in good food, and they are arguably cornerstones of sustainability for Gullah people. Veronica Davis Gerald (Gantt and Gerald 2003, 19), coauthor of *The Ultimate Gullah Cookbook* maintains:

> Love is one of the best-kept secrets but main ingredients in Gullah food. However, of all the ingredients, it is the most difficult to explain and to pass on in a recipe. For this reason, few books on this food culture attempt to give it consideration. Some call it cooking from the heart; others just call it "luv" […] Around the Gullah table, it is common to hear someone say, "e put e foot en um dis time" or "dey's a lot of luv in dis food." Expressions such as these mean that the cook has put so much of her or his energy and spirit into the preparation of the food, that they transfer the food onto the recipient.

For the Gullah, food is more than a necessity for survival. It is life. Since the beginning of the Gullah existence, food has played a central role in everyday life. Gullah food cannot be found in a store-bought package. It must be prepared with love, and perhaps more importantly, with hundreds of years of ritual behind each stir of the pot and pinch of spice.

NOTE

1. The names of these women have been changed to protect their privacy.

REFERENCES

Beoku-Betts, Josephine A. 1995. "We Got Our Way of Cooking Things: Women, Food, and Preservation of Cultural Identity Among the Gullah." *Gender and Society* 9, no. 5 (October): 535–555.

Carney, Judith A. 2002. *Black Rice: The African Origins of Rice Cultivation in the Americas.* Cambridge: Harvard University Press.

Cucinella, Catherine and Renee R. Curry. 2001. "Exiled at Home: *Daughters of the Dust* and the Many Post-Colonial Conditions." *MELUS* 26, no. 4 (Winter): 197–221.

Dash, Julie, dir. 1991. *Daughters of the Dust.* New York, NY: Kino International.

Dash, Julie. 1992. *Daughters of the Dust: The Making of an African American Woman's Film.* New York, NY: The New Press.

Deen, Paula. n.d. "Savannah Seafood Gumbo." Food Network. Accessed June 12, 2019. https://www.foodnetwork.com/recipes/paula-deen/savannah-seafood-gumbo-recipe-2117758.

Fitzgerald, Gerard J. and Gabriella M. Petrick. 2008. "In Good Taste: Rethinking AmericaHistory with Our Palates." *Journal of American History* 95, no. 2 (September): 392–404. https://doi.org/10.2307/25095625.

Foster, Gwendolyn Audrey. 1997. *Women Filmmakers of the African and Asian Diaspora: Decolonizing the Gaze, Locating Subjectivity.* Carbondale, IL: Southern Illinois University Press.

Gantt, Jesse Edward Jr. and Veronica Davis Gerald. 2003. *The Ultimate Gullah Cookbook.* Beaufort, SC: Sands Publishing Company.

Geraty, Virginia Mixson. 1992. *Bittle en' T'ing': Gullah Cooking with Maum Chrish'*. Orangeburg, SCouth: Sandlapper Publishing Co.

Littlefield, Daniel C. 1981. *Rice and Slaves: Ethnicity and the Slave Trade in Colonial South Carolina*. Baton Rouge: Louisiana State University Press.

Mannur, Anita. 2007. "Culinary Nostalgia: Authenticity, Nationalism, and Diaspora." *MELUS* 32, no. 4 (December): 11–31.

Morgan, Jennifer L. 2004. *Laboring Women: Reproduction and Gender in New World Slavery*. Philadelphia, PA: University of Pennsylvania Press.

Opala, Joseph A. 1987. *The Gullah: Rice, Slavery, and the Sierra Leone-American Connection*. Washington, DC: United States Information Service.

Robinson, Sallie Ann. 2003. *Gullah Home Cooking, the Daufuskie Way: Smokin' Joe Butter Beans, Ol' 'Fuskie Fried Crab Rice, Sticky-Bush Blackberry Dumpling, and Other Sea Island Favorites*. Chapel Hill: University of North Carolina Press.

Segar, Eva. 2006. *My Gullah Kitchen*. Beaufort, SC: You Should Write a Book.

Shange, Ntozake. 1982. *Sassafrass, Cypress & Indigo*. New York: Picador.

Sutton, David E. 2001. *Remembrance of Repasts: An Anthropology of Food and Memory*. Oxford: Berg.

The Nag Hammadi Library. 2011. The Gnostic Society (website). Accessed October 11. http://www.gnosis.org/naghamm/nhl.html.

The Summer of Food (Part 2) Marshview Organic Farm. 2011. Coastal Conservation League (website). Accessed October 11. http://coastalconservationleague.org/the-summer-of-food-part-2.

Theophano, Janet. 2002. *Eat My Words: Reading Women's Lives through the Cookbooks They Wrote*. New York: Palgrave.

White, Katie. 2009. "Stirring the Pot of Creolization: Women and the Culinary History of Gullah Communities on St. Helena Island, South Carolina." Master's thesis, San Diego State University.

CHAPTER FIVE

Decorating the Decorations

Daughters of the Dust and the Aesthetics of the Quilt

CORRIE CLAIBORNE

In addition to being the year Julie Dash's film *Daughters of the Dust* enjoyed a successful theatrical release, 1991 was also the year that brought us Lucille Clifton's collection of poetry *Quilting: 1987–1990*, from which the title of the poem "Quilting" was taken. The simultaneous arrival of Clifton's Pulitzer Prize-nominated collection and Dash's groundbreaking film doesn't seem to be accidental. Indeed, there was something in the air that asked that the story of Black women /Black people who were and are part of "this unknown world," as Clifton calls it, be told in a way that it hadn't previously. Change, as they say, had been coming. On March 2, 1991, Rodney King would be videotaped getting the beating of his life by the Los Angeles Police Department. In July, Mike Tyson was arrested and charged with raping a Miss Black America contestant. And in October 1991, the then unknown Arkansas governor Bill Clinton announced he would be running for president. Thus, when Dash's film, which depicted African Americans—specifically Gullah people—embracing their past and their African culture, it was the New World Black narrative for which Black people and the world were waiting. Dash's movie, which she produced, wrote, and directed, was a visionary change. Starring relative unknowns, it was an anti-narrative, anti-Hollywood film that sought to give life to a group of people who, in recent memory, had only been seen once before in a nationally or internationally distributed feature film.

The previous film, *Conrack* (1974), based on the book *The Water Is Wide* by Pat Conroy, told the story of Conroy's own experience as a teacher on Daufuskie Island, South Carolina, to Black children, all direct descendants of enslaved Africans, who, because of their isolation from white people and from popular culture, languished illiterate and broken under the guidance of a Black female principal who seemed more interested in having her charges beaten than educated. While Conroy's tale documents the powerlessness poor Sea Island Black people experienced in the 20th century, *Daughters of the Dust* elucidates the desire and push for agency and self-determination by Black people during the long period of Black resistance and the struggles for civil rights.

Instead of operating under what Toni Cade Bambara, in her essay "Reading the Signs, Empowering the Eye: *Daughters of the Dust* and the Black Independent Cinema Movement," called "the deficit model," Dash showed us Black women could love. And as Jacqueline Bobo points out, we LOVED *Daughters of the Dust*. By word of mouth, Black women managed to become 90% of the film's sold-out audiences (Bobo 1995, 9), happy to finally see their true selves and their true colors on the big screen.

Much like the Black woman quilter in Clifton's poem, Dash's women offer up a cacophony of 20th century Black women's experiences, identities, struggles, and triumphs. Further still, Dash's women have us ponder the social, personal, and collective trajectory Black women's identities has taken and continues to take, and how this trajectory shapes our movement in the world today. To get to this answer, we must examine Dash's use of layered images, much like the photographer Mr. Sneed's camera, then as kaleidoscope of history and future, and that of a quilt made new from fragments of past garments and memories, to sustain the Peazant family during the shifting terrain. More to the point, at the end of the film, we are left to wonder just how the Peazant family is going to survive in the new world of the North with their strange language and their "saltwater ways." Ultimately, the questions that Clifton's poem posits, "How does this poem end?" and "do the daughters' daughters quilt?" are the questions that we are still seeking to answer in the 25-plus years since *Daughters of the Dust*'s release.

The story Dash tells is not simply the story of Black people. It is, of course, the story of "unknown" Black people, the Geechees or, less pejoratively, the Gullahs, whose homeland, as William Pollitzer argues, spans 250 miles from North Carolina to Florida (199, 5). Interestingly, Gullah people were not unknown to me since my family originated from the Lowcountry of South Carolina. Although not from one of the coastal Sea Islands, my maternal grandmother's family recognized African retentions at work in their culture because of the relative low influence of white culture in Johnsonville, South Carolina. It was the pride in these African retentions that gave my grandmother, for example, the ability to defy convention and go to college and, until very late in her life, to refuse to let a white man or any "buckra" ever step foot on her property. It is the same strength and employment of African retentions—spiritual and natural—that allows Nana Peazant to reject the movement off the island. Indeed, Nana realizes everything important in life she already has: knowledge of the natural and the spiritual world, ancient cultural practices, and deep family ties. She tells her family, "we carry these memories inside of we"; in many ways, this is all the armor the family needs to protect them during their move north.

To be sure, memories and dreams, and giving voice to them, play a central part of the film. The narration at the beginning of the movie starts with the voice of Yellow Mary:

> I am the first and the last. I am the honored one and the scorned one. I am the whore and the holy one. I am the wife and the virgin. I am the barren one, and many are my daughters. I am the silence that you cannot understand. I am the utterance of my name. (Dash 1991)

By invoking the Black Gnostic Gospel, Dash speaks to the multiple selves at work in African people, but specifically Black women. "Daughters of the dust" recognize their connection to the land—their ancestors cultivated South Carolina soil to make Charleston the richest city in the South; and prior to that, their agricultural knowledge contributed to the thriving bounty of Africa's rice coast. More importantly, Nana Peazant makes the symbiotic connection between the womb, the ancestors, and those buried in the ground, and she admonishes her progeny to recognize this and to remember.

To be a daughter of the dust is to live in contrast to the images of Black women as mammies, maids, strippers, and prostitutes that have appeared in film since the beginning of American filmmaking. In fact, this narration recalls Toni Morrison's explanation of who the "beloved" is in her award-winning 1987 novel:

> Everybody knew what she was called, but nobody anywhere knew her name. Disremembered and unaccounted for, she cannot be lost because no one is looking for her, and even if they were, how can they call her if they don't know her name? Although she has claim, she is not claimed. (Morrison 1987, 274)

While it is clear at conclusion of the film that the name of the woman speaking is Yellow Mary, we also learn this is not, as Morrison argues, her actual name. Just as Sethe's community does not know the beloved's name, viewers, too, do not really know the women of Ibo Landing at the beginning of the film. The film then gives the opportunity to see and to know these women who have been "disremembered and unaccounted for," to name them. The images that accompany the opening lines of *Daughters of the Dust* are then about defining who these women are. Moreover, as frequently seen in the film, images do the talking when the words cannot. Jacqueline Bobo (1995, 135) argues the slow dissolve of images at the film's inception:

> [...] Mean something; it is more than a transition device signaling the passage of time. The dissolves are used to convey important information. [...] They are also a homage to [James]

Van derZee [*sic*] and the method he used to compose his photographs featuring the black inhabitants of Harlem in the early decades of this century.

While Van Der Zee is an important artist who, in many ways, defined the African American vernacular landscape through photography, it is more significant to locate the aesthetic Dash employs in the Sea Islands themselves. Instead of being solely an homage to the Harlem Renaissance photographer, Dash's photographic dissolves point instead to quilting as an identifying practice for both the fictional characters in Ibo Landing and for Julie Dash herself.

Quilts are everywhere in the frames of *Daughters of the Dust*. Very early we see the quilt that covers the bed of the lovers, as well as the walls of the houses—which are covered in images and newsprint. Along with the patchwork of colors seen in the kaleidoscope, in the clothing the people wear, and in the food they eat, Dash uses quilting to tell the people's story.

It is important, then, that when the Peazant family goes to their last supper on the beach, one woman is holding a collection of squares one knows she is going to piece together in order to tell about the family's journey off the island. Thus, what is most striking about the film is that the images remind one less of a Harlem photograph and more of the paintings of important Gullah artist Jonathan Green.

Although Viola brings the photographer with her upon returning from the mainland, it is the people who have yet to leave who truly tell the story of the family's migration, and by extension, the story of all Black people who have left their African roots to more fully assimilate into America. The quilt, then, becomes a part of "the medicine" or protection that the old ways offer. According to Robert Ferris Thompson, it is a West African belief that evil travels in straight lines. One of the reasons Black people in these isolated communities began putting newsprint on the walls (besides warmth) is they believed it slowed down evil spirits. The Gullah myth is that any "haint" would have to stop and read all the newsprint before they could attack the person. Here Dash privileges Gullah root culture to demonstrate the power and place of such traditions in Black Sea Island culture. Furthermore, Dash draws on superstitious beliefs many held about photography in its early years. This is evident in Mr. Sneed's interactions with members of the Peazant family as he tries to capture their images before their departure for the mainland. Dash uses the dialectic between modernity and Gullah folk ways to demarcate the shifting social and cultural tides at work at the turn of the 20th century.

The film and the narrative are multilayered just like the quilts and newsprint that adorn the modest homes of her characters. Further, this layering, of "decorating the decorations," is often seen in African Art, according to Robert Farris Thompson (1984), and in the language of the rural South, as Zora Neale Hurston argues in "Characteristics of Negro Expression" (2003). The "will to adorn" in speech is the most prevalent example of Hurston's theory in the Gullah context.

In the film, one sees the people of Ibo Landing using more ornate expressions like "day clean" to mean something simple like "sunrise." It is this embroidery of language that firmly situates the film in its Blackness, and, more specifically, in its Sea Islandness. Moreover, Dash uses the quilts in her film to add an extra layer of Gullah language, which is offered throughout the film without subtitles.

As William Pollitzer (1999, 180) points out in *The Gullah People and Their African Heritage*, the quilts are their own language on the Sea Islands:

> In the sea islands quilts communicate affection and celebrate family history—a marriage, birth, or departure for school. When one accompanies a departing family member, it is a reminder of kinship. Members of a family can identify the patches and tell whose clothing, drapes or household cloths they were before they did final duty in the quilt tops. [...] The quilts are cryptic chronicles, readable only by those who are initiated into the lexicon and context of the familial documents involved. They are a historical record, a primary source, coming directly out of the life of the family—only understood by them and possibly treasured all the more because of it.

Thus, the language of the quilt is then the most effective language the Peazant family and Dash can speak. This language is comprised of African symbols that hold meaning in the context of Ibo Landing and for the Peazant family. Further, Pollitzer (1999, 179–180) explains the significance of color in these strip quilts produced by the Gullah people:

> The colors in the quilts convey a deeper meaning than meets the eye, connected to the beliefs and values of the sea-island people, as they are in Africa. Red indicates danger, conflict, passion; blue repels bad spirits; white suggests innocence and purity.

The colors are not only seen in the quilts, but also in the clothing the characters wear. In particular, the white dresses are an important symbol that remains from the African continent. While the startling white dresses are reminiscent of baptismal gowns, as seen in older images from Spencer Williams's 1941 *The Blood of Jesus* (also released as *Glory Road*), they also remind us there is a startling lack of white faces in the actual movie. And some have argued, conversely, that the absence of whiteness or white images compromises the film's version of Blackness as W. T. Lhamon Jr. (2005) suggests in "Optic Black: Naturalizing the Refusal to Fit." However, Lhamon is shortsighted in his assertion that one can only comment on whiteness by depicting it and or/contrasting it to Blackness. Either way, whiteness *is* present in Ibo Landing in the form of the unseen man who rapes Eula, which causes tension between her and Eli. The white man is in the stories of both Yellow Mary and Nana. Lhamon implies the lack of true representation between Black and white people prevented Dash and her film from becoming popular with cross-cultural audiences, limiting her celebrity to marginal circles. However, just like Black women quiltmakers who used what they had in terms of materials to make their quilts—old dresses, work pants, and feed sacks—without a pattern, often ripping cloth instead of cutting with scissors, and showing the stitches instead of hiding the seams, Dash's art was never meant for mass consumption.

Toni Cade Bambara reminds us that Dash's work came out of "the insurgent activity" of students at the University of California, Los Angeles (UCLA) Film School. Bambara suggests Dash, like Haile Gerima and Charles Burnett, saw the importance of making film where accountability to the community took precedence over training for an industry that maligns and exploits, trivializes, and renders Black people invisible. The community, and not the classroom, is the appropriate training ground for producing relevant work; it is the destiny of our people that concerns us, not self-indulgent assignments about neurotic preoccupations. Our task is to reconstruct cultural memory, not slavishly imitate white models. Our task leads us to our own suppressed bodies of literature, lore, and history, not to the "classics" promoted by Eurocentric academia (Bambara 1993, 119).

In some ways, the limited popularity of the film is its message. It is the wisdom passed down by Nana when she said "we carry the memories inside of we" (Dash 1991). Surely, just like quilting was passed down from mother to daughter, the memories Dash evokes are of an internal, ethereal quilt. "Remember these will keep us warm," the narrator says in Lucille Clifton's poem. Like a quilt, Dash's film keeps us warm by reminding us of who we are. It is film that, like Alice Walker's short story by the same title, was to be put to "Everyday Use."

At the end of Dash's film, most of the family moves off the Island, while Nana and a few others remain. The viewer is left to ponder the future of the Peazant family. Clifton (1991) verbalizes this by asking, "How does this poem end?" and "Do the daughters' daughters quilt?" Although, I do not think we can truly know how the poem will end or what the story of Black people will be, it is clear Dash established a cinematic tradition that made it possible for Black women to recognize and really begin to see ourselves in American film. Clifton's question "will the daughters' daughters quilt" has important meaning within the context of film too. In essence, both Dash and Clifton muse whether Black women and Black filmmakers will continue to seem themselves through their own eyes, just as the UCLA film collective did by layer imaging and color to make us aware of ourselves outside of the typical Hollywood representations. In some ways, this insurgent aesthetic, this quilting aesthetic, is really *Daughters of the Dust's* greatest strength.

We have only to look at Ava DuVernay's 2010 film *I Will Follow* to know the daughters are quilting. The film revolves around a Black woman who moves in with her aunt to spend time with her as she is dying of cancer and the 12 people who come to visit after the aunt has died. Based in part on her personal history, DuVernay wrote, directed, and used her own money to make the film. Shooting in one location over 15 days made it possible for DuVernay to make the film for

$50,000. In a March 11, 2011, *Los Angeles Times* article, DuVernay makes plain part of her impetus for making the film:

> "I think when you look at the fact that this year, so far, the studios have released one film starring a Black woman, and it's 'Big Momma,' that statement to me is really profound," she said, referring to the third installment in the Martin Lawrence drag comedy franchise.

> It's really about the studios feeling what will sell to a mass audience, not developing films that appeal to niches and smaller groups. We all sit around and complain about the studio system, complain about men in dresses. The bottom line is, the energy I spent complaining about them is energy I can put into making a film about a happy black woman who is taking her destiny in her own hands. (King 2011)

> In fact, DuVernay founded an organization called the African American Film Releasing Movement (AAFRM) to make sure the struggles Dash had distributing her film are non-factors for other African American filmmakers. Moreover, she contends, "Those who make specifically black-themed movies […] should realize that 'no one is ever going to care about their film except the people it's made for, which is, Black folks'." (Cieply 2011)

DuVernay's film, like *Daughters of the Dust* 20 years before it, is visually stunning. Instead of having a strong plot line, the movie relies on gripping visual tableaus, beautiful color, and the stunning beauty of the main character, played by Salli Richardson-Whitfield. The main character's dying aunt is also covered in beautiful color, becoming a living quilt, who throughout the film reminds Richardson-Whitfield's character about the importance of music and storytelling. Moreover, as the synchronous arrival of Clifton's poetry and Dash's film is no accident, it seems *I Will Follow* is, as its title suggests, a way for a new producer-director to follow in Dash's footsteps. Further, DuVernay's AAFRM is reminiscent of the philosophy outlined by Black students at the UCLA film school. The aesthetic of *I Will Follow*, finally, gives us confirmation that when the Peazant family migrated north, they brought with them their memories and strong sense of identity. It is this unique Gullah identity Dash documents, a rich culture that continues to be passed down from hand to hand, from artist to artist, from mother to daughter.

REFERENCES

Arnett, Paul, Joanne Cubbs, and Eugene W. Metcalf Jr., eds. 2006. *Gee's Bend: The Architecture of the Quilt*. Atlanta, GA: Tinwood Books.

Bambara, Toni Cade. 1993. "Reading the Signs, Empowering the Eye: *Daughters of the Dust* and the Black Independent Cinema Movement." In *Black American Cinema*, edited by Manthia Diawara, 118–144. New York: Routledge.

Bobo, Jacqueline. 1995. *Black Women as Cultural Readers*. New York: Columbia University Press.

Cieply, Michael. 2011. "Building an Alliance to Aid Films by Blacks." *New York Times* (New York Edition), January 7, 2011.

Clifton, Lucille. 1991. *Quilting: Poems 1987–1990*. Brockport, NY: BOA Editions.

Conroy, Pat. 2002. *The Water Is Wide: A Memoir*. New York: Dial Press.

Dash, Julie, dir. 1991. *Daughters of the Dust*. 1991. New York, NY: Kino International.

Diouf, Sylviane A. 2009. *Dreams of Africa in Alabama: The Slave Ship Clotilda and the Story of the Last Africans Brought to America*. New York: Oxford University Press.

DuVernay, Ava, dir. *I Will Follow*. 2010.

Fry, Gladys-Marie. 2002. *Stitched from the Soul: Slave Quilts from the Antebellum South*. Chapel Hill: University of North Carolina Press.

Gantt, Jesse Edward Jr. and Veronica Davis Gerald. 2003. *The Ultimate Gullah Cookbook*. Beaufort, SC: Sands Publishing Company.

Hicks, Kyra E. 2003. *Black Threads: An African American Quilting Sourcebook*. Jefferson, NC: McFarland & Company.

Holloway, Joseph, ed. 1991. *Africanisms in American Culture*. Bloomington: Indiana University Press.

Hurston, Zora Neale. 2003. "Characteristics of Negro Expression." In *The Norton Anthology of African American Literature*, edited by Henry Louis Gates Jr. and Nellie Y. McKay, 1041–1053. New York: W. W. Norton & Company.

King, Susan. 2011. "For Ava DuVernay, Making 'I Will Follow' Is Personal." *Los Angeles Times*, March 11, 2011. https://www.latimes.com/entertainment/la-xpm-2011-mar-11-la-et-ava-20110311-story.html.

Leon, Eli. 2006. *Accidentally on Purpose: The Aesthetic Management of Irregularities in African Textiles and African-American Quilts*. Davenport, IA: Figge Art Museum.

Lhamon, W. T., Jr. 2005. "Optic Black: Naturalizing the Refusal to Fit." In *Black Cultural Traffic: Crossroads in Global Performance and Popular Culture*, edited by Harry Elam Jr. and Kennell Jackson, 111–140. Ann Arbor: University of Michigan Press.

Mazloomi, Carolyn. 1998. *Spirits of the Cloth: Contemporary African American Quilts*. New York: Clarkson Potter.

Morrison, Toni. 1987. *Beloved*. New York: Alfred A. Knopf.

Naylor, Gloria. 1989. *Mama Day*. New York: Vintage Books.

Opala, Joseph A. 1987. *The Gullah: Rice, Slavery, and the Sierra Leone-American Connection*. Washington, DC: United States Information Service.

Pollitzer, William S. 1999. *The Gullah People and Their African Heritage*. Athens: University of Georgia Press.

Thompson, Robert Farris. 1984. *Flash of the Spirit: African and Afro-American Art and Philosophy*. New York: Vintage Books.

Turner, Lorenzo Dow. (1949) 1974. *Africanisms in the Gullah Dialect*. Ann Arbor: University of Michigan Press.

Voight, Jon, Paul Winfield, and Madge Sinclair. 1974. *Conrack*. Directed by Martin Ritt.

Wahlman, Maude Southwell. 2001. *Signs & Symbols: African Images in African American Quilts*. Atlanta: Tinwood Books.

Williams, Spencer, dir. *The Blood of Jesus*. 1941.

Wood, Peter. 1974. *Black Majority: Negroes in Colonial South Carolina from 1670 through the Stono Rebellion*. New York. Alfred A. Knopf.

PART 3

The Sacred Emerge: The Witness, the Healed, and Daughters of the Dust

CHAPTER SIX

"I Arrived Late to This Book"

Teaching Sociology with Julie Dash's *Daughters of the Dust*, the Novel[1]

KAREN M. GAGNE

I arrived late to this book. It is more than ten years old and I feel as if I just missed a friend who had waited for me as long as they could, but had to leave.

—"Ysis" September 2004 reviewer of *Daughters of the Dust*, at Amazon.com

I finished the book in less than three days. This book gave me a closure I never knew I needed. In reading this book I was able to give my ancestors a proper burial and set all our souls free.

—Felicity Jackson, October 2006 reviewer of *Daughters of the Dust*, at Barnesandnoble.com

I picked up the hardcover edition in a discount bin at my university bookstore in 1998. It was on sale for $5.00. It was a clean copy, in good shape, and had a lovely picture on the jacket. It was an unknown title to me, but I was sold by the women on the cover. I envisioned I would enjoy reading it when I got around to reading a novel—post-Ph.D. I placed it on the shelf with others of similar classification. I'm glad I didn't wait *that* long. Just when I thought I was taking a break from my "sociology" work, the cover of *Daughters of the Dust: A Novel* caught my eye; I took it off the shelf and read it. It was hard to read, with some language barriers, but I still couldn't put it down. Each page demanded another. I tried to learn the language and keep the names of the African gods straight. Reading *Daughters of the Dust* proved to be an unforgettable journey.

Soon after I finished reading the book, I found a copy of the film by the same title. I was so thrilled that I would be able to see some of the scenes portrayed on the screen—especially those Saturday nights at Carrie Mae Johnson's backwoods juke joint, when Amelia and Elizabeth visit the place where Haagar (Amelia's grandmother) came from, and that most unforgettable scene when Lucy Peazant finds the skull and human leg bones with chains still on them while plowing in the field she intends to buy. Little did I know at the time that the book and the film were not one and the same; the book actually begins where the film ends. I didn't figure this out until toward the end of the film when I began to recognize the characters from the book. I started over and watched the film ("first") and then again read the book.

A few years later when I was teaching a class called "Images of the Family," I assigned all three works by the same title: the film (Dash 1991), the novel (Dash 1997), and the book about the making of the film (Dash 1992). What a trilogy! Dash makes an invaluable contribution towards the understanding of the lives of Africans in the New World. She makes plain the connection between the Gullah Geechee people of the Sea Islands and all Africans in the diaspora, those who moved North and those who live in the South—in the Caribbean and the Americas. In addition to consulting her own family for their histories, Dash did over ten years of research to prepare for this cultural production, at the Schomburg Center for Research in Black Culture in Harlem; at the National Archives, the Library of Congress, the Smithsonian, in Washington, DC; and at the Penn Center on St. Helena Island, off the coast of South Carolina (Dash 1992, 5). Sandra Grayson, in her analysis of the film, argues that when juxtaposed with other films such as Haile Gerima's *Sankofa* (1993) and Kasi Lemmons's *Eve's Bayou* (1997) Dash's *Daughters of the Dust* functions as a "continuous narrative about enslaved Africans and their descendents in North America, vignettes that represent experiences spanning from the antebellum period through the 20th century" (Grayson 2000, 2). Grounded in historical research, Dash uses spoken word and cultural symbols to present factual information that is "infused with an imaginative construction creating a mythic memory" (2).

However, while the film *Daughters of the Dust* has received considerable attention in academics circles,[2] the novel has received *no* attention at all. I thought it might have gotten lost to the dusty shelves of used bookstores—for a long time it was only available used at Barnesandnoble.com and Amazon.com. I am pleased however, that the book is again available. As a professor of sociology and anthropology, I would like to call attention to the powerful role this book can play in representing the human condition, in healing a community, and in "making the struggle irresistible," as Toni Cade Bambara suggests it is the job of a writer to do (Bambara 1982; Gagne 2006).

Through this powerful story, Dash makes a critical intervention against Western academia. The *novel* is not only a continuation of the story of the Peazants, the family portrayed in the film about to move north to the mainland. It does indeed pick up the story where the film leaves off and give insight into the characters we met in the film. *Daughters of the Dust*, the novel, is further a powerful cultural history all by itself. Through its "nonlinear, multilayered unfolding" (Dash 1992, xiii), the story connects African gods and goddesses (Ogun, Elegba, Oya, Osun, and Yemoja) and African ancestors to those Africans living in the present. It shows the importance of storytelling, regardless of the form or method one uses to tell stories, in carrying out the struggle of African peoples, as each new generation is connected to each other and to their ancestors by keeping collective memories alive.

Dash, like other Black women writers before her,[3] disrupts and rewrites "history." She offers a counter-narrative to the conventional and canonical stories of hegemonic discourse. Mae Gwendolyn Henderson argues Black women writers have encoded oppression as a discursive dilemma. In other words, these writers have consistently raised the issue of their relationship to power and discourse, and negotiate this dilemma by "entering into both 'testimonial' and 'competitive' discourses with their readers" (quoted in Brøndum 1999, 154). Regarding the film *Daughters of the Dust*, Lene Brøndum argues Dash speaks to Black women in an "intimate voice" by focusing on the stories of the Peazant women and by "mythologizing their past and their present." Brøndum adds that this is not merely a personal discussion. Dash "also enters into a public and political dialogue with the hegemonic systems" by subverting the traditional standards of historiography (Brøndum 1999, 154). In fact, Dash does two things. Firstly, she makes a film entirely about Black women's lives. This act *alone* blows up "History." Dash, in other words, rewrites the whole story (of "History") by writing Black women into the "canon" (154). Secondly, Dash writes a non-linear "composite history" of the Sea Islands by representing this history in a non-chronological manner—in which historical facts are "selected for representation according to whether they effectively reveal something about the 'essence' of a culture or a historical period, rather than according to 'objective,' historical demands for chronological accuracy" (Brøndum 1999, 154).

Writing about Paule Marshall's *Praisesong for the Widow* (1983), Abena Busia (1989, 198) argues it is crucial we not look at such texts by Black women writers as "abstractions." They must be understood as concrete aspects of the lives of Africans, "where our meaning—our story—becomes what we can read about ourselves and our lives." Reading texts like these is an active exercise in self-identification whereby one recognizes both life experiences and historic transformations that lead to celebration and a coming together "attainable only through an understanding and acceptance of the demands of the past, which are transformed into a gift for the future" (198). The impact of *Praisesong for the Widow*, for example, on Busia herself was a profound one:

> In many respects, the reason I am so powerfully attached to this novel is because when reading it for the first time, I experienced many powerful moments of recognition and could therefore feel the lyrical joy Avatara feels when she recognizes again elements from out of her childhood, which come also out of mine. The moment I first read the account of the Ring Shout, for instance, I recognized the outlines of the dance: I, like, Avey, had been a visitor to my home, watching on the sidelines while only the old people took part. The descriptions of the durbar in Ghana were so familiar, as were Lebert Joseph's ceremonies for absent children. Those supplications to the ancestors, performed for wandering children such as myself who seem to take a long time finding their way home again, have been done to ensure my safe return or to celebrate my safe arrival. My personal reading of this work then was in the first instance an "autobiographical" reading, which reminded me that all exiles can be transformed into homecomings. (Busia 1989, 240)

Avatara's private history of material acquisition and cultural dispossession is also the history of all Africans as a result of the enslavement-colonization process for 500 years.

Diaspora texts always begin and end with Africa. These works carry out the symbolic reversal of that Middle Passage for the writer *and the reader*, as well as for the people in the stories. Storytelling, Busia argues, "incorporates a wealth of nonwritten cultural forms that must be reinvested with meaning." Re-validation of these cultural forms, for the individual and for the collective, happens within the text and is part of the lifelong process of "African Reconnection" (1989, 197). The writer and the reader must engage in the same active process, as the protagonists, of recognizing and reassembling cultural signs; they must also actively take this journey and thereby reverse the Middle Passage in effect (1989, 196).

Through the journey of her protagonist Avatara, Marshall takes her readers on a journey both backwards and forward, toward a new "self-recognition and healing." This is, according to Busia, vital for the reconnecting of the scattered peoples of Africa—a trauma that is "constantly repeated anew in the lives of each new generation" (1989, 197). The trauma is reproduced by the conditions under which the people have to live, conditions which dictate that they sever from their African cultural roots. However, Marshall and Busia maintain that this is a sacrificial price much too high to pay.[4] To understand the magnitude of the sacrifice, it is necessary for Marshall's readers to take the journey along with Avey Johnson. Still, Marshall requires first that her readers have some knowledge of "diaspora literacy" (Clark 1990) so that all can see again the "fragments that make up the whole." In other words, readers must have an ability to read a variety of cultural signs of the lives of "Africa's children at home and in the New World" (1989, 197).

The journey Avey/Avatara takes in *Praisesong for the Widow* is the same journey that Amelia has to take in *Daughters of the Dust*. In both cases, this journey begins with a boat crossing, as I shall describe. Those who read these texts must also complete the journey—or "cross over." This is to say, again, Marshall's and Dash's readers must also "reverse the Middle Passage" (Benton 2000) if not literally by boat, and learn to read the cultural signs to become whole again.

Marshall's *Praisesong for the Widow* inspired Dash's idea for *Daughters of the Dust*. The central story in *Daughters* about Ibo Landing is borrowed from Marshall (Marshall 1983, 37–39; Dash 1992, 141; Brøndum 1999, 159; Benton 2000, 227). In giving Ibo Landing the central place in her text on Dawtah Island, Dash puts forth her stance like Marshall "regarding the great American afflictions, amnesia and disconnectedness" (Dash 1992, xi–xiii; Bambara 1996, 109). Both Marshall and Dash link the histories of all Africans in the Diaspora and their persistent resistance and revolt against their capture to that moment when the Ibos, seeing what was ahead of them when they got off the slave ships (and the many while still on the ships). Rejecting what would be the Carolina Sea Islands, they headed back toward Africa. The name "Ibo Landing" in the film and novel recalls stories still told on these islands *and* in the Caribbean. Toni Cade Bambara notes that this place, the site for the film, is called "the secret isle" because the land is both bloody and blessed: "A port of entry for the European slaving ships, the Carolina Sea Islands (Port Royal County) were where captured Africans were 'seasoned' for servitude. Even after the trade was outlawed, traffickers used the dense and marshy area to hide forbidden cargo. But the difficult terrain was also a haven for both self-emancipated Africans and indigenous peoples, just as the Florida Everglades and the Louisiana bayous were for the Seminoles and Africans, and for the Filipinos conscripted by the French to fight proxy wars (French and Indian wars)" (Bambara 1996, 94–95).

The last ship on U.S. record to have "imported" Africans to the United States is the slave ship *The Wanderer*. This ship transported four hundred Africans to Jekyll Island, Georgia, in 1858, fifty-one years after the importation of Africans as slaves had been banned in 1807 (Brøndum 1999, 159). The story of this ship is told to the young Peazants (and Dash's audience) by Nana, Bilal, and Eula in the film. Even Viola and Yellow Mary dismiss Mr. Snead's "official history" which counters the existence of this "too late date" ship. This important story, though, is retold to a new generation (and again to Dash's readers) in the book. Bilal Muhammad (and Paymore in the novel) arrived on this ship with the same Ibo peoples from whom the Landing received its name. In the novel, there is another ship called *The Sorcerer*. Evidence of *this* ship is found engraved on iron shackles that are accidentally dug up, still attached to human skulls and leg bones. The ship, Miz Emma Julia tells us, got its name because "it run so fast folks not sure dey see it. It come an go jus like dat!" This ship was constantly escaping the watch of the Yankees who, just before the War, in the waters between Beaufort and Charleston, looked for illegal transporting of new captives (Dash 1997, 234).

The film *Daughters of the Dust* represents a powerful and critical commentary on ethnographic film. This is suggested by the characters of Viola Peazant, a modern Jesus-saved woman who previously escaped her "heathenness" by leaving "this God-forsaken Island," and her hired photographer Mr. Snead (Dash 1992, 37–38). They come to the Island to record the movement of Viola's family from Island toward the "progress" that awaits them in the cities up North. Dash's commentary is palpable in the novel in the person of Amelia Varnes. The story of Amelia is a biting critique of the fields of ethnographic film and anthropology, their rise in the university, and the funding of these "sciences" by "benefactors" in the private sector who have interests in "developing" the land for their own profit.

Amelia is one of the first Black female anthropologists, studying at Brooklyn College. A graduate student in 1926, she would have been a contemporary of Zora Neale Hurston. Amelia has received word that the Foundation of Brooklyn College has provided her with a grant to complete her field research, which is to study "her people" of the Carolina Sea Islands. Amelia's benefactor wants to remain anonymous, but it is revealed to be someone who made a fortune dealing in land, railroads and other "investments." Her advisor, Professor Colby adds, "Actually I suspect he has an interest in the land down there; he's been talking about another summer home" (Dash 1997, 31).

Amelia is sent equipped with a 16mm, hand-cranked Akeley camera. In exchange for her testing out the old camera, her benefactor will pay for all the film and processing. The images, her professor suggests, will "add to the weight of her research."

Six months later, when Amelia finally returns to New York to complete her thesis, she is a completely different person. Fully intending to remain "objective" and "outside" her subjects of study when she began the project, Amelia finds out that this not only impossible, but increasingly undesirable. She sees the need to protect her family from encroachment of the kind of researchers of the type that she was—especially those sponsored by land-hungry "philanthropists." As she attempts to edit the film footage taken by her young cousin Ben she is reluctant to share these images of family and friends with strangers: "Contrary to everything that she had started out to do, she did not want their culture, their ways, how they talked to each other described in academic terms that would leave out the spirit and overlook the common heritage and stories that bound them so closely. She had winced when she read her thesis proposal with its distant perspective and cold language that attempted to describe people whose lives were filled with wonder, vibrancy, and an uncomplicated honesty. Life for them was hard, a struggle from one moment to the next, but it was filled with the natural pleasures that she was now just beginning to understand and appreciate" (Dash 1997, 283–284).

She carefully edits and provides only glimpses of the scenery and non-intrusive or more "impersonal" moments, although she is sure this is not going to sit well with her committee, or her benefactor. She does show a film at the end of a grueling defense meeting, where she is grilled about her thesis.

One committee member who has purportedly "completed the formative work on Negro communities, and [...] is not familiar with these people," poses the question, "What is it about these colored people that makes them different from any other colored people?" Amelia restates what she has been taught to be the requirements of a "culture," including a shared history. This interjection produces an uproar from Professor Anderson, who states, "They are simply stories. There is little there of historic merit. They have long since lost their ties to where they came from!" Professor Colby interjects with "Surely you're not going to dismiss the importance of oral tradition!" Anderson snaps, "Of course not!" But, he continues, "I'm just not sure that what these people have to say amounts to a history. Quite frankly, what you have described seems to me to be some kind of crude imitation of the old plantation culture, a patois derived from broken English and the flurried accents of Irish and Huguenot planters, all of which is the obvious product of European influence. Surely you're not suggesting that in the land of secession and large plantations, there can be anything else?" (Dash 1997, 289)

Amelia struggles to maintain her composure. Professor Rehnquist pipes in:

Mere vestiges, if anything, Miss Varnes. Not what would be acceptable in a scientific sense. Why, it is an established fact accepted by your own colored sociologists, that the colored people, bereft of a history, culture, traditions, have long since adopted the ways of the dominant culture, shedding all ties with the African continent. (Dash 1997, 289–290)

This exchange goes back and forth as Amelia struggled to defend her position, with Professor Colby's support, including her assertion that the people maintained a distinct *language* and not merely a *dialect* or simple form of English. When the others were not able to convince Colby or Amelia, they turned to more stylistic problems with her thesis:

"The writing [...]," Professor Anderson insisted. "There seems to be an inordinate amount of adjectives and adverbs. It's not as clean of personal [...] ah [...] feelings as it could be." It is at this point that Amelia shows them her film.

She had just completed it the night before, carefully, protectively choosing what she wanted to share with them and what she would share with her family when she and her mother returned. From the footage of Elizabeth and the children sprinting down the dunes, to the men cleaning the fish on the docks, to the churchgoers shouting in church, there was only the sound of the projector running as the images flashed on the screen. She had put together a pictorial story that ran through the lives of the people, never intruding, but showing their everyday realities and capturing their grace. She had chosen the footprints on the beach as the final sequence. (Dash 1997, 291)

Her committee was silenced. She passed with flying colors. A few days later, her advisor, breathless with exciting news, tells Amelia that she had been asked to present her paper at the yearly conference of the American Anthropological Society, which would guarantee that her work would be published in "at least two of the most preeminent journals in the country." He adds, "You have no idea of what you have started!" The committee was thrilled to hear about the film (291).

It is at this point that Amelia truly shows what she has learned in the last six months when she most emphatically rejects the path of fame and upward mobility that would be hers. She declines the invitation, first with "I can't present it" and then firmly, "I won't present it." When she is asked why she says:

> I'm scared [...] scared about the kind of change this is going to bring [...] What's going to happen to my family and my friends when everyone starts flooding in, asking about the details of their lives that are just natural to them? I know it's selfish, but they are a proud people, an independent kind of people. They've survived slavery, crop disasters, hurricanes, and floods, and I don't want them to lose what brought them through [...] The first class I took with you, you taught us about respecting what we were to study [...] but you also taught us about change and how as anthropologists we were not to introduce change. I can't help but worry that I've already brought change, and I'm afraid that if this paper gets published, it will bring about the worst kind of change. (Dash 1997, 294)

Dash's biting critique of this kind of research is illustrated in the passage that follows:

> "Miss Varnes, change is going to come to the Island," Professor Colby warned her. "If not through you, it will be someone else. You can't stop that. Why, your benefactor is sitting down with planners as we speak talking about what he's going to build down there in the next few years."
>
> "I know I can't stop change, but Lord knows, I don't have to be an agent of it."
>
> "But what of all your work?" Professor Colby argued. "It's wonderful! You deserve the acclaim it will bring."
>
> Amelia considered this and then smiled slightly. "I didn't write it for that, and I don't need that! I got so much more out of it than that."
>
> "It's a vital piece of work." He pressed her again. "It needs to be shared with others."
>
> Amelia stood to leave and extended her hand. "I understand what you're saying, but I don't want it published." They gazed at each other until he nodded with respect and understanding, then handed her the thesis.
>
> "You've done excellent work. When you're ready to take it further, you know how to contact me."
>
> She looked around the room and then turned to open the door. Professor Colby stopped her. "Will we have the pleasure of your company at graduation?"

When she turned to him, he was startled at the bright smile that lit her face. "No, I'm going back to the Island. My mother and I, we're going home." (Dash 1997, 294–295)

What happens on her six-month field trip to this gifted anthropologist, between the time she arrives at the train station in Charleston, South Carolina—dressed in a "city-smart suit and fashionably bobbed hair"—and when she returns to New York to finish her thesis? What would make Amelia give up such a promising career, only to return with her mother to that Island for good? As I suggested above, her real journey, just like Avey Johnson in *Praisesong for the Widow* (a journey that we, the readers, must also take), requires a purging and a cleansing, assisted by a boat ride to the Island.

Amelia managed to keep herself "together," through the choppy waters, suppressing the nausea and dizziness that swelled in her stomach (Dash 1997, 69). The water gets even rougher, the closer they get to their destination. Her cousin Elizabeth Peazant helps her get through:

> Amelia could sense the change in the mood as the men fought the current to get the boat close enough to the pier. They stopped singing and listened carefully for Willis George's commands as they pushed and waited, using the strength of the current to move closer. Amelia gasped when a wave slapped the side of the boat, spraying everyone with water. Elizabeth threw her arm around her and held her close as the men heaved together, sending the boat directly into the current. Fear shot through Amelia as she felt the current catch the boat and push it just past the pier. A shout from Willis George and the men heaved again, popping the boat out of the current. As they reached the calmer waters, the men grinned at each other, their white teeth flashing in the dark and at Willis George, nodding in satisfaction. They then rowed for pier at Ibo Landing. (Dash 1997, 71)

As she reached the edge of the pier, Amelia "bent double." Elizabeth "held her head until she had stopped heaving and then helped her to sit down." Amelia, like Avey Johnson in *Praisesong for the Widow*, slept for two days straight, rising on the third day. Eli Peazant notices this and says, "You sure she all right. She aint moved since her lay down. Her sleep like she dead." Eula Peazant understands, "She jus dat bone weary. Dat long trip and rough crossin. From what [Amelia's mother] Myown wrote, I spect dere was no peace to be had in dat house when her made known what her was gonna do" (Dash 1997, 72).

Getting the people of the island to tell their stories requires that Amelia shed her "baggage," layer by layer. Eliciting the trust of her relatives and their neighbors, especially when lugging the huge camera around, is a big feat. She eagerly gives over the filming to her eager cousin Ben, who right away has a knack and a desire for the job. Still, not all of her relatives are so thrilled with her presence. This includes her cousin Lucy, Elizabeth's younger sister. Lucy dismisses Amelia immediately and doesn't speak a word to her, even though the two share a bed during Amelia's stay.

At the beginning of the film, there is a magnificent shot of a young Nana Peazant's hands, as she holds some of the soil. A still photograph of this shot is reproduced in book on the making of the film. The elder Nana, throughout the film, reminds her departing family that the ancestors are in this soil; to leave it is to leave them behind. She begs them to stay, and if they cannot stay, to make sure to take a part of their ancestors with them, to keep the connection. She warns against leaving this soil and tells of those that came before them. In the novel, Lucy is the one woman who carries that appreciation for the soil with her. She works the land, speaks to it, and loves it each day. Not even she, however, was prepared for the *literal* presence of those ancestors in that soil.

What happens to Lucy in the story was one of the most self-transforming moments, so much so it is to be anticipated with much trepidation each time the story is revisited or read. Lucy Peazant is the second daughter to Eli and Eula Peazant.[5] She is someone who from early childhood has been committed to this life and community on the Island; she is an unflinching resister of the "new ways" and never considers these new ways as a desirable alternative to their life. Her father attempts to send her to the mainland for schooling, but after one term she refuses to go back. Instead she works the soil at the old Wilkerson place, the "piece of land that meant so much to [her]" (Dash 1997, 224) which she and her Charlie are saving up to buy. It had once been a large plantation where one "could still see the fire-scorched foundation stones of the Big House on the far edge of the pasture" (224) Trinity Wilkerson was the cook for the whites who owned the plantation and she got her "forty acres" after the War. She took some of the richest soil around. The land around this plot has long since been abandoned. All the Wilkersons except for Ol Trent have since left the place for good and Lucy is not only working the land, but is saving money to buy it.

The relationship between Lucy and Amelia remains distant. She has barely spoken a word to her cousin. Still, Lucy agrees to let Amelia help her plow the fields—mostly to give her a real taste of hard work. Amelia is determined not to let Lucy see her falter. Lucy fails to warn Amelia about how hard it would be to get their mule Homer to move. Amelia doesn't make it very far. Lucy finally makes her sit down. Amelia sits and watches in amazement at Lucy's command of Homer. Amelia turns to daydreaming about her mother and her life back in New York. She is sorry to have left her mother alone to deal with her father and grandmother. She snaps out of her daydreaming by Lucy's piercing screams. Lucy runs from the field. Amelia figures it is a snake, but Lucy is running in "wild patterns, waving and screaming." Pointing to where Homer stood, she bends over and clutches her stomach. "It evil. It evil back dere!" (Dash 1997, 227) Amelia goes over to the last spot Lucy had plowed. This is what happened next:

> She stared at the spot, then kneeled down and looked at an object that the plow had uncovered. She felt her heart begin to pound as she brushed the dirt from a pair of rusted

shackles, a chain running from them into the ground. Despite her misgivings, she grabbed a jagged-edged stick that lay in the furrow and began to dig. As she continued burrowing into the earth, her eyes filled with tears as she recognized a human leg bone. Dropping the stick, she jerked away and walked around to the front of the plow and saw, at last, what had sent Lucy spinning. A piece of skull was impaled on the front blade; a jaw-bone with several teeth lay in the scattered earth. She backed away and ran over to Lucy, who was curled on the ground, crying. She pulled Lucy up, slipped around her waist, and half-carried her home. (Dash 1997, 227)

In total, there are three sets of bones found. Eli states, "Three of dem, tied together like dogs." He adds, "We keep looking tomorrow" (230). Lucy is unable to leave her bed for days afterward. For years Lucy has been set on buying that meadow. Her sister Elizabeth worries that this discovery will crush her dreams.

The discovery of these human remains brings the folks from all over the Island. Word spreads like wildfire and the men, women, and children—old and young— make their way to the old Wilkerson place. Miz Emma Julia, one of Nana's oldest and closest of friends, arrives on a horse-drawn cart:

Upon seeing Eula, she immediately asks, "How Lucy?" Eula replies, "Her in a bad way." Miz Emma Julia says, "She come across dat evil buried dere in dat field! […] It up to we to make it right! Us got to claim our own, take dem back from de buckra!"

"You sound like my Nana," Eula nods. Miz Emma Julia snaps, "Us all of de same spirit!" When Miz Emma Julia is brought close to the bones now wrapped in quilts, she rubs the shackles and sees a faint imprint on the worn iron. She asks Elizabeth to tell her "what it say," and she responds, "The Sorcerer." Miz Emma Julia then tells everyone the story. (Dash 1997, ??)

The whole island comes together to prepare the bones for a proper burial. This takes place over several days. They construct an altar and prepare the burial ground. The women have missed this ritual; it has disappeared from the days when Nana and the others had passed on. Everyone tries to get Lucy to join them but she refuses to move from her bed.

But, Lucy does come to the final ceremony. As they begin, Miz Emma Julia orders the bones, wrapped in the quilts, to be brought to her. She lifts her arms and begins to chant so that the gods of "de many peoples of Africa" can hear her call. She asks them to hear the children calling them, the stolen children from "de lands of Ibo, Yoruba, Kissee, Dahomey, Angola, Gambia, Whydah!"

The ancestors answer with a sudden strong gust of wind that part the clouds and reveal the moon. Everyone feels their presence. Some fall to their knees. Lucy shrinks "as the wind seemed to circle her, moving along the edge of the group." Amelia feels the "soft caress of the breeze on the back of her neck, her body relaxing." Elizabeth holds out her arms and lets "the wind pass through her body." Then the wind stops as suddenly as it starts.

Lucy is beckoned by Miz Emma Julia to carry out the ceremony, "Come, chile, you brought dem to us. You gotta help dem go home." As if pulled by force, she reluctantly and slowly moves forward. "You a lil gal. You gonna need a helper to send dem home." This is a turning point in the relationship between Lucy and Amelia. Lucy looks to Amelia for this help and Amelia takes her place beside her cousin. Here is the passage in full:

> "Take de quilts an open dem up." Lucy took one end and Amelia the other and gently spread the quilt. They moved to the second quilt and opened it, Lucy turning her head from the bones that lay in the quilt. Miz Emma Julia held out her hand. "Spread out de shackles and de chain as dey lay in de ground." Amelia and Lucy picked up the pieces and strung them out best they could. Miz Emma Julia spoke, "Now, spread out de bones so we can see de old ones." Lucy looked as if she was about to flee. Caught by Miz Emma Julia's gaze, she began to sob. Eula pressed her hands to her mouth to keep from crying out to her daughter. Eli put his arm around Eula, holding her close.

> "Go on, gal. Let dem saltwater tears wash down and cleanse dem. Aint nobody cry for dem for years. Dey lay out in dat field for nobody know how long. Dat why dat field do rich wit de earth. Our elders give it dey life blood. Dey give to we what was took from dem." She gestured for Amelia to spread the bones.

> Amelia leaned down, hands trembling, and reached for a long piece of bone. When her shaking fingers touched it, she felt a jolt and pulled back. Miz Emma Julia nodded encouragingly. "Dey reachin out to you. Take what dey got to offer." Amelia wanted to refuse, then saw the fear in Lucy's eyes. Heart pounding and breathing heavily, she picked up the bone. She thought it was her imagination, the tingling that started in her fingers and began to spread up her arm. But as it spread over her body, she felt it in every pore as sweat broke out and her skin seemed to flush with blood. She felt the waves of fear, pain, and despair wash over her. The others flinched and moaned with her, while Lucy hid her face. Amelia slowly lowered her bone, her arms trembling, her clothes soaking. Miz Emma Julia placed Amelia's coat on her shoulders and stroked her head.

> The old woman then reached down and picked up a skull, crossing to Lucy, who cried out and shrank from her. Relentlessly, she grabbed Lucy's hand, struggling with her, and thrust the skull into it. She hissed at her, "Feel deir pain, gal! Feel deir hurt! Only when you feel de pain do de healin begin!"

> Lucy shook as she stared at the skull. Just as she was about to let it roll off her palm, her head snapped back as the force hit her. She jerked as if her body were receiving the blows, her head lolling and her arms flinging in every direction. Painfully she closed her fingers around the skull and struggled to bring it closer to her. Only when she clasped it to her chest did the force seem to take pity on her. Her head hung low; her body was limp. (Dash 1997, 240–241)

In words similar to Nana Peazant in the film, Miz Emma Julia reminds everyone:

> It take a strong people, snatch from de cradle, de wood, de village, put on de boat, and took cross de big water to land dey never know […] It take a strong people to keep dey all about

dem, to hold on de old ways, to keep de lies true, to know who dey be! It take a strong people to work from day clean to day over to clear de lan, build de house, plow de field, make
de indigo, sow de rice, pick de cotton, all to de good of de buckra. Some of we forget how
strong dem people was, us look past de old ways, put aside what dey was telling we bout
de right way to live. An now dey come back to we, de ancients who seed dis earth wit deir
tears, sweat, an blood! (Dash 1997, 241–242)

When Miz Emma Julia is finished speaking she holds up a skull and a large piece
of bone. Her whole body shakes as the forces moves through her. Those nearby
have to duck to avoid the spikes of electricity that emit from her body. They cry out
in fear, but Miz Emma Julia holds her head back and laughs. She then says, "Come,
chilren, dey telling you to rise up! Free de souls! […] We done took de pain an de
sadness! All dat lef is de healin!" (242)

Who among Dash's readers cannot join in this ceremony? Be right there to
feel the tingling in the fingers that spread up the arm, to feel the response of those
called upon by Miz Emma Julia, and feel the fear, pain and despair when Lucy
held the skull and received full force of the blows? Who cannot feel the healing
begin, as everyone rose up and began dance in celebration around the quilt that
held the bones?

The Peazants and their neighbors are joined in this story and in this journey
through their lives' unbelievable moments. Readers will meet Elizabeth, Eula
and Eli, Carrie Mae, Toady, and Yellow Mary (her whole story will be told),
Iona and Julien Last Child, and their children. We will meet Willis George,
Sallie Lee, and Sugarnun. Readers will understand why Haagar (from the
film), Amelia's grandmother, was in such a hurry to leave where she came from.
Finally, readers will learn why Ol' Trent spends his days walking from one end
of the Island to the other, combing the place for treasures and yelling out bible
passages.

The rest of the story should be saved for each new reader. Thankfully, there
has been enough to generate a new printing. I hope it will continue. Reading
Daughters of the Dust was more than my merely taking a break from sociology.
It was the beginning of my seeing sociology as a discipline in a new way—what
was missing and what was necessary for transforming it into what it *could be* as
purported study of humans. I read Dash *before* I read Bambara and Marshall,
before I read Morrison, and before so many more. As I read each new creative
production by a Black artist/community activist, I saw the connection and the
conversations between them as they "exemplify" what Joyce Ann Joyce identifies
as their "interdisciplinary nature" and suggest the critical role that the humanities
play in the Black Studies curriculum (Joyce 2006, 195), and hence the Human
Studies curriculum (Joyce 2004; Wynter 2006). Only through such works do we
as humans experience the "wonder" and the "mind's *heart*" that complement the
"mind's *eye*" that Sylvia Wynter argues "institute the processes of sociogenesis

through which we can alone come to experience ourselves as *human*" (Wynter 1994; Gagne 2007).

I have been using *Daughters of the Dust* as well as other Black literary productions in my sociology courses since 2009. In my Human Relations course, for example, students begin the same transformation that I describe above of myself and all those who engage in Diasporic texts. They participate in the telling about the reality of enslaved Africans and their descendants in North America—as a retelling and thereby a re-*constituting* of what it means to be human.

Julie Dash, together with Bambara and Marshall, has provided some of the most powerful works in Human Studies I have encountered to date. When we incorporate these cultural productions into the sociology curriculum, then we make a huge leap toward the study of and the re-writing of the human.

NOTES

1. This article is updated and reprinted with permission from *Human Architecture: Journal of the Sociology of Self-Knowledge* 6, no. 2 (Spring 2008): https://www.okcir.com/Articles%20VI%202/KarenGagne-FM.pdf.
2. In 2008, I counted fifty-seven articles that analyze the film, as listed in Gary Handman, "African American Filmmakers, African American Films: A Bibliography of Materials in the UC Berkeley Library" (2007). With the 20th anniversary of the making of this film and the papers given at the 2011 symposium "We Carry These Memories Inside of We: A Symposium Celebrating the 20th Anniversary of *Daughters of the Dust* and the Black Art Aesthetic of Filmmaker Julie Dash," I am so pleased that the number continues to grow. However, it is still the case that little attention is paid to the novel.
3. Zora Neale Hurston, Paule Marshall, Sylvia Wynter, Erna Brodber, Merle Hodge, Toni Morrison, Audre Lorde, and Toni Cade Bambara are but a few such writers.
4. This is suggested by both James Baldwin (1985, xiii) and Jacques Depelchin (2005, 154). Depelchin, citing Baldwin, argues in order to understand the source of this trauma, one needs to remember. However, there are overwhelming forces against this remembering. Baldwin writes, "It has something to do with the fact that no one wishes to be plunged, head down, into the torrent of what he does not remember and does not wish to remember. It has something to do with the fact that we all came here as candidates for the slaughter of innocents. It has something to do with the fact that all survivors, however they accommodate or fail to remember it, bear the inexorable guilt of the survivor. It has something to do, in my own case, with having once been a Black child in a White Country." Depelchin adds, "The pull to conform to the views of the dominant history would be irresistible, but for the fact of having seen the evidence. The witness cannot deny its existence if everything and everyone has conspired to claim they cannot see it" (154).
5. Eli and Eula Peazant, whom we get to know in the film, have six children. Elizabeth, the oldest, was the "Unborn Child" in the film, sent by the ancestors. Elizabeth, who went away for her education, has recently come back to be the island's only teacher. She lives in her great-great grandmother Nana's house deep in the forest. Then there is Lucy, Ben, twins Henry and James, and Rebecca, the youngest.

REFERENCES

Baldwin, James. 1985. *The Evidence of Things Not Seen.* New York: Holt, Rinehart and Winston.

Bambara, Toni Cade. 1982. *Toni Cade Bambara Interview with Kay Bonetti* (sound recording). Columbia, MO: American Audio Prose Library.

———. 1996. *Deep Sightings and Rescue Missions: Fiction, Essays, and Conversations.* New York: Pantheon Books.

Benton, Jacqueline. 2000. "Grace Nichols' *I Is a Long Memoried Woman* and Julie Jash's *Daughters of the Dust*: Reversing the Middle Passage." In *Black Women Writers Across Cultures: Analysis of Their Contributions,* edited by Valentine Udoh James, 221–232. Lanham, MD: International Scholars Publications.

Brøndum, Lene. 1999. "'The Persistence of Tradition': The Retelling of Sea Islands Culture in Works by Julie Dash, Gloria Naylor, and Paule Marshall." In *Black Imagination and the Middle Passage,* edited by Maria Diedrich, Henry Louis Gates Jr., and Carl Pedersen, 153–163. New York: Oxford University Press.

Busia, Abena P. 1989. "What Is Your Nation? Reconnecting Africa and Her Diaspora through Paule Marshall's *Praisesong for the Widow.*" In *Changing Our Own Words: Essays on Criticism, Theory, and Writing by Black Women,* edited by Cheryl A. Wall, 196–211, 239–240. New Brunswick: Rutgers University Press.

Clark, VèVè A. 1990. "Developing Diaspora Literacy: Allusion in Maryse Condé's *Hérémakhonon.*" In *Out of the Kumbla: Caribbean Women and Literature,* edited by Carole Boyce Davies and Elaine Savory Fido, 303–319. Trenton, NJ: Africa World Press.

Dash, Julie, dir. 2000. *Daughters of the Dust.* 1991. New York, NY: Kino International, DVD.

———. 1992. *Daughters of the Dust: The Making of an African American Women's Film.* New York: The New Press.

———. 1997. *Daughters of the Dust: A Novel.* New York: Dutton.

Depelchin, Jacques. 2005. *Silences in African History: Between the Syndromes of Discovery and Abolition.* Dar es Salaam, Tanzania: Mkuki Na Nyota Publishers.

Gagne, Karen M. 2006. "Fighting Amnesia as a Guerilla Activity: Poetics for a New Mode of Being Human." *Human Architecture: Journal of the Sociology of Self-Knowledge* 4, no. 3 (June): 249–264.

———. 2007. "On the Obsolescence of the Disciplines: Frantz Fanon and Sylvia Wynter Propose a New Mode of Being Human." *Human Architecture: Journal of the Sociology of Self-Knowledge* 5, no. 3 (June): 251–264.

Gerima, Haile, dir. *Sankofa.* 1993.

Grayson, Sandra M. 2000. *Symbolizing the Past: Reading Sankofa, Daughters of the Dust, & Eve's Bayou as Histories.* Lanham, MD: University Press of America.

Handman, Gary. 2007. "African American Filmmakers, African American Films: A Bibliography of Materials in the UC Berkeley Library in Media Resources Center." Accessed October 15, 2007. http://www.lib.berkeley.edu/MRC/africanambib2.html

Joyce, Joyce Ann. 2004. *Black Studies as Human Studies: Critical Essays and Interviews.* Albany: State University of New York Press.

———. 2006. "Toni Cade Bambara's *Those Bones Are Not My Child* as a Model for Black Studies." In *A Companion to African-American Studies,* edited by Lewis R. Gordon and Anna Gordon, 192–208. Malden, MA: Blackwell Publishing.

Lemmons, Kasi, dir. 1997. *Eve's Bayou.*

Marshall, Paule. 1983. *Praisesong for the Widow.* New York: G. P. Putnam's Sons, 1983.

Wynter, Sylvia. 1994. "But What Does 'Wonder' Do? Meanings, Canons, too? On Literary Texts, Cultural Contextst, and What It's Like to Be One/Not One of Us?" *SEHR* 4, vo1 1 (Spring): https://web.stanford.edu/group/SHR/4-1/text/wynter.commentary.html (Accessed June 13, 2019).

———. 2006. "On How We Mistook the Map for the Territory, and Re-imprisoned Ourselves in Our Unbearable Wrongness of Being, of *Desêtre*: Black Studies Toward the Human Project." In *Not Only By the Master's Tools: African American Studies in Theory and Practice (Cultural Politics & the Promise of Democracy)*, edited by Lewis R. Gordon and Anna Gordon, 107–172. Boulder, CO: Paradigm Publishers.

CHAPTER SEVEN

Conscious Daughters

Psychological Migration, Individuation, and the Declaration of Black Female Identity in *Daughters of the Dust*

SHARON D. JOHNSON

Carl Jung (1976) compares the psychological process of individuation, the identity-shaping process wherein we realize our full self-hood, to a journey (Jung 304, 316). Similarly, journalist and essayist Greg Tate describes African Americans as "nomadic souls" who live our identity "in a middle passage" (Dash 1992, 71). On the dedication page of *Daughters of the Dust: The Making of an African American Woman's Film*, Julie Dash quotes Jung: "Every woman extends backward [*sic*] into her mother and forward to [sic] her daughter" (Dash 1992; Jung 1969, 188). This paper re-examines the cinematic and literary texts of *Daughters of the Dust* (Dash 1990; 1992; 1997), and the act of geographical migration as a metaphor for psychological migration, the movement of the psyche as it necessarily separates from Mother, incubates as the Unborn Child, and informs, shapes, and defines the emergent Black female identity.

Personal identity, or *personality*, "the complete realization of our whole being [...] can never develop unless the individual chooses [her] own way, consciously and with moral deliberation" (Jung 1981, 172; 174). *Daughters of the Dust* (Dash 1991) depicts this truth lyrically and powerfully through the characters of Iona, Eula, and Yellow Mary. Their imminent geographical migration from Ibo Landing reveals the more difficult psychological migration away from Mother(s): Nana Peazant, Haagar, and Viola. The Peazant family's move toward the new horizons and new ways of life on the mainland are manifestations of the "forward-striving libido which rules the conscious mind [and] demands separation from the mother" (Jung 1976, 297).

THE JOURNEY TOWARD WHOLENESS

From its opening sequence, *Daughters of the Dust* (Dash 1991) cinematically depicts symbols of wholeness. Yellow Mary's voiceover recitation of "The Thunder, Perfect [Whole] Mind" (Baring & Cashford, 630–631) poetically unites opposing characteristics in to a whole being, "I am the first and the last. […] I am the whore and the holy one. […] I am the barren one, and many are my daughters. […] I am the utterance of my name" (Dash 1991, 00:02:24–00:02:54). She sails with Trula, Viola, and Mr. Sneed in a boat headed toward Ibo Island, evoking images of the Boat of Anubis as it makes its way to the Underworld, a necessary journey for the Kemetic soul's experience of the whole Osirian life-death-rebirth motif. As Dash has set up the shot, the seating of the four passengers represent a "quaternity" (Jung 1969, 235) arranged, suggesting a balance of psychic energy necessary for wholeness: Trula and a veiled Yellow Mary on one side of the boat, represent the mystery of unconscious instinctive feminine psychological energy, Viola and Mr. Sneed, facing them on the opposite side, represent the articulation of conscious discriminating masculine psychological energy.

Mr. Sneed's awe-filled description of the photographic process (Dash 1991) also intimates the process of becoming psychologically balanced and whole. He explains one object (the person), when placed between two mirrors (the unconscious and conscious psyche) set at right angles (in right relationship), "give the appearance of four symmetrically shaped objects" (00:08:54). Symmetry is balance and four is the number of wholeness or completion (Jung 1969, 372–373). Further, the number four is a feminine number (Jung 1969, 234). Thus, *Daughters of the Dust* (Dash 1991) is clearly set up to be a story about the psychological migration of women—of Daughters—toward wholeness.

NECESSARY SEPARATION FROM MOTHER

It is necessary for daughters to leave their mothers in order to individuate. Without this differentiation, the Daughter can not see herself clearly. The mother's voice, opinions, or limited vision interferes with the daughter's view of herself. As Iona basks in the verses of her love letter from St. Julian Last Child, who has asked her, "Please do not leave me in this flood of migration to the North" (Dash 1992, 90), her Older Cousin reminds her that "Auntie Haagar won't let you stay" (91). Conversely, the travelled, experienced, and independent Yellow Mary returns to Ibo Landing like a veiled mystery yet to be revealed, by those she has left behind. She is immediately subject to the judgment and disdain of the Mothers who have taken their image of her for who she is. Eula's uncertainty of her own voice is reinforced through her husband Eli's (Nana Peazant's great grandson) overarching proprietary claims over her and his simultaneous doubts about the paternity of their Unborn Child. In each case, the women's identities are obscured by some aspect of the mother and or motherhood.

The separation from Mother is also necessary so that *Mother* can see herself clearly. Nana Peazant, Haagar, and Viola each perceive that their respective actions are "done under the cloak of selfless devotion" (Jung 1981, 127) to the family, particularly to their daughters. However, they are actually totally unconscious of their controlling natures. Haagar, through her disapproving scowl and constant bark to summon her daughters, seeks to control their every move. Having control of her daughters, she believes, will protect them from being "ruin't." And then there is Viola. Through her overzealous clinging to a white patriarchal religious construct, Viola seeks to civilize and convert the girls' spontaneous, spiritually animated dance on the beach into controlled and rote activity, distanced from the waters and from the land (she recites "The earth belongs to the Lord, *not to us*, and the fullness thereof" [Dash 1991, 00:38:34; emphasis added]). Yet it is Nana Peazant who wields the greatest control over her daughters, even calling on unseen ancestral forces to help her maintain and protect her clan. Nana's intent is expressed from the very beginning of the film:

> North is what they wake up whispering in their husband's ears. [...] Now everything they own is all boxed up, and ready to head North. [...] But when they come today to kiss these old withered-up cheeks bye-bye, I'm going to have something more than farewell waiting on them. [...] I've been working on a plan. (Dash 1991, 00:11:46–00:12:08; 1992, 86–87)

Nana Peazant doesn't seem to care if her daughters want to leave Ibo Landing. Her intention is to influence their actions, imbue them with spiritual wisdom, even by supernatural intervention, if necessary, in order to make them do what she wants. Jung (1969) describes this as the mother's "stubborn persistence to [...] the right of possession over her daughter" (88). He continues, explaining, "The less conscious such a mother is of her own personality, the greater and more violent is her unconscious will to power" (88). This unconsciousness of the heroine, Nana, is evident in the tense contradictions between her words and her actions. For example, Nana tells Eli that Eula does not belong to Eli just because she married him (Dash 1991), yet she is reluctant to relinquish her own sense of ownership over Eula. In another instance, Nana curiously examines Yellow Mary's Saint Christopher medal and asks incredulously, "What kind of belief that is? He protect you?" (00:39:36–00:40:44). She does not recognize the medal is a cultural, spiritual relic and talisman much like the cultural, spiritual relics and talismans she carries in her can. Nana asserts to Eli that "we carry these memories inside of we" (00:22:06), yet Viola recognizes and can articulate what Nana cannot, that, "Nana is carrying a lot of luggage [...] she's old and she's frightened" (00:54:44–00:55:22). Nana's actions convey her sense of mistrust in that autonomous carriage of memory inside each member of her family as their time of migration draws near.

INCUBATION AS THE UNBORN CHILD

The daughters' forward-striving life force is greater than any personal will to power or to control because "the urge and compulsion to self-realization is a law of nature and thus of invincible power" (Jung 1969, 170). Once enlivened, this force's incubation and growth proceed, albeit hidden, undetected, or unrecognized. This is the daughters' inner incubation as the Unborn Child. "'Child' means something evolving towards independence," writes Jung (1969, 168). "As bringers of light, that is, enlargers of consciousness, they overcome darkness, which is to say that they overcome the earlier unconscious state" (169). This is a time of tension between the opposites of unconscious life within Mother, and natural progression toward life outside and separate from Mother. It is a time when the Mother archetype can either assist or assail the Child. Jungian analyst Robert Johnson (1995) describes a person's negative experience of the Mother archetype as a Mother complex. This complex causes the person to regress, become inert and sapped of life energy or libido. It coaxes the person to sleep or unconsciousness and feeds the tendency to remain stuck (81). The positive experience is the Mother Archetype (81), or a positive Mother complex (Jung 1969, 92), by which the person feels nurtured, supported, and inspired to move forward. This positive experience of the Mother archetype is generative and life-giving (Johnson 1995, 81). It is between these tensions of the aspects of the Mother archetype that the Unborn Child incubates.

For Eula, this is represented by the literal incubation and growth of the Unborn Child within her, and the joy of carrying new life versus the threat or danger of revealing the child's paternity. It is the movement between Nana Peazant's assurances to Eli that "you won't ever have a baby that wasn't sent to you. The ancestors and the womb [...] they one, they the same" (Dash 1992, 94), and Yellow Mary's admonition to Eula that, "He don't need to know. [...] There's enough uncertainty in life without [...] wondering what tree your husband's dangling from. Don't tell him nothing" (Dash 1991, 00:46:05; 1992, 123, 124).

Iona incubates in the intensifying love between her and St. Julian Last Child. This incubation, like the Child archetype, is "in continual danger of extinction" (Jung 1969, 170). Characteristically, the love growing during Iona's and Julian's stolen moments together is constantly interrupted by Haagar's murderous cries after her daughter (Dash 1991, 00:52:51–00:53:35; 1992, 127). It is also counterpointed by Viola's moral stiffness which threatens to diffuse Mr. Sneed's expressions of affection for her as they become more and more overt.

Yellow Mary gives voice to her inner incubation. As she enthralls Eula with stories about her life away from Ibo Landing, she at once defends it while articulating her lack of fulfillment with it, and her yearning for a return to life on the island. She tells Eula that, "I wish I could find a good man. Somebody I could depend on. Not that I'd want to depend on him. Just to know that I could if I had to" (Dash 1992, 121). Next, she longs for some of her family's gumbo because, "I had some in Savannah, you know, but they didn't put everything in it" (122). Finally, she talks about a musical jewelry box she wanted but did not buy. "I couldn't afford that case for myself, and I didn't ask anybody to buy it for me" (143). Instead, she held the box in her mind and "put all those bad memories in [...] and locked them there. So I could take them out, look at them when I'd feel like it, and figure it out. [...] But I didn't want them inside of me" (143). This is our first glimpse of a healthy differentiated personality of an "individual [who] must hold fast so as not to be thrown catastrophically off balance. [...] The holding fast can be achieved only by a conscious will, i.e., by the ego" (Jung 1969, 319).

THE EMERGENT BLACK FEMALE IDENTITY

As each daughter's ego forms a strong sense of Self, the mother makes way for the emergence, even if against her own will to power and to control. Viola leaves Ibo Landing still Christianized, but less puritanical. She allows Mr. Sneed's affection and Nana Peazant's ancestral custom to take up a little more space in her life. Nana Peazant surrenders to her family's decision to migrate North. She is upset, but surrenders to the force of change that is as real and powerful as the ancestors (Dash 1991, 01:38:28). Haagar believes she is victorious, as the boat prepares to leave Ibo Landing with both her daughters at her side. However, Iona's masculine energy (symbolized by Julian) comes to her rescue at the last minute. Iona disembarks and rides away into the depths of the island with Julian. This is "the *coniunctio* of male and female" (Jung 1969, 175). Iona does not migrate geographically, but does move away from her mother psychologically. By contrast, Haagar moves geographically, but not psychologically. She is left clawing at the earth, screaming Iona's name (Dash 1991, 01:46:08–01:46:32), declaring the same ownership over this daughter as Eli declared over Eula at the beginning of the film. Decades later, Haagar still seems not to have moved forward (Dash 1997). She, who disdains the "salt water negroes" of Ibo Island, has herself turned into a pillar of salt, psychologically.

Yellow Mary, no longer needing to enact her independence through constant movement away from Ibo Landing, now is able to "come home" (Dash 1992, 154) and *be* the independent woman who recognizes that *she* is the True Love she has been seeking. In this new consciousness, "all unnecessary objects are cleared"

(Jung 1969, 188). Accordingly, Yellow Mary is able to let go of *Trula*, the carrier of her projected true love of Self. Her declaration that "I am Yellow Mary Peazant!" (Dash 1991, 01:32:34–01:33:27) powerfully punctuates her emergence, her rebirth. Jung (1969) points out that, in some rites of rebirth, the "reborn [...] is given another name" (129). Yellow Mary is not given another name, but she proclaims it as if it is new because *she* is new. Her name, therefore, carries new meaning. It is no longer *de*meaned or associated with shame.

Eula gives birth to herself, to her own voice. Her emergence most symbolizes the "restoration [...] of the lives of her ancestors" (Jung 1969, 188). By speaking of the wounds and scars that keep mothers and daughters paralytically fused to, rather than in right relationship with, the past (Dash 1991, 01:37:04–01:38:28; 1992, 156–157), she frees and challenges the living mothers and daughters to "find new *interpretations*" of their ancestral commemorations "in order to connect the life of the past [...] with the life of the present" (157). Her words reach back tens of thousands of millennia even to heal the ancestral "original rejection" (Welsing 1991, 37). Frances Cress Welsing (1991) theorizes about the African (Black) mothers' rejection "of their albino (white) mutant offspring" (37; 23; 29) at the dawn of human civilization. These offspring were their own African children, whose skin was not black. Similarly, the Peazants revile and scapegoat Yellow Mary as much for her skin color (as her name suggests) as they do for her classification as a "ruin't" woman (Dash 1991). When Eula admonishes the family, "If you love yourself, then love Yellow Mary. She a part of you" (01:36:31), she is healing the original Maternal rejection in Africa as much as she is healing the women's rejection of Yellow Mary on Ibo Landing. Thus she powerfully "connect(s) the life of the past with the life of the present" (Jung 1969, 157).

Even the men have transformed their unconscious identification with Mother. Mr. Sneed expands his enchantment with *images* of the Peazants into participation in their lives and expression of human affection onto a *real* woman (Dash 1992, 162). Julian withdraws some of his identification as son of Mother Earth, "Son of these islands" (88; 91) and now identifies as an adult *man* embarking upon a new life with an adult woman. Eli, who identified with patriarchal ownership (of Daughter) and idealization/worship (of Mother) has learned surrender to and respect for the human and supernatural feminine, as expressed by Eula, Nana, and the guidance of his Unborn Daughter.

Nana Peazant's transformation also symbolizes the healing of the Original (African) Mother's rejection of children who did not mirror her image. Nana Peazant, now seemingly conscious of the rejection imbedded in her own actions, no longer loves her daughters conditionally, as she did at the beginning of the film, approving of them as long as they stay at Ibo Landing so that their lifestyle mirrors her own. Instead, Nana now proclaims to them unconditionally, "I love you 'cause you're mine!" (Dash 1991, 01:34:02; 1992, 161).

Through the film's depiction of the Peazant family's geographical migration, *Daughters of the Dust* expresses metaphorically the psychological migration of its key female protagonists. This paper has taken a closer look at the film's symbolism to illuminate the movement of their respective psyches as they separated from Mother, incubated as the Unborn Child, and informed, shaped, and defined their emergent black female identities. Their psychological migration, more so than their geographical migration, transformed them into truly Conscious Daughters.

REFERENCES

Dash, Julie, dir. 1991. *Daughters of the Dust*. 1991. New York, NY: Kino International.

——. 1992. *Daughters of the Dust: The Making of an African American Woman's Film*. New York: The New Press.

——. 1997. *Daughters of the Dust: A Novel*. New York: Dutton.

Johnson, Robert A. 1995. *Lying with the Heavenly Woman: Understanding and Integrating the Feminine Archetypes in Men's Lives*. New York, NY: HarperCollins.

Jung, C. G. 1969. *The Collected Works of C. G. Jung—Volume 9, Part 1: The Archetypes and the Collective Unconscious*. Edited and translated by Gerhard Adler and R. F. C. Hull. Princeton, NJ: Princeton University Press.

——. 1976 *The Collected Works of C. G. Jung—Volume 5: Symbols of Transformation*. Edited and translated by Gerhard Adler and R. F. C. Hull. Princeton, NJ: Princeton University Press.

——. 1981. *The Collected Works of C. G. Jung—Volume 17: The Development of Personality*. Edited and translated by Gerhard Adler and R. F. C. Hull. Princeton, NJ: Princeton University Press.

Welsing, Frances Cress. 1991. *The Isis Papers: The Keys to the Colors*. Chicago, IL: Third World Press.

CHAPTER EIGHT

Reading Nana Peazant's Palms

Punctuating Readings of Blue

TIFFANY LETHABO KING

In 1992, filmmaker Julie Dash spoke with scholar and cultural critic Houston Baker about her film *Daughters of the Dust*. During the interview she explained why the actor Cora Lee Day, who played Nana Peazant, and other Black women actors who depicted former slaves, appeared on screen with indigo-stained hands. Dash replied to Houston's inquiry by saying "It was important for me to show these indigo-handed people as a reminder, that these were the scars of slavery, this blueness. I needed to physically show the scars in a different way, because film is like poetry. You want to say something that has been said before, but in a different way."[1] Dash wanted to provide the audience with a new way of seeing and imagining the violence, scars of slavery as well as the kinds of blue-Black futures that the enslaved and their descendants crafted for themselves. While, the indigo embedded in the skin references the brutality of slavery in an unexpected way, the blue hands as a visual reference function in a way that exceeds mere scarification.[2] The flashes of indigo hands in the film function as a powerful punctum points that enable different ways of looking and alternative forms of vision. Further still, the lingering impact of slavery on African Americans has imbued their experiences with "a kind of blue" that permeates through every facet of life. One might essentially get the "blues" when confronted by spectacular and mundane forms of racism and or find comfort by listening to the Blues. Julie Dash's understanding of the transformative capacity of blue perforates the frames of the film and opens up multiple registers of meaning and affect for the viewer.

In *Daughters of the Dust,* Dash creates a textured and dense visual vocabulary that achieves what academic theory and language itself has not. Many Black movie goers are drawn to Dash's film because she presents penetrating visual moments that poignantly depict Black humanity. The stills and moving images of the film enable an alternative form of looking, perceiving, and sensing that calls attention to the limitations of Western colonial vision. Paying close attention to the way Dash uses the camera, styles and marks the bodies of actors, references Yoruba cosmologies, and marshals sound and other senses, one can discern a synesthetic visuality that runs counter to the imperious visual regime of settler colonial North America.

A number of scholars have analyzed Dash's work in *Daughters of the Dust* as a decolonizing and healing work of art. Toni Cade Bambara (Dash 1992, xi) credits Dash with attempting to "heal our imperialized eyes."[3] In analyzing the oppositional and decolonial cinematic work of Dash, Bambara draws our attention to the way that Dash explodes the Western "Hollywood protocol" (xiii). Dash uses "dual narration and multiple point-of-view camerawork, rather than a hero-dominated perspective" (xiii). Additionally, Dash's eschewing of a master narrative in favor of a non-linear, multilayered unfolding—one more in keeping with the storytelling traditions that inform African cinema—also allows for an oppositional notion of space to emerge (xiii). Bambara notes the following about the way that Dash's spatial sensibilities counter-hegemonic notions of space and geography:

> Dash's demystified and democratic treatment of space positions *Daughters* in progressive world film culture movements that bolster socially responsible cinema—Cuban, Caribbean, African, Philipino/Philopina, Cine Nuova, USA multicultural Independent. In *Daughters*, the emphasis is on shared space (wide-angled and deep focus shots in which no one becomes backdrop to anyone else's drama) rather than dominated space (foregrounded hero in sharp focus, other Othered in background blur); on social space rather than idealized space (as in Westerns); on delineated space that encourages a contiguous-reality reading rather than on masked space in which, through close-ups and framing, the spectator is encouraged to believe that conflicts are solely psychological not, say systemic, hence can be resolved by a shrink, a lawyer, or a gun, but not to say, through societal transformation. (Dash 1992, xiii)

As a scholar attending to the ways that conquest and settler colonial power, specifically the genocide of Native peoples and the commodification of nature through settlement finds meaning and expression through slavery, I find Bambara's reading instructive. Dash's visuality frustrates and at times ruptures settler colonial modes of sight. Settler colonial vision, or the vision of the Settler is organized around the acts of surveying, objectifying, taxonimizing and delineating the boundaries between bodies and nature. The Western, imperial eye is primarily an active eye that scans and reads from an all knowing vantage point of authority. The active eye mimics the all-seeing and all-knowing eye of God. In the essay,

"The Beholding Eye: Ten Versions of the Same Scene," cultural landscapes scholar D. W. Meinig presents human viewpoints or vantage points that describe the way that humans interpret the landscape with their eyes. Most of the vantage points rely on penetrating eyes that pierce the surface of the earth.

As penetrative masculine eyes, they read both land and bodies as systems and wealth generating commodities (Meinig 1979). The settler's vision would also instruct the colonial-eye to see and think about bodies as already marked and overdetermined by Western gender binaries of male and female, human and non-human. Further, the Settler delineates the spaces of slavery and Native geno-cide as bounded and separate forms of domination that do not touch. A number of Dash's visual moves disrupt this settler colonial visual order. By returning to the indigo-stained palms of Nana Peazant not as mere scars but as a punctum point that enables vision outside of settler colonial sight provides new vantage points and understandings.

IMAGES OF INDIGO

Minutes into the opening scenes of the film, the camera is gliding across a green river. In a boat, members of the Peazant family, Viola and Yellow Mary are accom-panied by companions Trula and photographer Mr. Sneed to their ancestral home on the Sea Isles off the mainland of Georgia. Viola is talking about the salt water Africans who were shipped to the islands right before the Civil War. The camera tightly crops and frames a wooden carving of the chest, upper arms, neck and head of Black male figure floating on the water. Within the soundscape of the shot of the carving, drums and what sounds like a female vocalist singing a Yoruba chant are audible. The camera then draws the eye into a dark forest. Once in the forest, the scene is a graveyard where an elder Black woman sits in front of a grave marking with a tin pail in her lap. The viewer learns later in the film that the elder women is Nana Peazant, the matriarch of the Peazant family.

The midrange shot of the Nana Peazant allows us to get a glimpse of her surroundings and hands. Clasped together and holding the bucket to her chest, we can see that her hands are darkened. Nana begins a monologue by stating "mi life not done done."[4] She then reflects upon her family members and community's plans for moving north. She indicates that she is upset about their move and will not be traveling with them. We also find out that when they come to say goodbye to her, she will give them a piece of her mind. She ends her monologue with "Ima work pon a plan."[5]

Shortly after this monologue, the audience gets another glimpse of Nana's hands which appear to be blue. They almost mimic the color of her dark blue dress. As the character Nana Peazant delivers her monologue a montage of the family and community making preparations for their migration unfolds on screen. The frames of the film move between various images of children and adults waking from sleep, men working in the front yards, and other interior and exterior spaces that look like they are in a state of transition. We also see other blue handed women engaged in various acts. The blue on the other women's hands is more pronounced and sharper than the blue on Nana Peazant's hands. As high priestess and family matriarch, Nana's hands are older and more worn from both physical labor, but also from the spiritual work she conducts to protect her family. Because the montage is shot as a series of close ups; there is a clearer shot of the blue that stains these women's hands partially due to fact that Additionally, the hands that are removing wax from an infant's ear, doing a teenage girls hair, ironing white fabric and holding a piece of bright red fruit are presented against another body or object that creates contrast. Another element of the scene that brings the indigo hands into sharp relief is that they are attending to the bodies and flesh of representations of youth, vitality and futurity (soft new skin, the neatly patterned hair of female adolescents and ripe fruit). Scarred hands with older stories of the terror of slavery tend to youthful bodies and their newer narratives of possibility and hope.

The indigo-blue that bled into the cuticles and the nail beds of Nana Peazant and the elder women of the Peazant family provide both proxmity to and distance from slavery at the same time. The indigo blue stained hands tell of a brutal violence that was intended to mark Black bodies as sub human forms of property. However, the indigo stains are also scars which render the violence that dyed them in the past.[6] The indigo stain holds a paradoxical story. It evokes all at once beautiful henna that tells a story of survival and at the same time a bone soaking violence that is arresting. The paradox of modern colonial violence is difficult to conceptualize and render effable in language and academic discourse.

Dash's optic of the indigo that stained formerly enslaved Black female bodies provides a visual vocabulary that also captures the ways that the violence of slavery and settler colonialism shape one another. Nana Peazant's hands become a location where plants, land and nature merge with human flesh. The sight of these bodies with blue hands and the indican plant's bio chemical components at one with human molecules crack colonialized eyes. The visual of the indigo-blue hands exceeds the capacity of the cognitive frames traditionally used to register the violence of slavery inflicted on Black bodies. These hands are a saturated and leaky image. They register more than slavery. Other types of violence, processes and people are on the scene.

The genocide of the Cherokee Nation was also made perceptible in these blue scarred hands. The violent removal of the Cherokee nation, the subsequent transformation of the Kiawasee Valley and the swamp lands of the Southeast, the violent commodification of indican plants and Black bodies into commodities can be rendered visible in the palms, fingers, lines and nail beds of Nana Peazant. The

Cherokee Nation, represented by St. Julien Last Child in the film, was targetted by various processes of systematic genocide which included their federally enacted removal during the 1830 Indian Removal Act. The ongoing settlement of plantations and the enslavement of Black people on the coasts and Sea Islands off of Georgia by settlers and slave holders (Settler-Masters) also constituted acts of genocide. Dash created a filmic moment where these processes all cohered and enunciated one another in the stained digits and palms of the formerly enslaved Black female.

Dash's poetics are important. They are what make the ineffable in academic theory visible and say-able. As an artist, Dash could make the invisible visible in her film. Dash's consultant, the historian and Gullah expert, Margaret Washington Creel insisted that though indigo would not have remained on the hands of the slaves that worked the indigo processing plants, the indigo was still poisonous (Dash 1992, 31). Creel's insight into the chemical elements of indigo and the incapability of indigo to stain the body is an example of why it is necessary to be aware of the limitations of the archive, particularly the body as merely an archive or repository of colonial violence.[7] Dash's representation of the invisible consequences of forced labor on indigo plantations through the embodied performances of plant-human hybrids seen on the actors' stained hands is a wonderful illustration of how the repertoire can make the hidden transcript of colonial violence visible. As a cultural production, Dash's film helps us think about how we might make the hidden power and violence of coloniality and slavery visible.

As an imaginative and creative artist Dash found ways to make an invisible poison render itself bare and mark the body for all to see. Dash's cinematic eye that uses sight as a synesthetic mode of knowledge production also pushes back against sight as a site of epistemic truth. Within cinema studies, the cinematic or cine-eye has been posited as a type of vision that emancipates the human eye. Dziga Vertov argued the cine-eye exceeded the human and camera eye due to its freedom from the constraints of "time and space" (1988, 93). Able to "juxtapose any points in the universe," supposedly the cine-eye can make visible things that "are inaccessible to the normal eye" (1988, 93). The cine-eye though heralded as a technological advance that enables sight still cannot make all things visible. The kind of knowing that the camera, or cine-eye could render bare for the eye is still only partial. Sight as an all knowing epistemology is not challenged or interrogated by the technological revolution of cinema.

For instance, the cine-eye in and of itself still cannot tell us what happened to the bodies of slaves who worked indigo. What kinds of slave bodies are produced by the simultaneous violence of slavery and settler colonialism? As Creel attests to, this question cannot be answered relying on sight as the entry point to knowing. Often knowledge of this nature is the embodied, oral and performative knowledge of communities targeted for genocide and social death.[8] What the eyes cannot see mutilated and oppressed subaltern communities know and experience. Creel's knowledge of the poisoning and death of slaves who worked on indigo plantations had to be brought into view as a form of subjugated knowledge by a filmmaker committed to altering sight. Dash had to manipulate vision, and make stained bodies appear where they would not have.

While using sight and the visual, Dash also critiques the regime of the visual in Western knowledge systems. Extending our vision into the realm of the invisible, Dash brings deadly processes that convert bodies into plant-flesh hybrids and interlocking nature of the often bounded spaces of the "Black" plantation and the "Native" settlement/clearing into one potent and poetic optic. The all-seeing imperial eye of the Settler-Master would look upon the indigo-stained body as evidence of its inhumanity. In the process of converting the indican plant into a commodity the Black slave body stains itself and marks itself as non-human. It loses its human capacity to maintain the boundary between the human body and the earth. Within liberal humanist nature/culture divide, this kind of violable body is a non-human body that cannot control nature. The Black female slave body becomes a part of the earth and settled space to the Settler-Master. While this kind of theoretical rumination on violence is made possible by Dash's film, it is not Dash's intent to render Black women as non-human in her film.[9]

In fact, Dash's film presents one of the most beautiful and humanizing depictions of Black life in the African Diaspora. Though terrifyingly haunting, the indigo blue stains on Black elder female hands in the movie are beautiful and senuous. There are other orders and depths of sight that indigo offers us. Dash's flash of blue enables one to gain knowledge of the paradox of indigo which also represents the paradox of modernity. In indigo I can see what New World violence produces and also what it cannot contain.

Dash's epistemology includes a simultaneous and contradictory form of sight that operates both inside and outside of colonial vision. Dash can hold the same scarred indigo-stained bodies in our line of sight and show us something more than dehumanization. The same indigo-stained hands contain something hidden in their blueness.

WHAT IS HIDDEN IN INDIGO

A cursory reading of the blue stained hands will not reveal the paradox of indigo. Catherine McKinley's pursuit of the meaning of indigo in her own life as well as in the lives of African diaporic people led to a life altering realization. McKinley (2011) documented her four year sojourn in her memoir and historical narrative, *Indigo: In Search of the Color that Seduced the World.* Her journey was one to "find of indigo what was hidden" (183). In order for McKinley to find what was hidden of indigo and what about the color consumed her, she had to undergo a transformation. She had to understand the reasons for her obsession with indigo before she could come to understand its role in her life and the lives of others in the African diaspora.

Toward the end of McKinley's four year pursuit of the meaning of indigo, she describes her breakthrough. She interprets the riddle given to her by an adopted Ghanaian aunt, "I understood now Eurama's riddles: Blue is black. Blue is life, mourning, joy, all at once. Life and death have exquisite symmetry. The symmetry is held in the color blue." Dash's use of indigo in *Daughters of the Dust* catalyses a similar realignment of one's sight and understanding. In order to perceive the symmetry, or the multivalent nature of indigo we must decolonize sight. Decolonization requires that we think about sight differently not pluck out our eyes. According to Renee Paulani Louis, "decolonizing [...] is not about the total rejection of Western theory, research or knowledge. It's about changing focus" (Louis 2007, 131). Linda Tuhiwai Smith (1999, 152) argues similarly that it is not a total rejection of the West but "rather it is about centering our concerns and world views and then coming to know [...] from our own perspectives and for our own purposes."

Rather than use the penetrating eyes of a settling, Western imperial subject; we must allow room for the receptive eye. This notion of the eye as a penetrating force that reads and deconstructs the landscape is a producet of imperial masculinity. Seeking a new vision, the eye that Catherine McKinley (2011, 60) ended up developing during her sojourn was an eye that could at times be penetrated:

> The beauty of the taglemust moving in the tide, knotting and unfurling, was mesmerizing. Indigo was a part of that Atlantic. If there was spirit at work, or an act of devotion to be made, mine would be bound to that history—my own and that of the people I was seeking. I hadn't made this journey simply to be a collector, but I needed indigo in my eye.

Mesmerized by the indigo garment in the water, McKinley connects indigo to the Atlantic, spirit, history and possession. For a moment, McKinley inverts the process we typically imagine as viewing. Rather than looking out with the eye to see indigo, McKinley pleads to have indigo in her eye. For McKinley, the eye can be entered, possessed even.

This kind of eye contests the vision of the imperial eye that projects its desires and fantasies outward toward objects. Here, McKinley reveals her own spiritual agency which enables her to allow indigo into her eye, her spirit, that she may see. The imperial eye is an inviolable eye of an inviolable human subject. The natural world does not alter it or possess it, the eye possesses the natural landscape.[10] However, McKinley needs to catch indigo as if she were catching the spirit. McKinley realizes at the end of her journey that she cannot possess indigo, she must be transformed by it. McKinley does not return from her trip with a beholding eye, but with an eye possessed by indigo. Her Aunt Eurama tells Catherine that she has a spirit that begs for blue. Auntie Eurama warns, "Blue-blue! Is all you think of" (Wahab 2008, 26).

Developing the capacity for your eye to be possessed or to catch indigo in it, is not the only step to decolonizing one's sight. The capacity to see does not stem from the power of the eye alone, or even the brain and the eye together. Sight happens due to a combination of senses. Oyeronke Oyewumi (1997, 14) argues in Yoruba cosmology, the senses work together. Sight was not privileged as the site of knowledge within pre-colonial Yoruba society; rather it is a complex array of the senses that need to be marshaled in order to make sense of the social world. Decolonial sight is a process of synthesizing multiple senses. Seeing on decolonial terms requires a recognition of the whole self and all of its capacity and ways of knowing. Decolonization requires a sight that can discern and be open to the multiple things that are occurring within oneself and others. With all other senses at play, decolonized sight seeks out integrity or holistic healing. What is crucial to see when viewing Nana Peazant's indigo-stained hands is that her hands were engaged in healing work. The indigo referenced the life and recuperative work of the formerly enslaved as much as it indexed the violence and dehumanization.

The montage of blue handed people in the beginning of the *Daughters of the Dust*, brings attention to women attending to the needs of the flesh. The erotic self-care, braiding of hair, cleaning wax from a baby's ear, pressing clothing, and preparing food all reference an attention to and love for the Black body. Within the context of an anti-Black world, caring for the body is a radical act for one formerly enslaved. However, it never works in a singular way. The body is a multitudinous site. Even the act of caring for the body through recuperating it implicitly references the violence it is healing from. In *Scenes of Subjection*, Saidiya Hartman (1997, 75) elucidates on what the recuperated slave body can reveal and make possible:

> Thus history is illuminated not only by the recitation of the litany of horrors that characterized the "commercial deportation of Africans," but also by performance practices that serve as a means of redressing the pained body and restaging the event of rupture or breach that engendered "the other side." The (counter) investment in the body as a site of need, desire, and pleasure and the constancy of unmet needs, repressed desires, and the shortcomings of pleasure are articulated in the very endeavor to heal the flesh and redress the pained body.

For Hartman, even moments when the pained body is being cared for (Dash's montages of the erotic activity of the hands) serve as moments that draw us back to the underside of modernity. However, when the film viewer witnesses violence and in the same moment is also seeing the recuperation of the slave body, the viewer does not have to be destroyed or paralyzed. This is the power of simultaneous vision. We are allowed to see and understand both parts of the paradox without being subsumed by the sentimentalism of romanticism or the horror of gratuitous violence. We can see multiple truths at one time in the blue handed bodies.

Dash's choice to stain her actors' hands blue was made in order to reference a variety of seen and unseen realms and meanings. Yoruba cosmologies could be accessed at a number of points in the film in order to interpret the multiple meanings of blue. In Dash's book, *Daughters of the Dust: The Making of An African American Woman's Film*, which chronicles the making of the film, Dash tells of multiple moments in the film when Yoruba cosmology was being evoked. Dash worked with composer John Barnes to score the film. Barnes evoked the sounds of West Africa at times and specifically wrote a closing theme for the movie entitled "Elegba Theme." The lyrics to the closing theme were "Ago Elegba, show the way Elegba" (Dash 1992, 16). Dash was explicitly referencing the cosmology through the actors she cast and the roles they served in the narrative.

The pages of the original screenplay are made available in Dash's *Daughters of the Dust: The Making of an African American Woman's Film*. Dash's margin notes are found throughout the pages of the script. In several places in block capital letters, Dash scribbled the coded meanings her characters held. The key characters of the movie represented Yoruba orishas. Each character, like the orishas who ruled over certain natural elements, are signified by certain colors and had specific roles in the community. On page one of the screenplay, Dash wrote NANA PEAZANT=O-BATALA. In these same handwritten notes on pages 2, 12, 25, 33 and 42 we find out that Yellow Mary is Yemaya, Trula is Oshun, Eli is Ogun, the Unborn Child is Elegba, and Eula is Oya Yansa (Dash 1992, 75–107). As these references are only explicitly revealed in the screenplay's margin notes, the references remain implicit in the film.

The film is coded. As a densely layered experience, people need to read and decipher the film on multiple levels. One of the systems that indigo references within Yoruba communities is the gendered work, status, spiritual competencies and capacities of female indigo workers. On McKinley's trip to the Yoruba art village, Osun-Oshogbo Sacred Grove, the writer explains how indigo work and the gender system are related in Yoruba culture. McKinley (2011, 173) writes:

> In Yoruba, everything has a spiritual significance. Even the most rudimentary work is guided by the realm of the spirits, and so as one works, one pays tribute. The goddess of Iya Mapo is the patroness of all exclusive women's work, trades like dyeing, pottery and soap making. She is the deity of sex. She guides all things erotic. She guides conception and birth. She guides the tricky realm of the indigo dye pot, and the hands of women and girls who design cloths, perform the intense preparation for dyeing, and undertake the many steps to finish a cloth.

As explained by McKinley, the realm of the indigo pot is guided by the goddess Iya Mapo. The deity of sex and "all things erotic" is also the deity of the indigo work gendered female or women's work.

By focusing on the erotic, it is also possible to expand the more rigid gendered reading that McKinley gives indigo work as erotic women's work. McKinley's important reading of indigo as erotic women's work aligns with the way the working hands function in Dash's montage. All of the indigo-stained hands are performing the gendered work associated with domestic space. They are cleaning, preparing food and caring for children and other female bodies. Angeletta Gourdine, who analyzes the film's representations of the Black body, specifically through the wardrobe choices that Dash made for the characters, argues that indigo work was gendered work. Gourdine (2001, 503) remarks on the various meanings of Nana Peazant's indigo-stained hands:

> Nana's dyed hands emblematize Blackwomen's labor under the yoke of slavery, their active participation in the consumer world, as most Black women on slave plantations were experts spinners, weavers, knitters, and dressmakers [...] This stain is particularly female, for women not only planted the cotton but also crafted the cloth from which they crafted their clothing. Nana's hands, then, reveal Black women's participation in the consumer cloth economy, partially enabled by the abundance of trees used for dying cloth on the coastal Sea Islands.

The indigo stain references multiple realms of the textile market and Black women's labor within it. Naming women's work, specifically women who work with indigo, as sacred and erotic in the way that Dash and McKinley do, rightfully infuses it with power and agency. However, I want to reframe the meaning of the erotic and subsequently reconceptualize how we think about the power of the erotic. By drawing on Audre Lorde's notion of the erotic, specifically the kind of power it enables women to access, I want to think about how the erotic power of indigo work can destabilize our naturalization and acceptance of Western constructions of gender. In the 1984 essay, "Uses of the Erotic," Lorde ([1984] 2007, 87) speaks about the erotic as an active position or space between two states and a powerful form of inertia that can move us to another place; into our strongest feelings. The erotic is a measure between the beginning of our sense of self and the chaos of our strongest feelings. Lorde's erotic power can lead into chaos. That chaos can help us access our strongest feelings, and our truest selves, which Lorde argues women are taught to fear. Chaos according to Lorde can also take us closer to knowledge and transformation. Lorde talked more extensively about this descent into chaos in her 1979 address delivered at a conference, "The Masters Tools Will Never Dismantle the Master's House." In this address, Lorde makes space for the productive tension of difference and challenges listeners to allow themselves to take a plunge into the depths of chaos:

> Within the interdependence of mutual (non-dominant) differences lies that security which enables us to descend into the chaos of knowledge and return with true visions of our future, along with the concomitant power to effect those changes which can bring that future into being. (Lorde 1983, 96)

Erotic chaos is a concept that is crucial to decolonization. I focus on the power of the erotic to take us into the space of chaos because chaos radically disorients us. I want to use Lorde's erotic route into chaos as a way of further destabilizing the Western concept of gender. I want to revisit the way that McKinley historicizes and frames indigo work as sacred women's work in the Yoruba culture. Drawing upon Oyeronke Oyewumi's text, *The Invention of Women*, I want to further destabilize what Oyewumi would call our sense of gender.

Taking Lorde's erotic journey into chaos in order to meet up with Oyewumi's deconstruction of Western gender constructions, I ask if indigo can offer us a road out of the territory of Western gender concepts? Rather than read indigo as McKinley does as women's work, can indigo reference gender chaos? Stated another way, rather than have indigo reference coherent gender categories like African woman or goddess could indigo reference a non-coherent personhood or being-ness? Lorde's jettisoning of the ordered and rational in favor of the chaotic and Oyewumi's work to make body reasoning strange can help us navigate our way out of the regulatory regime of Western gender constructions. I want to consider how Oyewumi's deconstruction and disengagement with Western body reasoning and gender construction can help me rethink gender when I make sense of Nana Peazant's indigo-stained hands.

Oyewumi (1997, 31) argues that "gender was not an organizing principle in Yoruba society prior to colonization by the West." Further, the Yoruba world-sense, rather than view, is not one that is ordered around sight and therefore the body (3). The body is at the core of Western constructions of gender. In the Yoruba world-sense, humans experience the physical, social and metaphysical world through a combination of senses. If we read Nana Peazant as Obatala, then we have to succumb to some of the chaos that Obatala's presence causes Western body-centric sight. Obatala is the creator of the world and humanity. Specifically, Obatala breaks up the water with land making the earth habitable. Obatala can express themselves as an ana-male or ana-female.[11] In Western terms, Obatala can show up in a feminine form or a masculine form.[12] Trying to rest ones eyes on the form of Obatala causes visual chaos. Nana Peazant as a reference for Obatala in Dash's movie could reference gender chaos and confusion.

Can Obatala's indigo also work to impede or obscure our vision and reliance on sight in order to reference other ways of knowing? As McKinley pursued indigo, she provided her own account of the capacity of indigo to confound the eye. McKinley states, "Indigo is not really a color, it is not cloth, I realized. It is only the tangible intangible. The attempt to capture beauty, to hold the elusive, the fine layer of skin between the two" (McKinley 2011, 81). Indigo is a veil or skin between the tangible and intangible. I argue that indigo has both the capacity to make the body visible and hide the body when placed on the hands of the actor Cora Lee Day who plays Nana Peazant. For a moment, I want to focus on its power to hide the body. Indigo placed on top of the skin has the power of opacity and creates chaos for the eye, specifically the active and all knowing imperial eye. For McKinley, indigo is an attempt to hold the elusive.

If indigo is only a veil between the tangible and the intangible then how might we read the body veiled or stained indigo? If indigo acts as a veil, could it be veiling or hiding the body in scenes where we see it staining hands and body parts? Changing indigo's part of speech and making it a verb here helps it to function better as an active process of making something opaque. Rather than function to further corporealize the body and make visible, indigo functions to create a layer between the body and the eye. Gourdine argues that the very first full body image of Nana, and for that matter any Black woman in the film, is one of a woman fully clothed in an indigo dress washing in the river. This is a scene and context in which one would expect nakedness (Gourdine 2001, 503). Gourdine reads this as an attempt by Nana Peazant and other Black women to cloak or shroud themselves from "invasive gazes" (503). Indigo-ing or obscuring the hands of Nana Peazant and other formerly enslaved women veils the body and confounds the all-knowing epistemology of sight that the Settler-Master relies on to survey bodies and land. By making the Black body opaque and non-transparent it cannot be easily known, objectified and turned into property. Indigo calls forth opacity and visual chaos.

Blue calls forth a decolonized cosmology. Blueness announces to the ears, mouth, nose, eyes and spirit other ways of knowing. Blueness, and indigo by extention, gives testimony of one's story—one's individual and collective trials and tribulations—documents just how "I got over." Even still, blueness can also usher in other times, spaces and worlds. Indigo-blue is a meeting place, a border. McKinley (2011, 81) writes of her knowledge of this:

> I was reminded again of the real power of the metaphor of cloth and especially indigo: that it merely materializes the very thin layer between what is seen and unseen, between what can be grasped and what can only be suggested, between the living and the spirit world. I was for the first time not able to assume my own protection. I was not the stranger with the notebook. I was no further from death than anyone.

The living world and the spirit world touch at the location of indigo. Nana Peazant, resilient, yet indigo-stained, was often the space where the Peazant ancestors and future descendants met. Nana Peazant is a location where the divine and the human touch. Land and human also touch and merge at the site of her hands. We can understand the natural world and the human world, indican plant and human skin as one. Various indigenous and non-Western cosmologies posit the plant and natural world as a relative of the human. Nana Peazant is a chaotic space of blurred lines that confound human, spatial and temporal coordinates that institute hierarchies and exclusions.

Indigo as a way of obscuring vision presents a space of incoherence and blurred boundaries. It is a space of fluidity, human-nature hybridity, flux, time travel, spatial disorganization and reorganization all at once. Nana's indigo is a site of transport, across waters, across times, across spaces. What we learn from the collapsing boundaries of Nana Peazant's body is that the body is not stable and coherent. The body is not the site of gender universally. Dash's engagement with Yoruba cosmology allows us to see that Nana's hands and body do not take us to gender truth. And sight in and of itself is not knowledge or truth.

With this reading of Yoruba society in mind, I appreciate the way that Dash is trying to convey and create a multi-sensory and multi-temporal experience for the viewers. When we see and experience Nana Peazant on screen, she is accompanied by a score played in the key of A. The theme song that composer Barnes created for Nana Peazant was done in the key of Aquarius, "representing the age that was imminent for Nana's family" (Dash 1992, 16). According to Oyewumi, for the Yoruba and other African societies sound is very important. The apprehension of reality involves more than perception. Apprehending the world is about "a particular presence in the world—a world conceived of as a whole in which all things are linked together. It concerns the many worlds human beings inhabit; it does not privilege the physical world over the metaphysical." (Oyewumi 1997, 14)

The way Dash linked the physical world to the spirit world, and the past to the future, effectively decolonizes the senses and forces a form of disorientation. The images, sounds, the feelings and non-representable elements of the film are refracted through the indigo strategically placed on the hands of Nana Peazant and other Black women. Rather than just see, one must also sense and feel what colors like indigo mean. As Oyewumi argues, "A concentration on vision as the primary mode of comprehending reality promotes what can be seen over that which is not apparent to the eye; it misses the other levels and the nuances of existence" (Oyewumi 1997, 14). Like McKinley (2011, 183), we need to "find of indigo what was hidden." Indigo cannot be known or experienced in the realm of sight alone.

Dash's cinematic vision enables the indigo scarred Black body to work on the imagination in a number of ways. Dash's blue handed people offer an encounter with the synesthetic and multisensory visuality required for making sense of unimaginable and confounding violence as well as the beautifully vexed lines and creases of human struggle and triumph.

NOTES

1. In her 1992 interview with Houston Baker Jr., Dash states she wanted to reference the scars of slavery differently than the iconic keloids on the back of a slave that had been whipped (Dash and Baker 1992, 164).

2. I learned this first hand while at a symposium called "We Carry These Memories inside a We," held at the College of Charleston's Avery Research Center for African American History and Culture, Charleston, SC, on September 14–16, 2011. There, Dash explained that the indigo stained hands referenced much more than just scars of slavery.

3. Toni Cade Bambara, "Preface" in *The Making of An African American Woman's Film*.

4. My transcription of the dialogue of the characters varies from the lines of the script in the screenplay. I present what I heard here rather than what is actually written in the screenplay. In the screenplay, you find "my life is not yet [...]" Actors do not read or produce the lines verbatim. I also do this in order to capture and depict my own sensorial experience with the film.

5. My own transcription of Cora Lee's monologue as Nana Peazant.

6. I'm appreciative to Lia Bascomb for providing comments for this chapter. Bascomb encouraged me to think about the temporal value of scars. A scar indexes past violence that a body has healed from. The indigo scarring does not merely reference slavery but the fact that one has survived slavery and found a way to live through it.

7. Diana Taylor (2003) argues an embodied practice of the repertoire is critical to hemispheric practices of memory work in the hemisphere. The repertoire provides a way of overcoming the various limitations of the archive.

8. In *Red, White and Black*, Wilderson (2010) uses genocided as an adjective to describe the onto-logical position of the Savage.

9. At the symposium "We Carry These Memories Inside of We," Julie Dash cautioned the audience that scarring her characters with the stains of slavery did not work to make them non-human. In no way did she intend to dehumanize her characters.

10. Amar Wahab (2008) argues the colonizing subject enacts a "surveying I" or "eye" as a way of looking and as a way of knowing the land and other as well as themselves. The surveying I/eye is a way of looking and a way of making a subject position.

11. These are the terms Oyewumi uses to index differentiation at the body as they pertain to repro-ductive functions. She does not use the terms male or female because they already carry the baggage of Western gender binaries and hierarchies.

12. See "The Orishas," Orisha Net Articles, accessed October 24, 2010, http://www.orishanet.org/ocha.html.

REFERENCES

Dash, Julie, dir. 2000. *Daughters of the Dust*. 1991. New York, NY: Kino International, DVD.

———. 1992. *Daughters of the Dust: The Making of an African American Woman's Film*. New York: The New Press.

Dash, Julie and Houston Baker. 1992. "Not Without My Daughters: A Conversation with Julie Dash and Houston A. Baker Jr." *Transition*, no. 57 (1992):150–166.

Gourdine, Angeletta K.M. 2001. "Fashioning the Body [as] Politic in Julie Dash's *Daughters of the Dust*." *African American Review* 38, no. 3 (Autumn): 499–511.

Hartman, Saidiya. 1997. *Scenes of Subjection: Terror, Slavery, and Self Making in Nineteenth-Century America*. New York: Oxford University Press.

Lorde, Audre. 1983. "The Master's Tools Will Never Dismantle the Master's House." In *This Bridge Called My Back: Writings by Radical Women of Color*. edited by Cherríe Moraga and Gloria Anz-aldua, 94–103. New York: Kitchen Table Press.

————. (1984) 2007. *Sister Outsider: Essays and Speeches.* Berkeley, CA: Crossing Press.

Louis, Renee Pualani. 2007. "Can You Hear Us Now? Voices from the Margin: Using Indigenous Methodologies in Geographic Research." *Geographical Research* 45, no. 2 (June): 130–139

McKinley, Catherine. 2011. *Indigo: In Search of the Color that Seduced the World.* New York: Bloomsbury USA.

Meinig, Donald W. 1979. "The Beholding Eye: Ten Versions of the Same Scene." In *The Interpretation of Ordinary Landscapes: Geographical Essays*, edited by D. W. Meinig, 33–50. New York: Oxford University Press.

Oyewumi, Oyeronke. 1997. *The Invention of Women: Making an African Sense of Western Gender Discourses.* Minneapolis: University of Minnesota Press,.

Smith, Linda Tuhiwai. 1999. *Decolonizing Methodologies: Research and Indigenous Peoples.* New York: Palgrave.

Taylor, Diana. 2003. *The Archive and the Repertoire: Performing Cultural Memory in the Americas.* Durham: Duke University Press.

Vertov, Dziga. 1988. "The Cine-Eyes. A Revolution." In *The Film Factory: Russian and Soviet Cinema in Documents 1896–1939*, edited by Richard Taylor and Ian Christie, 89–94. New York: Routledge.

Wahab, Amar. 2008. "Race, Gender and Visuality: Regulating Indian Women Subjects in the Colonial Caribbean." *Caribbean Review of Gender Studies* (2008):1–36.

Wilderson, Frank. 2010. *Red, White, and Black: Cinema and Structures of U.S. Antagonisms.* Durham: Duke University Press.

PART 4

The Power of Place in Shaping Identity and Artistic Cultivation

CHAPTER NINE

In Search of Solid Ground

Oral Histories of the Great Migration, from the Carolinas to New England

MARCELLA "MARCY" DE VEAUX

North, they say. North is what they wake up whispering in their husband's ears. That's the word that wets their lips in the nighttime. (Dash 1992, 86)

Julie Dash's 1991 theatrical film, *Daughters of the Dust*, portrays a period when rural families were leaving the Southern part of the United States in search of change. Millions of Blacks moved from the South to the industrialized North seeking freedom to live and work without the draconian restrictive racial codes placed on Black Americans who called the South home. Writer, producer, and director Julie Dash's seminal film provides a fitting backdrop to explore the experience of migration and displacement of land-based agrarian people of African descent who moved to industrialized manufacturing areas of the United States.

AMERICA'S GREAT MIGRATION

Beginning in the 1800s and well into the 20th century, millions of Black Americans migrated "within the boundaries of the United States—fleeing economic impoverishment, racial segregation, and state-sponsored oppression in search of something better" (De Veaux 2011, 2). The Great Migration was one of the most undocumented and underreported phenomena in the United States. The migration of African people from the rural farmlands of the American South settling in Northern cities close to the Canadian border and the Eastern shores of the Atlantic Ocean is one of the most significant demographic events to ever take place (3).

The story of the Great Migration has been studied and documented by historians and researchers who focused mostly on facts and figures around this migratory pattern. Many spoke of this mass movement in biblical terms, equating it with the Israelites leaving Egypt, headed for "The Promised Land" (Baskerville 2001). The impact on both the North and the South was substantial. The South lost much of its native-born Black population who cultivated food and tobacco for the nation. For the North, the concentrated migration created an intensive shift of economic, political, and cultural importance on the Northern cities, changing their way of life. Residents of Boston, Baltimore, Buffalo, Chicago, Cleveland, Detroit, Indianapolis, Newark, New York, Philadelphia, Trenton, and Washington, DC, where the African American population moved, struggled in welcoming their new neighbors. "These new locations offered harsh, brutally cold winters—coupled with noise, speed, and accelerated movements of an urban center. Once north, these former farmers were required to adjust to stacked tenement apartment living, void of any green space" (De Veaux 2011, 62).

THE NEW ENGLAND STATES

Most of this history has been placed on states in the Midwest region of the country. Black migration into the New England States—Connecticut, Rhode Island, Massachusetts, New Hampshire, Vermont, and Maine—is, however, mostly unknown.

In 2009, I began conducting research on the experience of migration, displacement, and dislocation for African Americans during the Great Migration period. Specifically, I interviewed families who migrated from North and South Carolina to cities in New England. I used my own family's journey from the South to Haverhill, Massachusetts, a small city located on the New Hampshire border, as an entrance into the experience of migration for other Black families who headed North. Piecing together oral histories, myths, legends, and some official documents, I have established that my maternal family tree begins in Virginia in 1838 and also in Nova Scotia, Canada, where my maternal grandfather's grandparents were free people:

> Their locality before Canada is assumed in Virginia. However, the actual facts remain a mystery. The family legend as it is told begins in New England and, although there are official government records that were found in Canada, those remain suspect to me. (De Veaux 2011, 7)

A piece of the story that is known is that my maternal grandmother's family migrated from the Charlottesville, Virginia area to Massachusetts at the turn of the century. Similar to millions of African Americans, I also have ties in South Carolina. My father's family has roots firmly in Charleston, South Carolina, where records report the birthplace of both of his parents and grandparents. "According to South Carolina's Department of Archives & History, at least half of the current African American population in the United States has ties to South Carolina" (De Veaux 2011, 4).

Along with moments from *Daughters of the Dust*, this paper incorporates the voices of African American family members from my previous research who tell their own story of migration using the West African tradition of oral storytelling "just like the African Griot, who would hold these records in his head, the old souls in each family, could recollect all the births, deaths, marriages and sales" (Dash 1992, 147)

A PSYCHOLOGY OF PLACE

Daughters of the Dust documents the phenomenon of migration and dislocation experienced by the Gullah people—a cloistered group of African Americans living in the lowcountry of South Carolina and Georgia—who although accustomed to an agrarian life, decide to leave the land of which they have become attached in search of opportunity. Eco-psychologist Janine Canty suggests, "for African people bonded by proverbial landscape, sacred soil—and earth—displacement creates a traumatic disconnect from the land, their ancestors, and ancestral burial grounds" (De Veaux 2011, 19). Nana Peazant asks: "how can you leave this soil [...] this soil. The sweat of our love, it here in this soil, I love you 'cause you're mine, you're the fruit of an ancient tree" (Dash 1992, 154). For Nana, the soil represents her connection to her ancestors. Similarly, for descendants of West Africa, the relationship to the living and spiritual world, the land, the landscape, and its natural resources are a basic condition for such a spiritual connection. According to cultural eco-psychologist Carl Anthony (quoted in Canty 2000), the connection to geography is critical to indigenous cultures, who model their customs and laws according to the landscape they inhabit. Along with Nathan Huggins, Anthony and Canty contend that the life force of African people links the present life with the past through the ancestors and the landscape. Dash's family matriarch, Nana Peazant, bears witness to this fact in her daily visits to tend the grave of her husband. She tells her great grandson, Eli:

> I visit with old Peazant every day since the day he died. It's up to the living to keep in touch with the dead, Eli. Man's power doesn't end with death. We just move on to a new place, a place where we watch over our living family. (Dash 1992, 93)

IN SEARCH OF HOME

Daughters of the Dust opens with tension between the matriarchal character, Nana Peazant, and her grandson. She pleads with him in her native patois to remain on the island just off the coast of South Carolina where Africans first landed in this country, "when you leave this island, Eli Peazant, you ain't going to no land of milk and honey" (Dash 1992, 97). Her granddaughter, Viola Peazant, who has returned to Ibo Landing as an escort for other family members to make the journey, tells her niece that the North holds "the beginning of a new life" (97). Dash presents this pursuit for a place to belong in Nana Peazant's granddaughter, Yellow Mary, who is searching for a place where she is not judged. While she talks of going to Nova Scotia: "I like the sound of that place [...] Nova Scotia [...] Nova Scotia will be good to me" (144–145), she ultimately she discovers and discloses her desire is for home--for the place where the people know her name. For Yellow Mary, home was with the living family who knew her and could call her name and the ancestors who continued to watch over her and her family. Employing the word *home* in this context requires expanding the definition from only a geographic location to "a place where one is emotionally attached, in harmony with surroundings, and acclimated to the environment" and "home, the center of consciousness or sensitivity" (Gove 1993). As she makes her decision to remain on Ibo Landing, Yellow Mary says, "but I need to know that I can come home [...] to hold onto what I came from. I need to know that the people here know my name" (Dash 1992, 154).

Daughters of the Dust was released at a time when an emerging area of research was exploring the effects of displacement specifically in African American communities. This research was expanding on anthropological theories of attachment between individuals and their intimate environments that included communities of people and place (Fullilove 2004). The migration from the South resulted in a dislocation from the land and familiarity of place for descendants of African people. Fullilove argued for "a 'psychology of place' that is principally concerned with the sense of belonging to a locale" (9). In *Daughters of the Dust*, the burial grounds of Ibo Landing were a vital locale for Nana Peazant; her psychology of place was the burial grounds of the departed and she pleaded with her family to keep the ancestors close.

AN ARCHETYPAL JOURNEY

The film culminates with members of the Peazant family leaving Ibo Landing heading north to the mainland of South Carolina. We have a glimpse of what the next chapter for this family might have been through the earlier experiences of Viola Peazant: "When I left these islands, I was a sinner and I didn't even know it. But I left these islands, touched the mainland and fell into the arms of the Lord" (Dash 1992, 115). The Great Migration was an archetypal journey and through developing oral histories of Black families who made the journey from the Carolinas we can surmise how the Peazants might have fared.

In developing oral histories, I chose to conduct interviews with the Griots who told stories of their leaving the South and their desire to remember and recall home. These interviews, conducted in 2011, provide the source for the material that follows in this chapter. One elder, Leahnora Turner Hill, migrated from "Carolina" into Massachusetts, a state that lies at one of the most northeastern points of the United States, in 1929:

> Her maternal grandmother left North Carolina at the turn of the century for the Village of West Newton, near Boston, Massachusetts. West Newton has a vibrant Black community that dates back to 1875 when freed men and sons of former slaves who settled there established a Black church. (De Veaux 2011, 99)

In the 1940s, Leahnora returned to Warren County, North Carolina for the first time since her departure to reunite with her paternal grandparents who had remained in the South. Just past her teen years, she had anxiety about returning to the South to reunite with grandparents she could not remember, but was anxious to see the farm country that she and her parents had left:

> My parents kept talking about grandpa this and grandma that, but I could not remember them, as a youngster I could not remember them. I was anxious to see this farm. Having attended schools in Newton and reading books I saw pictures of farms […] I had grandiose expectations […] I thought of a farmhouse with a white picket fence! I laugh at myself now. They didn't have books to tell you about a real rural farm or what a cotton field was like. I will never forget that I imagined a white farmhouse with a white picket fence; and then I got there, in the rural area and saw a real rural area with dirt roads, a distance from the highway but I was anxious to see "from whence I came." (99)

She reported to me her family's stories told frequently by her mother and father, aunts and uncles, who had migrated to Massachusetts. Those stories were with pleasant memories of "down home." She said:

> My mother and father, aunts, uncles, and my grandmother, the cluster of them, would always talk about it with pleasant memories; they would always talk about "down home" and I wanted to see what "down home" was. They talked about the good times; they yearned for the family and the camaraderie of people. It was what they had known all their life. But they also said that [farming] was hard, backbreaking work and they never said that they were sorry they left it. (De Veaux 2011, 99)

In developing these oral histories, the most compelling emergent theme came from the desire of these migrants to be near loved ones, living and deceased. According to author Dwayne E. Walls in *The Chickenbone Special*, people went up North and "sent back home for relatives—sometimes even for long dead relatives, who were disinterred and shipped North for reburial because North was home now, and a man liked to have his kin buried at home" (Walls 1970, 25).

Leahnora's younger brother, Samuel Turner, talked of the family's desire to have the ancestors buried in the local cemetery of the Village of West Newton, Massachusetts:

> My maternal grandmother and her husband are buried in Newton. They didn't send the bodies back. When my father died, my father's father was still alive and all his brothers and sisters. They wanted my mother to send his body back and she did, to North Carolina. That was something she always regretted, I can hear her saying it, many times. "If I knew then what I know now, I never would have done that. Because all of his family is here and it's people here that would be interested in visiting the grave.

> My mother died in 1967 in July, in December she was going to be 70 years old, so we thought this was remarkable that this woman was going to be 70 years old. She decided that she was going to have a big, big 70th birthday bash. So we started putting money together for this bash. And before we could get [the party] on, she died. And we had put together a sizeable amount of money at the time. One of her dreams, if she had her druthers she would have my father's remains [here]. We had [my father's remains] exhumed and brought him back to the cemetery and had them buried together. Why was that so important? Because she said that we should know where our parents were buried, or children should know that, that was a part of history. (De Veaux 2011)

Mr. Turner went on to say that he followed his mother's desire for his children and his children's children to know where the family was buried:

> I never was a disciple of this but some of my brothers and sisters are, you know visiting the grave, visiting the gravesites. For my parents' graves we have perpetual care. Some of my brothers and sisters on Decoration Day or Memorial Day, they will be there and stop to visit the grave quite a bit. Once and a while, I might do that, if someone wants to see it. When my kids were small we would go over there. I would take them over to see where Ma [Turner] was buried. (De Veaux 2011)

For some families who migrated, the connection to the ancestral burial ground is there, but has lessened over time. Miriam Grigsby Bates migrated to Connecticut from North Carolina and her being included in the family burial ground has become a question. Born in Prairie View, Texas, her family migrated north to North Carolina in 1926 when she was three months old. After college, Miriam migrated to Connecticut to further her education and spent 30 years "up north" only to return to Charlotte where she continues to live today. She struggles with the question of joining the ancestors in the family burial ground:

> I have a plot in the same cemetery as mother and dad. My brother sort of convinced me. My brother's wife is buried there and my [other] brother is buried there. I don't know and I don't even know if that's my choice, or whether cremation is the way to go. I've even had a plaque made for mine, but over the last couple of years I've seen cremations that are almost more appealing to me. I think economically, that made sense. I don't see putting all that money in the ground when it could be used someplace else. (De Veaux 2011)

Her memories of her parents and grandparents are not in the cemetery; however, Miriam says she is not sure she would like to be memorialized or remembered as a place in the ground. "I don't know. My first feeling is in 50 years, who will care? I remember [the ancestors] in other ways other than the cemetery. It's not because of a plaque in the cemetery; it's because of them and what they did." And yet she worries about what will happen to her two adult children, "I got three lots, not knowing what would happen [...] but I just wanted it to be a place" (De Veaux 2011).

THE MIGRATION NARRATIVE

The remembering of these stories enriches the understanding of this period in America's history, which is considered one of the most under-reported and undoc-umented migrations within the borders of the United States (Wilkerson 2010). These memories fill the gaps of missing history during a time of significant histor-ical and cultural change. Also, they provide an unfiltered perspective of those who lived the experience, offering a more complete and complex picture of America's history (De Veaux 2011).

For these reasons, I advocate for the creation of oral histories as a way to explore and preserve American history. As Featherstone wrote, the "telling of stories can be a profound form of scholarship, moving serious study close to the frontiers of art in the capacity to express complex truth and moral context in intel-ligible ways" (quoted in Lawrence-Lightfoot and Hoffman Davis 1997, 11).

In the telling of this particular story of migration, I maintain that an art form known as the migration narrative is a most useful practice to document a phe-nomenon that is essential to understanding. Visual artists, playwrights, poets, and both fiction and non-fiction writers who tell the story of America's Black migra-tion, have employed this form of artistic expression. The first was Paul Lawrence Dunbar who wrote *The Sport of the Gods* in 1902 and focused on American urban Black life for families who encountered the harsh realities of city life in the North. The literary narrative form is mostly found in humanist discourse with a plat-form of telling an event in the form of a story in which the subject migrates to a metropolitan area. Farah Griffin, the author of *Who Set You Flowin'?: The Afri-can-American Migration Narrative* (1995), presented an exhaustive review of an artistic migration narrative. Griffin found her title from Harlem Renaissance poet, Jean Toomer, and his poem, *Seventh Street* (1923), which asks the question "Who set you flowin'?" in reference to the Great Migration of African Americans (De Veaux 2011). In addition to Dash's film *Daughters of the Dust*, documentation of this migration came from dance with Liz Lerman's *Dance Exchange* (1955), and on stage with August Wilson's production of *The Piano Lesson* (1990). The preservation of history, specifically American history, through artistic expression must be supported. Employing oral histories as well as these artistic practices may eliminate the overpowering interpretative approach that seeks weakness and pathology in the exploration of communities of color. Moving away from the "tradition-laden effort to document failure" (Lawrence-Lightfoot and Hoffman Davis 1997, 9), these stories fill in the missing gaps of the "self motivated activities of peoples of African descent to remake themselves and their worlds" (Dodson and Diof, 1). Encouraging individuals to tell their own stories without interpretation is a relevant method for inquiry, analysis, and understanding. The stories of those who lived the experience of migration or who can tell of this experience are essential in the understanding of African American life and the ongoing social and cultural shifts that resulted from this mass movement.

REFERENCES

Baskerville, John D. 2001. "African American Migration." Accessed April 10, 2006. http://www.uni.edu/historyofblackhawkcounty/peopimmigrants/African-AmericanMig/HeadingNorth.htm.

Canty, Jeanine Marie. "Cultural Ecopsychology: Issues of Displacement and the Urban African American Community." Master's thesis, Prescott College, 2000.

Dash, Julie. 1992. *Daughters of the Dust: The Making of an African American Woman's Film.* New York: The New Press.

De Veaux, M. 2011. "In Search of Solid Ground: Oral Histories of the Great Migration, 1920–1960." Ph.D. diss., Pacifica Graduate Institute.

Dodson, H. and Sylviane A. Diof. 2004. *In Motion: The African-American Migration Experience.* New York: The New York Public Library.

Fullilove, Mindy Thompson. 2004. *Root Shock: How Tearing Up City Neighborhoods Hurts America and What We Can Do about It.* New York: Ballantine.

Gove, P. B., ed. 1993. *Merriam-Webster's Third International Dictionary.* Springfield, MA: Merriam-Webster.

Griffin, Farah Jasmine. 1995. *Who Set You Flowin'?: The African American Migration Narrative.* New York: Oxford University Press.

Lawrence-Lightfoot, Sara and Jessica Hoffman Davis. 1997. *The Art and Science of Portraiture.* San Francisco: Jossey-Bass.

Walls, Dwayne E. 1970. *The Chickenbone Special.* New York: Harcourt Brace Jovanovich.

Wilkerson, Isabel. 2010. *The Warmth of Other Suns: The Epic Story of America's Great Migration.* New York: Vintage Books.

CHAPTER TEN

Motherlands as Gendered Spaces

Cultural Identity, Mythic Memory, and Wholeness in Julie Dash's *Daughters of the Dust*

SILVIA CASTRO-BORREGO

This paper will analyze post-colonial and Black feminist points of view the project of historical reconstruction and revision that deeply affect the thematic and formal features of the work of African American filmmaker Julie Dash, and her 1991 award-winning film *Daughters of the Dust*. My paper will demonstrate how Julie Dash consciously created her characters to challenge the icons of the dominant Western culture. My critical study departs from the post-colonial condition of the contemporary United States, since for African Americans there is a situation that critic Michelle Wallace describes as "internal colonization". The paper will also refer to Julie Dash's eponymous novel *Daughters of the Dust* published in 1997, since in both the film and the novel, the Carolina and Georgia Sea Islands—off the U.S. mainland—become *motherlands* where identity and family history can be traced through memory, storytelling, ancestry and myth. The presence of these elements in the film and the novel allow the characters to enter into spiritual journeys towards empowerment and wholeness.

Ancestry, a deep sense of spirituality, a style that establishes symbiotic bonds with both the past and the present, reveals a mastery in a figurative use of visual language that enlarges the initial project of historical reconstruction towards the connecting and healing understanding of wholeness as spiritual return. Claiming the space know as Ibo Landing in the Sea Islands as a sacred one, a place where the archetypal African memory is secured, *Daughters of the Dust* follows the project depicted by Paule Marshall in her 1983 novel *Praisesong for the Widow*, because both the novels and the film emphasize the diasporic identities of their characters who seek history within themselves, defining the links among Black women worldwide. The diasporic identities these works of art delineate, enable them to experience distinct but related cultures—the North and the South of the United States, while retaining a special sense of home—Africa, as the locus of self-definition and power. They develop the capacity to survive whole, to embrace contradictions, and to affirm self across continents and generations.

> [...] When they realized there wasn't nothing between them and home [...] they got so tickled they started in to singing [...]

> Paule Marshall

Both Marshall's *Praisesong for the Widow* and Julie Dash's film *Daughters of the Dust* have at the core of their thematic and narrative/technical structures the myth of the Ibo Landing. It is obvious that the presence of African American myths in contemporary literature is strong for they provide a system of knowledge that allows contemporary African Americans to connect with their common roots. Furthermore, it presents a possible channel for achieving wholeness and a strong sense of identity. Both the novel and the film strongly emphasize the importance of the re-telling of African American myths that exist in the African survivals in the southern Sea Islands where the first slaves "fresh off the boat," the Ibos, landed. The main character in *Praisesong for the Widow*, Avey Johnson, goes through a process of acculturation, guided by her great-aunt Cuney. Cuney demands that as a child, Avey be sent to her on the Sea Island of Tatem. There, every summer, Cuney tells Avey the story of the Ibos implicit in the myth of Ibo Landing.

In *Daughters of the Dust*, the Peazant family goes for a picnic to Ibo Landing on the Sea Island where they live, on the symbolic day the Peazant family leaves for the North. In both cases, by explicitly choosing the piece of land known as Ibo Landing as the setting to tell their mythical story, both authors reinforce the cultural connections between the Sea Islands and Africa. They present the Gullah and Geechee cultures from the Sea Islands as distinctive and original, with imaginative settings.

Both Marshall and Dash assume the position of storytellers in an effort to develop a sense of the collective history that, as African Americans, they feel has been denied to people of African descent in the Western hemisphere. Each begins with the observation that the history of people of African descent in the United States and the diaspora is fragmented and interrupted, and that history must be reconstructed in a way to be a resource for the present. In pursuing the idea of *Daughters of the Dust*, Julie Dash investigated her family history in South Carolina and their migration to New York. Also, writer Paule Marshall, born from Bajan parents, spent her childhood between Barbados and Brooklyn, thus her emphasis on the African diaspora. Such writers and artists consider as their mission the creation of texts and the construction of images that pass on stories. The stories then enable readers to recognize and meet the challenge of reconstructing their own history. Marshall, however, not only refers to the project of historical reconstruction, but she also highlights a spiritual reconstruction, a connection and ultimately, a return.

Interestingly, although Marshall and Dash embrace the same project of re-integration and regeneration, Marshall begins with the historical fragmentation and interruption experienced by the people of African descent in the United States and the rest of the African diaspora, and Dash situates her story at the turn of the century, a time of fearful anticipation of the fragmentation that it is to come. Thus, the argument of wholeness is conceived and developed as a strategic point in both Marshall and Dash's work. Spiritual wholeness for African Americans, as explained by Professor Johnnella E. Butler, consists of an understanding and embracing of the African American past that interacts with the present in order to give sustenance for living and understanding the present and to remain hopeful towards the future.

Paule Marshall's *Praisesong for the Widow* and Julie Dash's *Daughters of the Dust* enter into the dynamics of what Edward Kamau Braithwaite calls the "literature of Reconnection." Kamau Braithwaite sets the beginning of this type of literature in the mid-sixties during the Black Power Revolution and defines it as "a recognition of the African presence in our society not as a static quality, but as root—living, creative, and still part of the main" (1974, 99). Indeed, contemporary African American writers and artists of the eighties and nineties do find the African presence in their culture as a powerful source of inspiration in order to draw valid connections that reinforce their cultural identity as a recognizable and viable ethnic group. Through the interaction of myth, history and fiction, these authors create imaginary settings that, with the help of southern locations—the Sea Islands of the Georgia and South Carolina coast—enable them to construct and present situations where the characters are inevitably compelled to return to their African roots in what has been called the reversal of the Middle Passage.

Ancestral spirituality is linked to the process of re-memory in the novel and translates in flashbacks in the film. In other words, it is comprehending the present by looking into the past and gathering the "scraps of memories" that could be either mental or psychological. In *Praisesong for the Widow*, Avey's remembrances of her Aunt Cuney and Ibo Landing come strongly to her through dreams and in unconscious ways. In *Daughters of the Dust*, Nana, the Peazant's great-grandmother carries her tin can full of her "hands," talismans for protection that contain a lock of her mother's hair. Here this ancestral spirituality is reflected in deliberately conscious and simultaneously psychological ways. It is usually by the influence that the figure of the ancestor has on the characters and through his/her memory that contains the whole African tradition, that the ancestral spiritualism is evoked in these works. Ancestral spiritualism transforms the materialistic North American setting into a place of meaningful connection to African Americans with ancestral Africa, thus revealing to the African American individual a sense of belonging to a spiritual homeland. As Paule Marshall points out, "a spiritual return to Africa is absolutely necessary for the reintegration of that which was lost in our collective historical past and the many national pasts which comprise it" (Williams 1986, 53). She emphasizes the role that Africa plays in determining African American historical identity, an aspect of their personality that she feels has been "systematically de-emphasized." Therefore, Marshall points out that it is the task of African Americans, as people of African descent, to "reinvent" their own image, a process in which the role of Africa is essential.

While Marshall emphasizes the need for a spiritual return to Africa by means of ritual and remembrance, with *Daughters of the Dust*, Dash emphasizes the southern Sea Islands as a place where African ways and beliefs survived, sustaining the slaves, and later the African Americans living in that region. The myth of Ibo Landing at the core of both stories, tells us how African captives of the Ibo tribe refused to live in slavery when they were brought to the new world. They walked onto the water, and then on top of it, returning in this way to Africa.

The structures of myths function as devices for these women writers to think with, ways of organizing their reality. The more we know about our myths, the more we will be able to assess the function of spirituality. As Julie Dash points out, "myth is very important in the struggle to maintain a sense of self and to move forward into the future" (Dash 1992, 30). The presence of mythopoetics in both the novel and the film allows the writers to present historical events recognized in traditional historiography, and to enlarge them by infusing them with an imaginative construction. Thus, the message is very strong, powerful, and sustaining to the tradition of resistance. This is shown in the fact that every Gullah community embraces this myth of the Ibo Landing, and every Gullah community has a part of the island considered Ibo Landing. Therefore, the construction of a mythic memory, one that insists on a balanced interaction among reality, accuracy, and authenticity, utilizing as well the realm of the spiritual, is of great importance in the healing process in which these texts are engaged. The way in which important concepts such as memory, space and time are conceived in these texts and images recalls spiral circularity. The specific time and location, the chronotopes that for Bakhtin are the basis of all representation combine in Dash's movie to orchestrate complex interactions, linking the threshold of change at the turn of the century, with the symbolic threshold of Ibo Landing—"between the land and the sea, island and mainland, between the world of the living and that of the spirits" (Finke 2003, 130).

Underlying this rhetorical strategy is the need for modern African American artists to redefine history, and redefine mythic history as well in a project that revives African American's collective history, ultimately healing the fragmented identities and psyches in the effort to achieve wholeness. Therefore, history is redefined and reconstructed within the frame of memory. The chronotope emerges from a structure of memory, simultaneously sensual and visceral, and encourages the writer to reconstruct a logic of repetitive spiral complexity rather than a binary linear polarity. The chronotope of the threshold mediates, according to Finke, between two other chronotopes: the linearity of everyday life interacts with the chronotope of the spirits representing the traditional African concept of time as a two-dimensional phenomenon, with a long past, a present and virtually no future. The linear concept of time in western thought, with an indefinite past, present and infinite future, is practically foreign to African thinking (Mbiti, 16–17). Thus, the "African belief system that survives in this Gullah culture is in dialogue with the beliefs and values of European Christianity" (Finke 2003, 130).

Through the project of spiritual reconstruction, the nature of the text is redefined, insisting on a theoretical articulation that recognizes the energy of the community formed by writer, reader, viewer and text. As Karla Holloway suggests, there is an important and noticeable difference between an African thesis of mythologies as literature (the presence of myth in the text or story), and a western thesis of mythology as an aspect of literature. Holloway encourages the critics of African American literature to use this distinction as a point of genesis, in understanding the literary trajectories of Black women's texts (Holloway 1992, 85–100). The presence of mythology in the African American text becomes a very important element within the text and within the story because of its proximity to what Morrison understands as "re-memory" in her novel *Beloved* (1987).

Such a synchronic view of time definitely alters our western understanding of history. Time from the African perspective must be experienced in order for it to become a reality, and experience suggests a generative action between the past and the present. As Denniston points out, through their oral traditions, Africans look back to their origins, using various myths to explain the existence of deities, the creation, and other aspects of their universe (1995, x–xxii). The immediate and remembered past, which goes back several generations, affirms that the rhythms of life remain continuous and intact. By choosing the Ibo Landing myth and through the use of ritual, Marshall and Dash confront questions of geographical and cultural alienation and conflict within a hostile society. They incorporate African uses of myths into African American life and spirituality, preserving links to the past and reassuring African American cultural history.

I approach the film *Daughters of the Dust* as being part of what Vèvè Clark calls "Diaspora literacy" from an Afrocentric perspective as an alternative interpretative mode for literary analysis. Cheryl A. Wall and Avena P. Busia both argue that we readers must develop diaspora literacy "and learn to read the various cultural signs and performances that signify an underlying bond" (Busia 1988, 1–43; Wall 2005,

183). The past, for people of the African diaspora and for African Americans, remains fragmentary, since they live in a world where cultural knowledge must be retrieved and negotiated between the demands of material well-being and the pursuit of spiritual wholeness. Vévé Clark approaches "Diaspora literacy" from an Afrocentric perspective as an alternative interpretative mode for literary analysis. She uses this term to refer to "the reader's ability to comprehend the literatures of Africa, Afro-America and the Caribbean from an informed, indigenous perspective" (Clark 1991, 41). Vévé Clark urges readers of African American literature to think beyond linear Hegelian dualities. These frame the world in eternal irreconcilable positive and negative axioms, in order to cope with the complexities, the differences, the borders, the fragmentation, and multiplicities inherent in the realities and shared experiences of the African Diaspora. To comprehend the African Diasporic sphere, one needs to reclaim the cultural differences and to redefine unity in transnational terms. In order to do this, we need to acknowledge and to understand the dynamics of wholeness, or rather the search for it, as a theoretical tool to read African American texts. The search for wholeness stands as a key theoretical concept for African American literature and culture, together with double-consciousness, re-memory, and ancestral spiritualism. Re-memory and ancestral spiritualism are two intimately related concepts. Ancestral spiritualism consists of the connection among past, present and future, and the life force that makes it possible for the physical and the spiritual worlds to be one. Johnnella E. Butler develops this idea in her essay "African American Literature and Realist Theory: Seeking the 'true-true'" where she states that "rememory and double consciousness hold the key to understanding the dynamics of wholeness" (Butler 2006, 171). As the concept of re-memory connects with the past through the ancestor figure, they both establish a vital link with myth since the ancestors are "timeless people whose relationships to the characters are benevolent, instructive, and protective, and they provide a certain kind of wisdom" (Morrison 1984, 343). They function as bridges between history and myth because they join present experiences with those of the past, affirming cultural continuity and "instructing new generations in survival techniques" (Pettis 1995, 117) which are vital for the achievement of wholeness and for spiritual and moral growth. Ancestors, according to African views, are a "collective repository of wisdom rather than a group of heroic individuals." They provide guidance and inspiration because they establish moral and ethical standards (Woods 2007, 190).

Those 18th century Africans [...] the watchers [...] the keepers [...] the ancestors.

Nana Peazant

Nana Peazant is a central figure in the film *Daughters of the Dust* whose name is one of the many African derived words in the Gullah dialect. It means "elderly woman" or "grandmother." The first images of the film *Daughters of the Dust*, introduced by Nana Peazant's words, draw on complexity, on opposition and contradiction, carrying Nana's introductory incantation reveals what it means to be an African American woman in America, creating a space for many meanings to emerge. They allow us to enter the complex psyche of the Black woman. Along with the words, the images on the screen introduce us into the Gullah world of the Sea Islands where the film *Daughters of the Dust* takes place. Images significant to the content of the movie are presented: the blue stained hands of the ancestor, Nana Peazant, the oldest woman in the Peazant family, the great-grandmother; Nana and the sandy dust of the island's soil, running through her indigo-blue stained fingers. Following this, we are introduced to Ibo Landing, an emblematic place in the island, a space where African American mythmaking reflects "the muddy waters of history" in an effort to explain the slavery origins of the Peazant family. Nana Peazant, carrying the spirit of those drowned Ibos, rises from the water, fully dressed and wearing two belts—just like Aunt Cuney from *Praisesong of the Widow*—on her walks into Ibo Landing. Ibo Landing symbolizes "rebirth and the integral connection of the old with the new" (Bobo 1995, 136).

The story is set in 1902, on the day on which the Peazant family meets for their "last supper," since all of its members will leave the next day in search for a new life in the mainland. According to Viola, the missionary who comes to visit the island accompanied by Mr. Snead, the photographer, to see and document her family's passing, the mainland represents "progress, culture, education and wealth" (Dash 1992, 79). However, for Nana Peazant the family's elder, the passing to the North means the loss of the family's roots, traditions, and beliefs rooted in their African heritage. The matriarchal Nana uses her spiritual means to "keep the family together up North" (Dash 1992, 96), to give them strength and cultural identity, and to solve Eli and Eula's problem. Nana calls on the ancestors, by daily visiting their graves, and by carrying a tin can full of her magic "hands" and bits and fragments of small objects that connect her with the past. By praying to the ancestors for help, she beckons the "unborn" child into this world. The Unborn Child represents the ancestral spiritualism which connects the "otherworld" of the ancestors, those who have lived before and are now dead, and life in the present. This five year-old girl, dynamically represents the "sacred belief that those who reside in the realm of the spiritual are vitally connected to the people in the present" (Bobo 1995, 147). With the creation of this character who literally remembers and recalls, a return to certain parts of the past is mandatory for the understanding of the present and the knowledge to be gained by the ancestors, because in the movie the "first and the last," the Unborn Child and Nana, are one, and they both have the same purpose: to help those travelling up North to preserve cultural memory and retain a sense of identity rooted in the Gullah and Geechee communities of the Sea Islands.

Nana Peazant's granddaughter by marriage, Eula, is pregnant after being raped by a white landowner. Eula's husband, Eli, is alienated from his wife because he believes that the child that she is carrying is fathered by the white rapist. In fact, the word rape is only used once in the movie to describe what has happened to Eula, and the action itself is deliberately concealed. This is because Dash considered that "the sexual carnage" of Black women at the hands of white men has been referred to so many times in the history of slavery, that Dash feels "it has lost its potency and its ability to enrage." The movie then, focuses mainly on the post-trauma of rape, "to show how the couple and the family handle it; therein lies their demonstration of the strength needed to survive" (Bobo 1995, 137).

Nana's spiritual power is affirmed when Eula and Eli's Unborn Child comes to the family reunion through a ritual of communion with the family's ancestors. Through the presence of the Unborn Child, Eli is reassured of his paternity because the Unborn Child is in fact, his daughter.

Nana's spiritualism, however, is in contest with that of Haagar, a member of the Peazants by marriage, who is leading the move North and who refers to Nana's beliefs as "hoodoo mess." She names both her girls Myown and Iona, and claims that her children "ain't gonna be like those old Africans, fresh off the boat" suggesting that anyone determined to buck progress and stay on Ibo's Landing is old-fashioned and ignorant. However, Iona will never go to the mainland; she remains in the island with her Native American lover. And Myown, much at her mother's dismay, remains connected to the realm of the spiritual and to Nana (as we know from Dash's novel of the same title as the film) passing on her spiritual knowledge to her daughter Amelia, who through the lenses of her camera, her intellect and her commitment to her academic research as an anthropologist vindicates her right to reconnect with the cultural roots of the island, and her own historical and spiritual inheritance. Amelia eventually returns to Datwuh island, 22 years after her mother left, and guided by her cousin Elizabeth—the Unborn Child, who grows to be the teacher there—will recover her severed ties to her own people and to ancestral Africa. In fact, Myown's resistance to the sense of disconnection and fragmentation instilled in her by her mother, allows her to pass her true feelings to her daughter who is charged with the mission of becoming the carrier of cultural memory, claiming those people in the island and its traditions as part of her own heritage, just as her cousin Elizabeth had done 22 years before in the island as the Unborn Child.

Viola is not the only member of the family who lives in the mainland, for Yellow Mary, accompanied by her girlfriend Trula, also comes to visit Nana in this time of mixed tribulations. Yellow Mary had gone to Cuba as wet nurse for a white family, but after being raped by her white master, resolved to achieve economic independence by becoming a prostitute. Yellow Mary visits Nana and the island to stake a claim for inclusion in the family history, providing "shrewd snubs" to the family's dreams of crossing to the mainland (Jones 1993, 21). The film concludes with a ritual of spiritual regeneration designed by Nana to preserve the family ties and as means for protection from the dangers they will face in the cities of the North. Nana is to remain on the island where all her ancestors are buried. Eli and Eula, and Yellow Mary also choose to stay behind with Nana.

This special day in which the whole family gets together is a day of celebration of the old days, the days in which Nana and her husband started a new life upon North American shores. As such, traditional culture, the distinct ways of the Gullah with their African message of resistance is celebrated.

> I came up with the idea of structuring the story in much the same way that an African griot would recount a family's history.
>
> Julie Dash

Daughters of the Dust is a groundbreaking film within the history of Black filmography in the United States. Categorized by the late writer Toni Cade Bambara as "oppositional cinema," (Dash 1992, xiii). The film presents, the story under dual narratorship. The story unfolds, led by the voices of Nana Peazant, and the Unborn Child, simultaneously both characters and ancestors. Thus, the film's story has two points of view: that of a child who has not yet been born, and that of a great-grandmother who has seen it all, and who can see the coming of the child in the future. Ancestry evolves in the film as a narrative structure that claims that the story needs to be told in a non-western way. This is reflected in the multiple-point-of view camerawork that reveals a non-linear, multilayered presentation. The story unfolds then within a non-linear structure that resembles the storytelling traditions which inform African American literature and cinema. Within such tradition, many voices intertwine, emerging from both memories from the past and from other worlds and the present, in a fashion which folds in the old with the new, and that functions as evidence of an Afrocentric grounding. As Bambara points out, the film *Daughters of the Dust* is claiming its place within the progressive world film culture movements that "bolster socially responsible cinema" (Dash 1992, 13). This is represented in the innovative techniques that Dash displays in *Daughters of the Dust* such as shared space (wide-angled and deep-focus shots in which no one becomes backdrop to anyone else's drama) as opposed to dominated space which foregrounds the hero in sharp focus while the rest are "othered" in a background blur. Bambara further points out that Dash uses socialized space rather than idealized space. This delineated space encourages a contiguous-reality reading and suggests the resolution of a situation or episode through societal transformation rather than through masked space in which, through close-ups and framing, the spectator is encouraged to believe that conflicts are solely psychological, not systemic and thus can only be resolved by a gunshot, "a lawyer or a shrink" (Dash 1992, 13).

Another distinctive feature of the film is its post-colonial nature. *Daughters of the Dust* sets out to revoke the colonial history that has obscured the past of African Americans through that of the Peazant family. One of the few first images that we see following the credits is a light-skinned, well dressed woman wearing a hat with veiling, standing up near the front of an open barge. This image strongly reminds us of dominant cinema's colonialism; however, we notice that the woman does not pose as a sitting down, well-mannered lady might have done. Rather, she stands hip shot, chin cocked, one arm akimbo. The viewer perceives a message of freedom, an attitude that breaks with the rules and we clearly see "a new kind of woman" (Dash 1992, 123). Toni Cade Bambara describes Yellow Mary's gestures as "ebonics," and in doing so she suggests that Dash has "appropriated the image from reactionary cinema for an emancipatory purpose" with the intention to heal our "imperialized eyes" (Dash 1992, 12).

As such, *Daughters of the Dust* aims to show a Black family, and especially the women of this family in a way never done before. This is achieved by presenting a narrative construction that evokes the concept of defamiliarization by redefining the history of Black people. This means in the film, not only maintaining historical events and issues concerning the people and Sea Island region, but also inscribing their mythic history in their story. Describing how the film defamiliarizes our western conventions, filmmaker Julie Dash affirms that it is not only how the scenes are set up, but also the places where the camera is placed—the closeness that allows the viewer to belong inside the group, to listen to intimate conversations between the women, who are placed at the center. In fact, this sense of closeness that recalls a sense of community among the women in the movie, and between characters and audience, is informed by the principles of Afro-American ritual drama—together with a call for authenticity—being formalism the main stylistic concern. Formalism, according to Carlton Molette, intends to project and ideal form, so the actors do not need to pretend to be somebody other than themselves. This effect is reached in *Daughters of the Dust* by using a stepped camera, as when shooting the Unborn Child. The smooth effect of slow motion "produces a sense of manipulation other than the conventions of realism, implying a subjective or psychological dimensión of time and reality" (Allen 1992, 44). The stepped camera effect takes "the viewer from the chronotope of the everyday to the chronotope of the spirits" implying not only a subjective apprehension of time and space but as Finke points out, suggesting "a mythic one that is designed to replicate the storytelling of the African griot in dialogue with the western technology of vision that constitutes Dash's medium of film" (2003, 131).

Afro-American ritual drama also calls for "soulful behavior" which consists of the building of emotional intensity through rhythm, creating a total spiritual involvement with a proper purgation of emotions. Viewers are invited to witness the building of a community, its survival strategies, their crisis, losses and changes, and the productive interaction between cultures without losing sight of the power dynamics between them (Finke 2003, 132). Thus, the purpose of being functional, validating and strengthening those values that although existing among African Americans need to be revised and expanded so that they make sense in contemporary U.S. society.

The movie is told from the point of view of a woman, and relegates the men to the periphery. The decolonized context of *Daughters of the Dust* and its commitment to "de-center the white patriarchal gaze" brings the Black woman, arguably the most "othered" and the "object" to full view. The focus is on restoring images of Black women who, as bell hooks points out, are "truly on the bottom of this society's race-sex hierarchy" (Dash 1992, 40).

We are all good women.

Eula Peazant

Remembering the history of Black women in 19th century North America, Julie Dash explains how "African American women never had the luxury of being a woman. She had to always be so much more: the keeper of secrets, the provider, the nurturer, all of this" (Dash 1992, 50). Therefore, women are represented with great variety in the movie, suggesting images that Dash feels are more in tune with their real culture because the film explored the ways Black women "responded to images of themselves as sexually immoral" (Bobo 1995, 158). At the center remains the great-grandmother, Nana Peazant, emerging from the soil as a powerful omen, as a mythic totem pole. She shows that even in the midst of the denigration of Black womanhood, there was the veneration of the Black woman as elder. In the scene when Nana and Eli are talking on the grave of Nana's husband, Eli says to her, "I really believe you were a goddess" (Dash 1992, 95).

Surrounding Nana are the rest of the women of the Peazant family whose strength, beliefs, circumstances, and sense of self and community are as varied as the colors of a shiny rainbow, arguing for new standards for judging womanhood and selfhood. As Eula pleads to the rest of the Peazant women: "If you love yourself, love Yellow Mary" (Dash 1992, 157). Eula, has become "ruint" just as Yellow Mary was before her. However, Eula's powerful and moving soliloquy, almost at the end of the movie, makes a case for all women whose honor and dignity have been plundered. She wonders:

Am I ruined too? As far as this placed is concerned, we never enjoyed our womanhood [...] Deep inside, we believed that they ruined our mothers, and their mothers before them. And we live our lives always expecting the worst because we feel we don't deserve any better. (Dash 1992, 156)

The validation ritual that Eula begins evolves around Yellow Mary, who is despised by some women of the Peazant family, Hagaar, and the hair braider among them. Eula recalls the traumatic experiences of Black women in the Sea Islands and elsewhere under slavery. Eula recounts: "we couldn't think of ourselves as pure women, knowing how our mothers were ruined. And maybe we think we don't deserve better, but we've got to change our way of thinking" (Dash 1992, 156). In this way, Eula joins the elder Nana in reaffirming the family need for connection, first of all among themselves, secondly to their ancestral African roots, not letting "their inheritance from enslavement rob them of their heritage of resistance and survival" (Bobo 1995, 161). As Nana exclaimed: "You're the fruit of an ancient tree" (Dash 1992, 154).

I am trying to teach you how to touch your own spirit.

Nana Peazant.

Nana Peazant fears that with the new will come the loss of memory and the disappearance of the strength that family provides, particularly necessary for Black people. The migration that the Peazant family is about to undertake will be both a physical and spiritual project in which they will have to reconcile simultaneous forms of retention and integration in order to maintain their cultural sustenance. In the film Nana, representing African American women, deliberately takes on the role of oral historian—the one who remembers.

Situating the Unborn Child as co-narrator, Dash clarifies her perspective as Afrocentric instead of deriving theme and action from European, Western ways. For instance, the Unborn Child is Elegba: one foot on this world, one foot on the other. Dash affirms that although Elegba is usually male, she made it female because he has the power to be anyone in his role as mediator between the sacred and the secular worlds: "the one we appeal to overcome indecision" (1992, 25). The Unborn Child then, connects Eli and Eula to an African world view. Esu-Elegba, the mythical West African trickster figure makes possible that connection. In Marshall's novel *Praisesong for the Widow*, the elder man who guides Avey towards Carriacou island and the "Beg Pardon" dance, Lebert Joseph, is also Esu Elegba.

Take my "hand." I am the one that can give you strength.

Nana Peazant.

Nana, Eula, the Unborn Child, and later on Eli, link their identities to the space of Ibo Landing, placing it against the North, which is a place that represents the fragmentation of the family, disconnection from the ancestors, and the loss of identity for the children. As Manthia Diawara points out, "Ibo Landing is Africa in America." As the place where the slaves landed and remained isolated from mainland America, the film argues that the members of the Peazant family "must learn the terms of their belonging" because this place will be an example of African Americans associating with Africa, and must use the space known as Ibo Landing to validate their identities as Americans emerging from a distinct culture (Diawara 1992, 15).

Daughters of the Dust negotiates the spaces of colonized terrain and family as liberated zone, the themes of women as a source of value, and history, as interpreted by Black people, led by their experiences and memories. As Toni Cade Bambara observes, *Daughters of the Dust* asks that the viewers enter a triple process of recollecting the dismembered past, recognizing and acknowledging cultural icons and codes, and recentering and revalidating the self, demanding our recognition of Black complexity (Bambara 1993).

The spiritual basis of the film *Daughters of the Dust* allows us to enter what Diawara calls "a Black structure of feeling" (quoted in Mellencamp 1994, 96). Spirituality, the powerful character of Nana, together with the Unborn Child, the wind, the music—all of *Daughters of the Dust* images carry with them a unifying effect that draws the viewer to experience the spiritual dimension of African American culture, which is strong, enduring, and sustaining.

REFERENCES

Allen, Jean. 1998. "Looking Through 'Rear Window': Hitchcock's Traps and Lures of Heterosexual Romance." In *The Female Spectator: Looking at Film and Television*, edited by Deirdre Pribram, 31–44. London: Verso.

Bakhtin, Mikhail M. 1981. "Aspects of Time and Chronotope in the Novel." In *The Dialogic Imagination*, translated by Michael Holquist and C. Emerson, 84–258. Austin: University of Texas Press.

Bambara, Toni Cade. 1993. "Reading the Signs, Empowering the Eye: *Daughters of the Dust* and the Black Independent Cinema Movement." In *Black American Cinema*, edited by Manthia Diawara, 118–144. New York: Routledge.

Bobo, Jacqueline. 1995. *Black Women as Cultural Readers*. New York: Columbia University Press.

Braithwaite, Edward Kamau. 1974. "The African Presence in Caribbean Literature." In *Slavery, Colonialism, and Racism*, edited by Sidney W. Mintz, 99–108. New York: Norton.

Busia, Avena P. B. 1988. "Words Whispered over Voids: A Context for Black Women's Rebellious Voices in the Novel of the African Diaspora." In *Studies in Black American Literature Vol. III. Black Feminist Criticism and Critical Theory*, edited by Joe Weixlmann and Houston A. Baker Jr., 1–43. Greenwood, FL: Penkevill.

Butler, Johnnella E. 2006. "African American Literature and Realist Theory: Seeking the 'true-true.'" In *Identity Politics Reconsidered*, edited by Linda Martín Alcoff, Michael Hames-García, Satya P. Mohanty, and Paula M. L. Moya, 171–192. New York: Palgrave.

Castro-Borrego Silvia. 2009. "The Search for Wholeness in the Construction of Diasporic Identities in Contemporary African American Women's Literature." In *The Dialectic of Diasporas: Memory, Location and Gender*, edited by Mar Gallego and Isabel Soto, 53–72. Valencia: Biblioteca Javier Coy d'Estudis Nord-americans.

Clark, VèVè A. 1991. "Developing Diaspora Literacy and Marassa Consciousness." In *Comparative American Identities: Race, Sex, and Nationality in the Modern Text*, edited by Hortense J. Spillers, 40–61. New York: Routledge, 1991.

Dash, Julie, dir. 1991. *Daughters of the Dust*. 1991. New York, NY: Kino International.

———. 1992. *Daughters of the Dust: The Making of an African American Woman's Film*. New York: The New Press.

———. 1999. *Daughters of the Dust: A Novel*. New York: Plume.

Denniston, Dorothy. 1995. *The Fiction of Paule Marshall: Reconstruction of History, Culture, and Gender*. Knoxville: University of Tennessee Press.

Diawara, Manthia. *Black American Cinema*. Bloomington: Indiana UP, 1992.

Finke, Laurie. 2003. "Aspects of Time and Chronotope in Cinematic Life Narrative: *Daughters of the Dust* of the Dust." In *American Mirrors. (Self)Reflections and (Self)Distortions*, edited by Mª Felisa López Liquete et al., 125–132. Guipúzkoa: Universidad del País Vasco.

Holloway, Karla. 1992. *Moorings and Metaphores: Figures of Culture and Gender in Black Women's Literature*. New Brunswick, NJ: Rutgers University Press.

Jones, Jacquie. 1993. "The Black South in Contemporary Film." *African American Review* 27, no. 1 (Spring): 19–24.

Marshall, Paule. 1983. *Praisesong for the Widow*. New York: Plume.

Mellencamp, Patricia. 1994. "Making History: Julie Dash." *Frontiers: A Journal of Women Studies* 15 no. 1 (1994): 76–101.

Molette, Carlton. 1973. "The Way to Viable Theater? Afro-American Ritual Drama." *Black World* 22 (April): 4–12.

Morrison, Toni. 1984. "Rootedness: the Ancestor as Foundation." In *Black Women Writers (1950–1980): A Critical Evaluation*, edited by Mari Evans, 339–345. Garden City, New York: Anchor.

———. 1987. *Beloved*. New York: Alfred A. Knopf.

———. 1977. *Song of Solomon*. New York: Alfred A. Knopf.

Pettis, Joyce. 1995. *Toward Wholeness in Paule Marshall's Fiction*. Charlottesville: University of Virginia Press.

Wall, Cheryl A. 2005. *Worrying the Line: Black Women Writers, Lineage and Literary Tradition*. Chapel Hill: University of North Carolina Press.

Williams, John. 1986. "Return of a Native Daughter. An Interview with Paule Marshall and Maryse Condé." *Sage* 3 (Fall): 52–53.

Woods, Tim. 2007. *African Pasts: Memory and History in African Literatures*. Manchester: Manchester University Press.

CHAPTER ELEVEN

Making *Daughters of the Dust*

(Revised)

JULIE DASH

It has been over 26 years since the release of *Daughters of the Dust*, but it some ways, it feels like just yesterday. The world—people and the technology that keeps our lives in perpetual progress—have evolved in what sometimes feels like light speed. So too, has the film industry. In some ways, it is now easier than ever to make a film. The accessibility of fairly inexpensive camera equipment and easy to use programs like iMovie puts the magic of filmmaking in just about everyone's hands. Seeing my film students' creativity and innovation come to life in their final film projects gives me hope about what's on the horizon.

And while film technology continues to advance, until very recently, Hollywood has been reticent to change, to become more inclusive of people and projects that fall outside of the dominant culture. Throughout the years, this has been a painful reality to see and, of course to experience.

More recently, however, with the critical acclaim of talented filmmakers such as Dee Rees, Justin Simien, Nate Parker, and of course, Ava DuVernay, there has been a long-awaited shift. Changes won't happen in some distant future any longer. Change is here.

I never planned a career as a filmmaker. As a child growing up in the Queensbridge Housing Projects in Long Island City, New York, I dreamed of some typical and not-so-typical career choices. None of the images I saw of African American people, especially the women, suggested that we could actually make movies. We were rarely even in them. No, I never dreamed of filmmaking when I was little. At that time, I wanted to be in the secretarial pool, typing away and having fun like the women I saw on TV and in the movies. I had no idea that the images I saw didn't depict the real life of working women.

Later, I turned my attention to something much more glamorous—roller derby. I was amazed by the motion, speed and power of women flying around the roller rink in competition and combat. Yeah that was going to be me. The Roller Derby queen of New York. A child's dreams. A young girl's fantasies, shaped by the limitations imposed by my environment. My ambitions, like those of most children growing up in African American neighborhoods, in projects, in inner cities, were stifled by what I thought possible for me as a Black child. My dreams were also molded by the cinema and television stories, where the likes of me didn't even exist.

I don't know if I would have survived the secretarial pool long-term. I did learn some office skills, and at different points in my career as a filmmaker I had to take temporary secretarial jobs in order to eat while I continued making films. As for Roller Derby, the television show didn't last long, and I'm not sure I would have survived that, either.

My introduction to filmmaking began at the Studio Museum in Harlem when I was seventeen. I was just tagging along with a friend who had heard about a cinematography workshop there and thought she could learn to take still photos. We joined the workshop and became members of a group of young African American discovering the power of making and redefining our images on the screen. It was fun. As I became involved in the workshop, I enjoyed it and was drawn more and more to it. I'd found something that was creative and exciting and intellectually challenging, but I still didn't think this could be my work.

I made my first film when I was about nineteen. An animation film about a pimp who goes to an African village and is beaten and dragged out of the village by the people there. It was called *The Legend of Carl Lee DuVall*. I used picture I had cut out of a *Jet* magazine, glued them to pipe cleaners, and shot them with a super8 camera. I was really beginning to love filmmaking—but still, when I went to college I initially majored in physical education. I was going to be a gym teacher.

While at City College in New York, a special program, the David Picker Film Institute, was set within the Leonard Davis Center for the Performing Arts. I went there and interviewed because it sounded like fun, and I already had some film experience from the Studio Museum. I was accepted and wound up graduating from CCNY with a degree in film production.

At that point I knew my course was set.

LOS ANGELES

As soon as I finished at CCNY, I moved to Los Angeles. My plan was to get into the UCLA film school. I had read about Charles Burnett, Haile Gerima, and

Larry Clark making narrative films out in L.A., and that's what I was interested in. At the time, the West Coast seemed to be more involved with narrative films than the East Coast where a lot of Black filmmakers, including myself, were making documentary films.

I was very excited about the prospect of UCLA. Considering my previous work and experience, as well as my degree from CCNY and good recommendations, I was sure I would get in. I didn't [...] because of a technicality.

Applicants to the film school at UCLA had to submit, among other things, three letters of recommendation. I had been promised these letters by three of my teachers (two of them white and one Black). To my surprise however, one of the letters was never sent, and as a result I wasn't accepted. I was stunned. I was even more hurt when I found out that both of the white professors had sent their letters supporting me. I thought getting into UCLA would be a triumph and an advance not just for me as a young African American, but also for other Black filmmakers. Instead, I learned a bitter lesson, one that I would remember throughout my career.

A great part of filmmaking is overcoming various kinds of obstacles. What I learned then was that I would sometimes have to face sabotage, often from "my own people." I would have to feel the pain over and over again. While making, *Daughters of the Dust* I encountered this to an extent that I had never suspected.

After the UCLA rejection, I had to figure out what I would do next. I had no other plan because I had been sure I would be in school. Fortunately, Larry Clark was about to begin shooting his film *Passing Through*. I joined his crew and went out into the California desert. One of the actresses I met on *Passing Through* was Cora Lee Day, whom I would cast years later as Nana Peazant in *Daughters of the Dust*.

Working on a film in the desert helped to heal me. I began to get strong again. And one again I stumbled into the next phase of my training. One afternoon in Los Angeles, my friend and I heard about grants that were available for filmmakers at the American Film Institute (AFI). We went there looking for the grant applications. It all felt very strange to me, because the atmosphere was so relaxed, and AFI was in this beautiful house in Beverly Hills.

We were standing in the hallway looking lost when this young Black man dressed in jeans came down the stairs. He said, "My sister, how can I help you?" I thought the brother must work there, you know, maybe he was the janitor (we are all infected by the stereotypes). I told him that we were there to get the grant applications. He listened, asked some questions, and then gave me some of the best advice I was ever given.

He told me to apply for a fellowship instead of a grant. He said that I should be attending AFI, not just seeking some small cash to make a short film. I took his advice, applied for the fellowship, and became one of the youngest fellows to attend AFI.

Later I discovered that the young man was Ted Lange; he would later be known as Isaac on *The Love Boat*. I also found out that he had been the co-writer on Larry's film *Passing Through*. I always knew I wanted to make films about African American women. To tell stories that had not been told. To show images of our lives that had not been seen.

The original concept of *Daughters* was a short silent film about the migration of an African American family from the Sea Islands off the South Carolina mainland to the mainland and then the North. I envisioned it as a kind of "Last Supper" before migration and the separation of the family. The idea first began to wander throughout my head about 1975, while I was still at AFI. I was making notes from stories and phrases I heard about my family, and became fascinated by a series of James Van Der Zee photos of Black women at the turn of the century. The images and ideas combined and grew.

In 1981, I received a Guggenheim grant to research and write a series of films on Black women. In 1983, I completed my short film, *Illusions,* with Lonette McKee in the lead role as a studio executive who passed for white during World War II. This is also when I began intensive research for *Daughters of the Dust*.

Daughters of the Dust

The stories from my own family sparked the idea of *Daughters* and formed the basis for some of the characters. But when I probed my relatives for information about the family history in South Carolina, or about our migration north to New York, they were often reluctant to discuss it. When things got too personal, too close to memories they didn't want to reveal, they would close up, push me away, tell me to go ask someone else. I knew then that the images I wanted to show, the story I wanted to tell, had to touch an audience the way it touched my family. It had to take them back, take them inside their family memories, inside our collective memories.

Soon I was off, running faster and faster, trying to find more and more information that would allow me to uncover this story. I spent countless hours in the Schomburg Center for Research in Black Culture in Harlem reading and looking at images from old newspapers, magazines, and books. I went to the National Archives in Washington, D.C., as well as to the Library of Congress and the Smithsonian Institution. UCLA also has a wonderful research library that provided much needed information. And finally I went to the Penn Center on St. Helena Island, off the coast of South Carolina.

The research was fascinating. In fact, if I were not making films, I would probably be glad to spend the rest of my life digging around libraries. I learned so much about the history and experiences of African American people. One of the most fascinating discoveries I made was of the existence of over 60,000 West

African words or phrases in use in the English language, a direct result of the slave trade.

As I poured through the documents, taking notes and developing the story line for *Daughters*, it became clear that a short film would not be large enough for the story. I knew I would have to make a feature. There was too much information, and it had to be shared.

THE ELLIS ISLAND FOR AFRICANS

The Sea Islands of the coast of the Carolinas and Georgia became the main drop-off point of enslaved Africans brought to North America in the days of the trans-atlantic slave trade. It became the Ellis Island for the Africans, the processing center for the forced immigration of millions. It also became the region with the strongest retention of African culture, although even to this day the influences of African culture are visible everywhere in America.

Many of the images seen in *Daughters of the Dust* parallel the action and behavior of African Americans today. For instance, the hand signals given by two of the men in *Daughters* is a reference to the nonverbal styles of communication of ancient African secret societies which have been passed down across thousands of years and through hundreds of generations. Today these forms are expressed in the secrets of fraternities and in the hand signals of youth gangs.

As a young girl growing up, I remember watching young men on a basketball court or at other gathering places, and before they would drink together, they always poured a little on the ground. I always thought that was a strange and funny ritual. Later, during my research for *Daughters*, I discovered the West African ritual of pouring libations, a show of respect to the ancestors, to family and to tradition. As the men on the basketball court would say, "This is for the brothers who are no longer here or couldn't be here today."

In 1984, while I was still writing, my daughter N'Zinga was born. Her birth revealed to me the need to see the past as connected to the future. The story had to show hope, as well as the promise that tradition and family and life would always sustain us, even in the middle of dramatic change. N'Zinga's arrival in our lives also brought the "unborn child" into the script. I hadn't seen her until I saw my own daughter.

By 1985, most of my research was completed, and I began to write the script for *Daughters of the Dust*.it would go through five complete rewrites and two polishes. In fact, I even rewrote some of it while shooting. Although I did most of the primary research myself, I'm indebted to several people who gave me important help along the way, especially Dr. Margaret Washington Creel, Oscar Sims, and Worth Long.

SHOOTING *DAUGHTERS OF THE DUST*

By late 1986, when I was finally ready to begin shooting, I was faced with another problem: financing the film. Originally I thought it could be done for about $250,000. I had some production money from the National Endowment for the Arts, but it was not enough to begin production. I applied for and received several grants, one from the Fulton County Arts Council (GA), another from the Georgia Council on the Humanities, and another from Appalshop, Southeast Regional Fellowship (SERF). But by the standards of feature productions, it was still not enough, and I soon realized that I just have to begin, and hope that more money would come when we had something to show.

I knew that it would be difficult to get other people to understand the vision of this unusual film. I knew it would be different from the films most people were used to, and there weren't many people willing to invest in an "untraditional" Black movie. I needed to create on screen what I had in my mind. I knew exactly what it should look like. After hours and days of discussion with Arthur Jafa (A.J) my coproducer and director of photography, I was confident that we could capture exactly the feelings and memories I wanted to invoke in the mind of the audience. If I could show people a piece of this—literally, give them a piece of my mind—I was sure that I could raise enough money to finance the film. With the grant monies available, and after scraping together unused film stock from friends like Charles Burnett, I decided to shoot a sample of the film.

In the summer of 1987, I took a crew of ten and four cast members, Adisa Anderson, Barbara-O, Alva Rogers and VertaMae Grosvenor (who also served as a technical adviser) to St. Helena Island to shoot for five days. While there, I also conducted screen tests for Unborn Child.

After the initial shooting, we returned to Atlanta, once again broke, and faced the dilemma of trying to find money to edit the sample.

I began to do small projects for various organizations, like the National Black Women's Health Project (the people at NBWHP were extremely supportive of my work and very helpful), and put all of my earnings, beyond basic living expenses, toward editing the sample. Finally, after several months, it was ready to show.

With a completed script, a sample, and a filmography of my previous work, we renewed our search for funds. I had also revised the budget, based on our experience on St. Helena, and knew that we would actually need around $800,000 to complete the film. We sent packages to a variety of American and European sources. The responses were as interesting as their sources were varied.

Hollywood studios were generally impressed with the look of the film, but somehow they couldn't grasp the concept. They could not process the fact that a Black woman filmmaker wanted to make a film about African American women at the turn of the century—particularly a film with a strong family, with characters who weren't living in the ghetto, killing each other and burning things down. And there weren't going to be any explicit sex scenes, either. They thought the film would be unmarketable. They believed that they knew better than we did about what moved Black people. They figured it would be a pretty, artsy European sort of film that no one would come to see. Every major studio either passed on it or didn't respond at all.

We didn't do much better in Europe. Most of the European sources couldn't understand what we were trying to do any better than their Hollywood counterparts. One told us the film sounded too much like a typical American film. Another said it was too radical in its concept for their audience. Still others said perhaps next year, if we were still looking for funds by then.

Our most sympathetic response came from the New York-based organization, Women Make Movies Too, which held a benefit fundraiser in 1987. They raised $5,000 for the production. But these funds, as badly needed as they were, only covered the expenses of sending out all the samples. It was beginning to look like we had exhausted all our sources, when a break came that sent us flying into production.

In 1988 I was attending the PBS Rocky Mountain Retreat in Utah. There I met a woman named Lynn Holst, who happened to be the director of program development for American Playhouse. Lynn was interested in the project and we spent many hours discussing it. I liked her immediately, and felt that even if nothing came out of our meetings in terms of funding, I'd made a friend. Well, I was rewarded twice. I did make a friend, *and* American Playhouse wound up providing most of the money for *Daughters of the Dust*. Finally, we would be able to make the film.

We entered a two-phase process with American Playhouse. The first was to rework and develop the screenplay even further. We added dialogue and some additional scenes. During this process, I worked closely with Lynn, and I think we learned a lot from each other. Unfortunately, a lot of what we added to the script was ultimately lost due to time and budget constraints.

The second phase was production. American Playhouse insisted we shoot a union film. (We found out later that we didn't have to.) This is often an unfortunate dilemma for independent filmmakers, who want to respect the unions, but are rarely able to afford to complete a film in accordance with union guidelines. We would up striking a deal with the Screen Actors Guild (SAG) under a special contract for minority, low-budget projects. Even with the special terms, we started shooting $200,000 over budget.

We entered the second phase in August of 1989. I met Steven Jones, our line producer and production manager, and Pam Jackson our associate producer, in Beaufort, South Carolina, to scout locations. We planned to begin shooting by October but nature had something else in mind for us.

In those days, of preproduction, I found myself nauseous and easily fatigued. At first I thought that it was the heat and the humidity, until I learned that I was pregnant. I had to quickly make a decision as to what I was going to do. I had two choices—to put off the production for at least another year or to have an abortion. I made my decision to go forward with the filming of *Daughters*. I flew back to Atlanta to have the abortion. This was a painful decision many women have had to face, especially women who must rely on their physical as well as mental stamina to perform professionally. Unfortunately, many women do not have the same options that I had. At least I could still make a choice. *Daughters* would become the child that I would bear that year.

The week we were to start, Hurricane Hugo slammed into the coast of North and South Carolina. We had just moved our production crew to St. Helena when we were told that the island had to be evacuated immediately, that Hugo would come crashing in on us within a matter of hours. We heard the news about four in the afternoon, and by 10:00 P.M we had packed all of our equipment and were headed back to Atlanta in a long caravan of cars, trucks, RVs, and vans. We would have to wait out the storm. It was not our first obstacle, and I knew it would not be our last.

When Hugo finally finished feasting on the coast, we returned to shoot *Daughters of the Dust*. Fortunately, it had missed our main locations on the islands. Unfortunately, it hit Charleston and other cities, causing severe damage. Part of our good luck was that some of the relief workers who had helped in Charleston came down later to work with us on the film, some as production assistants and some as cast members. Gloria Naylor, the author of *The Women of Brewster Place* and *Mama Day*, lived in the area, and she joined the crew as production assistant. It was great to meet her and have her on the set.

When we finally began shooting we knew we had only twenty-eight days to complete all the principal photography. Our main beachfront location (Hunting Island) was a one-mile hike to the coast from base camp. Due to environmental restrictions, we couldn't take a four-wheel-drive vehicle on the nature trail or along the coastline, so all the equipment had to be carried in each morning. We also couldn't bring in a generator, so A.J decided to shoot with natural light—sunlight—only. Therefore, we needed to squeeze in as much shooting time every as the sun would allow. Often we would be in the middle of setting up or shooting a particular scene when the sun would suddenly cast perfect and beautiful light in another spot. We would hurriedly change directions and capture the unscheduled scene with only a moment's notice. Sometimes this would work, sometimes it failed comically; but we kept shooting.

For the most part, the crew and actors all worked in the same spirit, everyone appreciating that we were doing something different, something special. But, there are always those who cannot or will not see what is being done. Two particular incidents stand out as perhaps the most damaging.

After the shooting had already begun, when we couldn't possibly stop or recast, one of the lead actresses felt that she should be paid more money. Perhaps she had heard the budget was $800,000 and thought that we were underpaying her, or that I or the other producers were making a lot of money. In fact, all of us were working practically for nothing. She and some of the others in the cast apparently didn't understand that $800,000 was an extremely low budget and that I would be heavily in debt when the film was finished. She decided to get the union to force us to pay her more money. When I found out what she was up to, I was hurt and angered. I felt that I had been ambushed by someone whose career I was, after all, helping to promote by casting her in a major role in a feature film.

In independent film, we are never able to pay top salaries. None of us are adequately compensated for the work we do, not the writers, the producers, the directors, the crew, the actors, not one. We do it to create the work. We do it to sharpen our skills. We work with the hope that if the film is good, someone will offer us a bigger budget the next time, and then we'll be able to hire and compensate adequately those who sacrificed on the low-budget projects. We work as a community of artists, collaborating to create a work of art. I was wounded, but had to stifle my emotions and get the best performances out of the actors, while trying to keep the crew focused and motivated.

On another occasion, I was confronted one morning by an actor who refused to put on his costume. We were ready to shoot a scene that included him, and for whatever reason, he decided that this was time to assert the fact that even though I was the director, he was a man and no woman could make him do anything. This man, a Muslim, who had been telling us all about the need for unity among Black people, stood there in the middle of the set, in front of the crew, and confronted me, physically. He knew that he could intimidate most people because of his size (about 6'4") and demeanor. I knew that if backed down from him the entire project would come crashing around me. Any authority or control I had on the set would be completely undermined. We were seconds away from actually fighting, but I made my stand. What he hadn't anticipated was my willingness to take an ass whipping rather than let him take over my film. I was ready to fight. The seconds passed by, full of tension. I could see his eyes searching for my face, looking for signs of fear or weakness. The crew and cast all stood frozen, shocked unsure. Finally, A.J. intervened and the actor took the opportunity to back away and save face. In the end, he knew that he had too much to lose if he attacked me. He put his costume on. I'd won, but secretly I was shaken for days after.

A twenty-eight-day shooting schedule for a feature film is incredibly punishing. We were all exhausted from working long hours day after day, in addition to our constant fight with nature. We were in areas heavily infested with mosquitoes and other biting insects, and were often caught in the middle of sudden and violent sandstorms.

But through it all, we kept shooting. We pushed on, all of us, crew, cast, everyone. We became friends, enemies, lovers, coconspirators and family. Toward the end, we ran short of money and had to wrap some of the cast early. But the spirit of the project had infected some so deeply that they stayed on and worked for nothing for days afterward. Adisa Anderson, Bahni Turpin, and Vertmae Grosvenor were some of those who stayed, helping out where they could, and their help was greatly appreciated.

When we finally wrapped the shooting of *Daughters* there was a great sense of relief, and some sadness. We all felt like we had contributed to something special, something new, something important. It would be a while, almost two years, before we would be able to measure the impact of it on an audience, but we knew it would be special.

We gave a party with food and champagne and music. We showed slides of the crew and cast at work and everybody got a kick out of seeing themselves at some pretty funny moments. I was pleased. We were a good group of hardworking filmmakers, and in spite of quite a few problems, we had all forged ahead and made something beautiful. As I enjoyed myself at the party, though, my mind began to run ahead anxiously to the next part of the process. The film now had to be edited, but we had no funds for postproduction and were already heavily in debt.

When we got back to Atlanta, I was physically and emotionally exhausted. Not only had I been consumed with the normal grind of directing a feature film, but I had been constantly fighting for money, managing personalities, and worrying about the next wave of fundraising. I also felt guilty about being away from my daughter for so long while I shot the film. Now I would be home for a while, but the pressure and stress did not end. I still had to edit the film. I set up my living room as an editing room and watched as 170,000 feet of film was unloaded at my house—a mountain of work, an almost unsurmountable task. Keith Ward, Tommy Burns, and Angela Walker did the syncing of the film, and I began editing in January 1990.

I did what I could with whatever money became available. After the first month I brought in Joseph Burton to help with the editing, and later Amy Carey came on board to help complete it. In June, I was fortunate enough to receive a Rockefeller Fellowship for $45,000 which went immediately into the film. The National Black Programming Consortium also contributed money for postproduction. By December we finally had a fine cut. Now it was time to look for a distributor.

Amy Carey, the editor, and I took the fine cut to Los Angeles to begin producing the original music score with John Barnes. We had already scheduled and rescheduled the sound mix, so we had only two weeks to complete the music before the final sound mix. John Barnes worked throughout the Christmas holiday to compose and score seventy-two musical cues for the film.

For the soundtrack of *Daughters of the Dust*, John assembled an impressive collection of musicians and styles to evoke the film's magic and mystery. He used a myriad of instruments, including the synclavier, the Middle Eastern santour, African bata drums and African talking drums, and he successfully mixed synclavier-based percussion with authentic music from Africa, India, and the Middle East.

We wanted to depict various religions—including traditional West African worship rituals, Santeria, Islam, Catholicism, and Baptist beliefs—through musical expression. John drew from his own spiritual beliefs, which include a respect for astrology, in composing the music. For instance, he wrote the Unborn Child's theme in the key of B, the key of Libra, representing balance and justice. "This character was coming into the world to impart justice, a healing upon her father and her mother and her family." Similarly, he wrote "Nana's Theme" in the key of A representing the Age of Aquarius, or the new age that was imminent for Nana's family.

The closing theme, called the "Elegba Theme," was written in the key of Taurus, D sharp (or E flat). John told me, "It is the key of the earth, the key ruled by love." The lyrics, "Ago Elegba [...] show the way, Elegba," he says, are about people who are moving forward after having been given love and dignity, and who are now facing the crossroads.

While we were recording the score, we began the final sound mix at Sound Trax Studios in Burbank, California. We recorded at night and mixed during the day. The whole recording session went on for ten continuous days in which we barely slept a wink.

I was certain that now that the film was completed, distribution would not be a problem. It had been hard in the early days to convey in words the idea of this film. But now that it was done, I figured there'd be no more blank looks. They wouldn't have to imagine a film about African American women at the turn of the century. Here it was, right in front of them. I was wrong. All of the distribution companies turned it town.

I was told over and over again that there was no market for the film. The distributors talked about the spectacular look of the film and the images and story being so different and thought-provoking, yet the consistent response was that there was "no market" for this type of film. Again, I was hearing mostly white men telling me, an African American woman, what my people wanted to see. In fact, they were deciding what we should be allowed to see. I knew that was wrong. I knew they were wrong.

One of the ongoing struggles of African American filmmakers is the fight against being pushed, through financial and social pressure, into telling only one kind of story. African American have stores as varied as any other people in American society. As varied as any other people in the world. Our lives, our history, our present reality is no more limited to "ghetto" stories, than Italian Americans are to the Mafia, or Jewish Americans are to the Holocaust. We have so many, many stories to tell. It will greatly enrich American filmmaking and American culture if we tell them.

In order to secure distribution for *Daughters* I decided to start showing it on the festival circuit. The first one we were able to present at was the prestigious Sundance Festival in Utah, in 1991.

The film was well received, as we thought it would be, and won the festival's award for cinematography. I was very happy, not only for the success of the film, but for the recognition given to A.J. for his works as cinematographer.

I took it to festival after festival, from January through September 1991. At the Black Light Festival in Chicago, *Daughters* sold out every showing. I went to Germany, to the Munich Film Festival of Women in Spain, the response was the same. *Daughters of the Dust* provoked the audience. Most liked it, some did not. But it provoked them, and that made me see that I had created something important, a film that caused its audience to think and react and come to grips with their own memories.

During this period I was commissioned by Alive From Off Center to direct *Praise House*, a performance film featuring the Urban Bush Women I was glad to do the work; I was always moved and intrigued by the work of the Urban Bush Women. Also, the money helped me pay off my debt.

Finally, in September 1991, a small company operating out of New York, Kino International, agreed to act as the distributor for *Daughters of the Dust*. I was relieved, but concerned, because they only agreed to distribute the film on a staggered schedule throughout 1992. I had hoped for a simultaneous release in key markets throughout the United States. I think it is important that African American filmmakers get maximum exposure for their films during the initial release period. If not, they're often pulled before the audience has a chance to find them. This is what happened to Charles Burnett's excellent film, *To Sleep with Anger*.

The other concern that I and other African American filmmaker are faced with is the amount of money that the distributor will spend on prints and advertising. When a film is released on a staggered schedule, it often means a very small budget for promotion, thereby limiting the exposure and the potential revenues of the film.

In this case, however, I was lucky and Kino International made a big push for the opening of the film. They also had the wisdom to hire a new African American public relations firm, KJM 3, to arrange publicity for the film. KJM 3 worked hard, and I soon found myself swamped with requests for interviews. Suddenly, I was appearing in national magazines and newspapers all across the country.

Daughters of the Dust opened January 15, 1992, at the Film Forum in New York. It sold out every show. The day of the opening the Coalition of One Hundred

Black Women of New York gave a fashion show and reception in support of the film. I was overwhelmed. People were asking me how it felt to be the first African American woman filmmaker with a feature film in theatrical release. It was a thought that had never crossed my mind. I had always considered myself one of a community of some very talented, powerful women filmmaker—women such as Neema Barnett, Ayoka Chenzira, Zeinabu irene Davis, and Michell Parkerson. Now people were saying, "Oh you're Julie Dash."

Daughters of the Dust had finally made it to the screen. As I watched people file out of the theatre on opening night, I felt all kinds of emotions. I was happy to see my work so well received; I was moved by the emotion on the faces of the people, especially older African Americans; I was proud to be contributing to the growing power of African Americans filmmakers, telling the stories of our people; and I was relieved that the voices of our women were finally being heard. But I didn't bask in the success of *Daughters* for too long. By the time it opened, I was already promoting the next film.

Daughters of the Dust is always with me. In many ways, the film birthed me just as I gave birth to it. By writing the script, I found my voice. By directing and producing it, I learned to use it to tell my people's story—Black people, Gullah kinfolk, but especially Black women's stories. Since that time, a myriad of other projects and important life lessons have helped hone my voice.

Recently, I became a grandmother. The reality that my daughter, N'Zinga—who was a child while I was shooting *Daughters*, who traveled with me as I promoted the film—is now a mother—reminds me of Nana Peazant's words and wisdom, as well as her protective spirit. I recognize and honor the fact that the ancestors and the womb are one. Life is cyclical. Making *Daughters of the Dust* was a life-changing cycle in my life and career—the experience, the friendships I made along the way, and the blessings I have received as a result continue to propel me forward to uncharted territories.

Epilogue

FARAH JASMINE GRIFFIN

In this quiet place, simple folk kneel down and catch a glimpse of the eternal.

Nana Peazant, *Daughters of the Dust*

As mesmerizing now as it was upon its release, *Daughters of the Dust* has earned its place as a classic. It is therefore fitting the film inspired this collection of original and innovative essays. Drawn from a diverse array of fields, the essays do not offer a definitive interpretation but instead open up a space, issue an invitation, for ongoing dialogue, conversation, and continued viewing of this great work. As such, the essays herein demonstrate the continued significance of Julie Dash's vision in creating a work that can withstand multiple interdisciplinary interpretations and analyses. *Daughters of the Dust* is both a work of its time and of ours.

As with literary works that preceded it—Toni Cade Bambara's *The Salt Eaters* (1980), Paule Marshall's *Praisesong for the Widow* (1983), Toni Morrison's *Song of Solomon* (1977) and *Beloved* (1987), Gloria Naylor's *Mama Day* (1988), and Alice Walker's *The Color Purple* (1982)—*Daughters of the Dust* dared to reconceptualize the way we saw, thought about, and experienced Black life by placing Black women at the very center of its aesthetic vision and narrative form. If it looked back and grounded itself in these literary works, it also looked forward and helped clear the space for films like Kasi Lemmons's *Eve's Bayou* (1997) and Benh Zeitlin's *Beasts of the Southern Wild* (2012), both of which owe much to *Daughters of the Dust*.

Daughters of the Dust asks us to slow down, to stop, to be quiet, and to attune ourselves to the rhythm of our breath. Focusing on a moment in time—the eve of a family's migration North, on the winds of the first Great Migration—the film unraveled history and myth. Instead of situating itself in the movement of the journey or the chaos and confusion of the urban destination, it bathed us in the sweeping landscapes, the marshes, the trees and beaches of the Sea Islands. It whispered, "Be still." Like those grandmothers who used to turn off the lights and have us sit in silence during thunderstorms out of respect and awe for the powers of God, Nana Peazant, and by extension the entire film, tells us, "In this quiet place, simple folk kneel down and catch a glimpse of the eternal." To be still is to be open to the divine. Julie Dash reminds us that stillness and contemplation are also part of Black folk tradition.

In this way, she anticipates a recent turn in African American cultural criticism. In *The Sovereignty of Quiet: Beyond Resistance in Black Culture*, Kevin Quashie (2012, 6) calls for "an aesthetic of quiet [...] that is neither motionless or without sound," but as a metaphor for "the full range of one's inner life: one's desires, ambitions, hungers, vulnerabilities, fears." Two decades before the publication of Quashie's work, *Daughters of the Dust* introduced an aesthetic of quiet, one that allowed for representation of the inner lives of the people of Dataw Island. The film famously celebrates not only Black women's diverse and hypnotic physical beauty, but also Black people's moments of rest, contemplation, prayer, anguish, and pleasure. Alone and in groups, they revel in stillness.

The opening scenes are framed by two such moments: an indigo tinted dawn where Nana Peazant takes a spiritual bath in the waters of Ibo Landing, waters that may hold the remains of Africans, and where Bilal Muhammad issues the Adhan (the call adhan to prayer) before offering an open-handed prayer over the blowing pages of the Koran. In between these two sacred moments, these very distinct religious practices, we witness the arrival of a boat bearing the missionary, Viola Peazant; the photographer, Mr. Snead; and the worldly, traveling women, Yellow Mary and Trula. Consequently, Christianity is situated as the religion of conversion and the modern, transported with the technological modernity of photography and cosmopolitan identities. But the prayer rituals ground us in place and sensibility. As Kevin Quashie reminds us, "The emphasis in prayer is not so much on the deity who is listening as it is on the subject who is praying and his or her capacity and faithfulness" (2012, xx).

The religious traditions of Ibo Landing include those the enslaved Africans brought with them: a reverence for the natural world and the ancestors, and for that other holy book, the Koran. These are traditions that require constant communication with the divine, be it through five daily prayers or the care and feeding of ancestral altars. Although Bilal is a presence, Nana Peazant is the spiritual center of the family and the film. Like Morrison's Baby Suggs in the Clearing or Naylor's Mama Day in the woods, Nana Peazant is the one who communes with the ancestors and calls upon the unborn. Throughout the early part of the film, we see her sitting pensively before the tombstones of departed family members, quietly stitching talismans for her family. Peazant shares her spiritual wisdom with individual grandchildren who seek guidance, love, and nurturance, and, at times, who challenge her and her beliefs. She is the spirit guide, the keeper of history, and the bearer of tradition.

These moments are all rendered in a quiet, near stillness. The camera moves in sweeps and brushes over bodies that walk, practice capoeira, sway in the wind, and engage in ring games that are founded in spiritual practices like the ring shout and induce a state of spiritual euphoria. The only figure who runs is that of the unborn child, who gallops with pleasure, not unlike the wild horses that also populate the landscape. It is the stillness and the pacing that most seemed to jar some critics upon the film's release, a true shortcoming of the critical eye in this instance.

The insistence on pacing, on stillness, on interiority did not sacrifice a complexity of emotions. In his moments of solitude, Eli must fight with himself over his feelings of powerlessness to avenge the rape of his wife, Eula. Haagar Peazant rails against Ibo Landing, which she see as a godforsaken place. These moments of solitude allow each person to honestly come face to face with the intensity of their emotions.

Stillness and waiting in *Daughters of the Dust* is not passive. It is the space of healing and of preparation—healing from wounds inflicted by the world and preparation for engaging it. Both Jesus and the Buddha retreated, sought solitude, listened, and emerged from doing so to change the world. In the stillness of her dreams, Eula Peazant meets her deceased mother and feels the presence of her unborn daughter. Is it any wonder she is given the responsibility of relaying the story of the Ibos who walked on water or, more importantly, of delivering the healing sermon, which links Yellow Mary's trauma to the historical trauma of Black women in the West—their persistent raping, which has even challenged their ability to love themselves or believe God's love is available to them. Eula seems to say "I am she and she is me." Her sermon resonates with the wisdom of the Nag Hammadi, quoted at length by Nana Peazant at the film's opening:

> For I am the first and the last.
> I am the honored one and the scorned one.
> I am the whore and the holy one.
> I am the wife and the virgin.
> I am the mother and the daughter.
> I am the members of my mother.
> I am the barren one and many are her sons.

In this quiet place, the women of *Daughters of the Dust* confront themselves, each other, their ancestors, and their future, and together they reveal to us a glimpse of the eternal.

So, too, does Julie Dash. Throughout the film, she juxtaposes the ancient with the modern, only to reveal them as part and parcel of the same eternal continuum, informing and shaping each other. Ancient texts like the Gnostic Gospels, the Bible, and the Koran pepper the narration alongside quotations from Paule Marshall's *Praisesong for the Widow*, which is the source of Eula's remembrance of the Ibos, and Sylvia Ardyn Boone's *Radiance from the Waters*. Nineteenth-century optical devices like the kaleidoscope and the stereoscope—both associated with modernity—along with Mr. Snead's camera, represent technological innovations, yet they also serve to narrow our vision. At the same time, the film brings us the colorful star-like designs of Black women's quilts whose patterns echo those made by the kaleidoscope. The quilts are made from scraps of memory, and therefore embody the past while providing beauty and comfort in the present. The stereoscopic lens provides black-and-white newsreel images of crowded urban streets teeming with immigrants, which contrasts with the wide open spaces of Ibo Landing. And yet, lest we too easily make the distinction between modern technology and the old-fashioned needle and culinary arts of Black women, we should recall all of these images are brought to us through the medium of film. Julie Dash's vision, and that of her cinematographer Arthur Jafa, make use of the camera to tell this tale. Film—like the novel, the song, the quilt, the ring game—is yet another medium for rendering Black people's story. In the hands of a gifted artist like Dash, the very medium itself is transformed, capable of rendering not only seductive images, but also deep spiritual truths.

Daughters of the Dust calls for viewing and reviewing. It invites inquiry and analysis. But most importantly, it provides an opportunity to experience the very beauty, complexity, and contemplative insight that it both documents and imagines.

REFERENCES

Bambara, Toni Cade. 1980. *The Salt Eaters*. New York: Random House.

Boone, Sylvia Ardyn. 1986. *Radiance from the Waters: Ideals of Feminine Beauty in Mende Art*. New Haven: Yale University Press.

Marshall, Paule. 1983. *Praisesong for the Widow*. New York: Penguin.

Morrison, Toni. 1997. *Song of Solomon*. New York: Alfred A. Knopf.

———. 1987. *Beloved*. New York: Alfred A. Knopf.

Naylor, Gloria. 1988. *Mama Day*. New York: Random House.

Quashie, Kevin. 2012. *The Sovereignty of Quiet: Beyond Resistance in Black Culture*. New Brunswick, NJ: Rutgers University Press.

Walker, Alice. 1982. *The Color Purple*. New York: Harcourt Brace Jovanovich.

Contributors

Silvia Pilar Castro-Borrego is Lecturer of English and North American literature and culture at the University of Málaga (Spain). She has edited the volume *The Search for Wholeness and Diaspora Literacy in African American Literature* (Cambridge Scholars, 2011), and published the articles "Re(claiming) Subjectivity and Transforming the Politics of Silence through the Search for Wholeness in *Push*" in the journal *Atlantis* (2014) and "Integration, Assimilation, and Identity in Lorraine Hansberry's *A Raisin in the Sun* and Barbara and Carlton Molette's *Rosalee Pritchett*" in the *Revista Canaria de Estudios Ingleses* (2015). Recent publications include the article "Claiming the Politics of Articulation through Agency and Wholeness in Two Afro-Hispanic Postcolonial Narratives" in *JIWS* journal (2016). In June 2017 she organized the 12th CAAR conference at the University of Málaga under the theme "Diasporic Encounters, Subjectivities in Transit: Race, Gender, Religion and Sexualities in the African Diasporas" and is now a member of the Research project "Bodies in Transit" at the Universities of Huelva and Vigo.

Corrie Claiborne is a dedicated cultural theorist and digital humanist with a 20-year commitment to higher education. Originally from Columbia, South Carolina, she has extensive experience in organizing exhibitions, teacher trainings, and community programs, as well as in creating innovative courses, publications, and grants around African-American and American culture and literature. Dr. Corrie Claiborne is currently an Associate professor of English and American Literature.

She received her undergraduate degree in English from Syracuse University, an M.A. in English from the University of South Carolina, and a doctorate from The Ohio State University. In 2010, she partnered with the Myrtle Beach Museum of Art and the Richland County Library in Columbia, SC to deliver a series of lectures about the similarities between the Quilts of Gee's Bend, Alabama and the cultural artifacts of the South Carolina Low Country. She is also currently working on several publications related to Gullah/ Geechee Culture, including an edited collection of oral histories with Samuel Livingston entitled *Framing Gullah Geechee Culture: An Interdisciplinary Approach*.

In addition to serving on numerous university and community committees, in 2013 Dr. Claiborne and Jamila Lyn developed a service learning project with the Morehouse Bonner Office of Community Service entitled "Re-imagining Black Masculinity, Ending Sexual Violence." This project looked at ways to get students to discuss the images of men in the media and to mentor younger men to change their actions surrounding violence in their communities. In 2009, she was awarded a UNCF/Mellon Fellowship at Harvard University.

Julie Dash is an award-winning filmmaker, television director and writer, and scholar. In 1991, Dash broke through racial and gender boundaries with her acclaimed film *Daughters of the Dust*. Written, directed, and produced by Dash, *Daughters of the Dust* was the first feature film by an African American woman to have a wide theatrical release. At the Sundance Film Festival, *Daughters of the Dust* won Best Cinematography. In 2004, the Library of Congress selected the film for inclusion in the National Film Registry, the first film by an African American woman to join this distinguished list. In 2012, *Daughters of the Dust* was placed with the Sundance Institute Collection at UCLA.

Dash has written and directed for CBS, BET, ENCORE STARZ, SHOWTIME, MTV Movies and HBO. She directed the multi-award-winning movie *The Rosa Parks Story*, which earned two NAACP Image Awards, an Emmy nomination for Angela Bassett, and a DGA Best Directorial nomination.

Dash's additional films include *Incognito*, *Funny Valentines*, *Love Song*, and *Subway Stories: Tales From the Underground*. Her work as a film director has also encompassed media design for museums, a theme park pavilion for Disney's Imagineering, and The National Underground Railroad Freedom Center Museum's environmental theater presentation of *Brothers of the Borderland*. Her work includes music videos, documentaries, public service announcements, industrial documentary films, and commercial spots for Fortune 500 brands, including Coca Cola and GMC.

In October 2015, Dash was a part of Turner Classic Movies' (TCM) *Trailblazing Women* series, co-hosting an evening with Illeana Douglas. Dash is currently developing a feature- length documentary about Vertamae Smart Grosvenor, a world-renowned author, performer, and chef from rural South Carolina who has led a remarkably unique and complex life. The film is based upon Grosvenor's best-selling work, *Vibration Cooking: Or the Travel Notes of a Geechee Girl.*

Recent retrospectives of Dash's narrative film work have been held in Beijing and Hong Kong University, China; Charleston, SC; Creteil, France; Taipei, Taiwan; and Philadelphia, PA. Dash also served as chair of the International Jury at the Kerala International Film Festival, India.

Dash is the Distinguished Professor of Documentary Filmmaking at Spelman College. Prior to this post, she was Distinguished Professor of Television and Emerging Media (CTEMS) at Morehouse College. From 2013–2015 she was a Visiting Assistant Professor at the College of Charleston, in the department of African American Studies, and with the Avery Research Center for African American Studies. in 2013 she held the Bob Allison Chair in Media at Wayne State University. She earned her MFA in Film & Television production at UCLA, received her BA in Film Production from CCNY, and was a Producing and Writing Conservatory Fellow at the American Film Institute's Center for Advanced Film Studies.

Daughters of the Dust: A Novel, a sequel to the film, was written by Dash and published in 1997 by Dutton Books. Dash also wrote *Daughters of the Dust: The Making of an African American Woman's Film* (The New Press, 1992).

Marcella "Marcy" De Veaux, Professor of Journalism at California State University, Northridge, is an educator, media expert and diversity consultant with more than two decades of experience in entertainment public relations. She holds a doctorate in Depth Psychology, a discipline that examines what lies "below the surface" of conscious awareness. Currently, De Veaux arranges workshops on diversity, equity, inclusion, and cultural competency for faculty, staff and students around the split that divides our nation - race, class, gender, geography, and generation. In addition, she conducts workshops for businesses, non-profit organizations and media companies towards building a culturally competent work environment.

Karen M. Gagne teaches in the Department of Gender and Sexuality Studies at St. Lawrence University. She received her PhD and MA in Historical Sociology from Binghamton University in New York, and her BA from Hampshire College, in Amherst, Massachusetts. She is interested in social movements (such as the anti-colonial, indigenous, and Black Power movements of the 1950s and 1960) and connecting those movements to our present moment; Africa-New World Studies; and applying Sylvia Wynter's "Black Studies Alterity Perspective" as a model for rethinking knowledge, cognition, education, and human studies in general in the 21st century. Previously, Dr. Gagne taught sociology, anthropology and ethnic studies at the University of Wisconsin-Platteville.

Dr. Gagne also serves on the Board of the Deep Root Center for Self-Directed Learning in Canton, New York, whose mission it is to provide the environment, resources, and support for young people who choose to live and learn without school. Deep Root Center is a member of the Liberated Learners Network that strives to provide all young people with access to interest-driven, life-long learning practices outside of a formalized school setting.

Farah Jasmine Griffin is the inaugural Chair of the African American and African Diaspora Studies Department, and Director of the Institute for Research in African American Studies at Columbia University. She is also the William B. Ransford Professor of English and Comparative Literature. She is a past Director of the Schomburg Scholars in Residence Program. Professor Griffin received her B.A. from Harvard and her Ph.D. in American Studies from Yale. Griffin is the author of *Who Set You Flowin?: The African American Migration Narrative* (Oxford 1995), *Beloved Sisters and Loving Friends: Letters from Rebecca Primus of Royal Oak, Maryland, and Addie Brown of Hartford Connecticut, 1854-1868* (Alfred A. Knopf 1999), *If You Can't Be Free, Be a Mystery: In Search of Billie Holiday* (Free Press 2001) and co-author, with Salim Washington, of *Clawing At the Limits of Cool: Miles Davis, John Coltrane, and the Greatest Jazz Collaboration Ever* (Thomas Dunne 2008). Her most recent book is *Harlem Nocturne: Women Artists and Progressive Politics During World War II*, was published by Basic Books in 2013.

Griffin collaborated with composer and pianist, Geri Allen, and director and actor, S. Epatha Merkerson, on two theatrical projects, for which she wrote the book. The first, *Geri Allen and Friends Celebrate the Great Jazz Women of the Apollo*—featuring Lizz Wright, Dianne Reeves, Teri Lyne Carrington, among others--premiered on the main stage of the Apollo Theater in May of 2013. The second, *A Conversation with Mary Lou*, featuring vocalist Carmen Lundy, premiered at Harlem Stage in March 2014 and was performed at The John F. Kennedy Center in May of 2016.

Heike Raphael-Hernandez is Associate Professor of American Studies at the University of Würzburg, Germany and Adjunct Professor of English at the University of Maryland University College, Europe. Among her recent publications are *Migrating the Black Body: The African Diaspora and Visual Culture* (with Leigh Raiford, U of Washington Press 2017) and a special issue (with Pia Wiegmink) for the journal *Atlantic Studies* about "German Entanglements in Transatlantic Slavery" 14.4. (Fall 2017), which was republished as a book (Routledge, 2018). In addition, she is the editor of *Blackening Europe: The African American Presence* (Routledge 2004), and *AfroAsian Encounters: Culture, History, Politics* (co-edited with Shannon Steen, NYU Press 2006). She is author of *Contemporary African American Women Writers and Ernst Bloch's Principle of Hope* (Edwin Mellen Press

2008) and *Fear, Desire, and the Stranger Next Door: Global South Immigration in American Film* (U of Washington Press, forthcoming 2019). Together with Cheryl Finley (Cornell U) and Leigh Raiford (UC Berkeley), she was awarded an American Council of Learned Societies Collaborative Research Fellowship for 2015–2017 for their joined research project "Visualizing Travel, Gendering the African Diaspora."

Sharon D. Johnson is a screenwriter and scholar of film, television, and African American arts and literature. She is currently part-time faculty at Emerson College's Los Angeles Center in the Department of Visual & Media Arts, where she teaches her original senior seminar on race and gender in literary adaptations for feature film. She has also been part-time faculty at California State University, Northridge in the Department of Africana Studies and the Department of Cinema and Television Arts.

Dr. Johnson has been a published journalist for almost 30 years, as well as a produced television writer and member of the Writers Guild of America, West, Inc. (WGAW) since 1993. She served as Chair of the Writers Guild Committee of Black Writers from 1999 to 2003 and has been a featured guest on news and information programs on ABC, BET, KCAL, KCET, NPR, and Telemundo discussing race and diversity issues. She holds a BA in the Program in the Arts—Writing from Barnard College, an MA in Media Studies from the New School, and a PhD in Depth Psychology from Pacifica Graduate Institute.

Ayana I. Karanja is an Associate Professor in the Department of Sociology at Loyola University Chicago where she teaches courses that include women in film, race and ethnicity, critical race theory and postcolonial studies. Dr. Karanja is the author of *Zora Neale Hurston: The Breath of Her Voice* (Peter Lang 1999).

Dr. Patricia Williams Lessane is Associate Vice President for Academic Affairs and Associate Professor in Sociology and Anthropology at Morgan State University. Prior to this post, she served as Associate Dean for Strategic Planning and Community Engagement and Executive Director of Avery Research Center for African American History and Culture at the College of Charleston where she taught Anthropology, African American Studies, and First Year Experience courses and was a tenured faculty member in the library. She is a cultural anthropologist who has worked at The Field Museum and The Museum of Science and Industry in Chicago. She holds a BA in English from Fisk University, a MALS from Dartmouth College and a PhD in Anthropology from University of Illinois at Chicago. Along with Violet Showers Johnson and Gundolf Graml, she is the co-editor of *Deferred Dreams, Defiant Struggles: Critical Perspectives on Blackness, Belonging and Civil Rights* (2018) published by Liverpool University Press. She is a producer and humanities scholar on Julie Dash's latest documentary, *Travel Notes of a Geechee Girl* currently in production. She served co-PI on the Race and Social Justice Initiative at The College of Charleston. Her 2015, *New York Times* editorial, "*No Sanctuary in Charleston*" gave personal and social commentary about African American life in Charleston following the massacre at Mother Emmanuel Church. She has written opinion pieces about the intersection of race, gender, and class in Black life in the United States for *The Post and Courier*, *The Baltimore Sun*, and *Skirt Magazine*. She is a Fulbright Specialist and in 2016, she was a Fulbright scholar at University of Málaga in Málaga, Spain. In 2018, she was honored as The College of Charleston's Administrator of the Year and was one of eleven women honored that year at the Charleston YWCA's inaugural What Women Bring awards for her work as a non-profit leader. She is the mother of two amazing teenagers: Osayende, a 19 year old son who is a student at NYU's Tisch School of the Arts, Aniyah Ruth, a sixteen year old daughter, who is a sophomore in high school, and a loving Boxer/Hound named Sadie Mae.

Tiffany Lethabo King is an assistant professor in the Institute for Women's, Gender and Sexuality Studies at Georgia State University. She is the author of *The Black Shoals: Offshore Formations of Black and Native Studies* (Duke University Press 2019).

Katie M. White is the Director of Social Action at Stone Ridge School of the Sacred Heart in Bethesda, MD. Her research interests include Gullah history and culture, feminist food studies, and social justice pedagogy.

Index